RED POWER RISING

New Directions in Native American Studies
Colin G. Calloway and K. Tsianina Lomawaima, General Editors

The National Indian Youth Council, 1964. (Center for Southwest Research, University Libraries, University of New Mexico, MSS 703 BC, box 1, folder 15)

RED POWER RISING

*The National Indian Youth Council
and the Origins of Native Activism*

Bradley G. Shreve

Foreword by Shirley Hill Witt

University of Oklahoma Press : Norman

All author royalties from the sale of this book are donated to the National Indian Youth Council and the American Indian College Fund.

Publication of this book is made possible through the generosity of Edith Kinney Gaylord.

Library of Congress Cataloging-in-Publication Data

Shreve, Bradley Glenn, 1970–
    Red power rising : the National Indian Youth Council and the origins of Native activism / Bradley G. Shreve ; foreword by Shirley Hill Witt.
        p. cm. — (New directions in Native American studies ; v. 5)
    Includes bibliographical references and index.
    ISBN 978-0-8061-4178-7 (hardcover : alk. paper)
    1. Indians of North America—Politics and government—20th century. 2. Power (Social sciences)—United States—History—20th century. 3. Indians of North America—Civil rights—History—20th century. 4. Civil rights movements—United States—History—20th century. 5. National Indian Youth Council—History—20th century. 6. Indian activists—Southwest, New—History—20th century. 7. Indian youth—Southwest, New—Political activity—History—20th century. 8. Indian students—Southwest, New—Political activity—History—20th century. 9. Student movements—Southwest, New—History—20th century. 10. Decolonization—History—20th century. I. Title.
    E98.T77.S49 2011
    323.1197—dc22   2010033799

Red Power Rising: The National Indian Youth Council and the Origins of Native Activism is Volume 5 in the New Directions in Native American Studies series.

For Winter Sequoyah

CONTENTS

Illustrations

FOREWORD

A letter from Dr. Edward F. LaCroix somehow smuggled its way to me in a State Department diplomatic pouch in 1995 or 1996. I was a career Foreign Service officer posted to Lusaka, Zambia, serving as the cultural affairs officer. The letter informed me that he was the historian of the National Indian Youth Council and, as such, was compiling documents, photographs, and memorabilia relating to NIYC's past activities. He also sought names and contact information for NIYC alumni if I had any to share.

I thought at first that I would not be much of an informant for him since my formal connection with NIYC had ended decades earlier. My closest contact then was with Herbert C. Blatchford, a cherished friend as well as the true initiator of the NIYC.

No sooner than my Zambia tour was completed at the end of 1996 and I retired to my home of record—Albuquerque, New Mexico—I was shocked and deeply distressed to learn that Herb had been killed in a house fire weeks before. The tragedy also saw the incineration of his vast collection of NIYC materials.

When my household effects from Zambia were delivered to Albuquerque some months later, I was surprised to find that my small file of NIYC documents and photos had survived. (In my transfer from Paraguay to Somalia in an earlier posting, the shipping container with all of my personal items had flooded while on the transport ship, ruining much of my library, papers, . . . and even my ratty fur coat.) In view of the loss of Herb's collection, I decided to turn mine over to the Special Collections at the Zimmerman Library, University of New Mexico. And that is where Bradley G. Shreve found me.

Brad sent me a copy of his doctoral dissertation, "Red Power Rising: The National Indian Youth Council and the Origins of Intertribal Activism" (University of New Mexico, 2007), the basis for the present book. What a delight to read! Brad asked me to ruminate about the NIYC years, and I hope that in my vignettes the reader will feel some of the excitement and, yes, frustrations that challenged us at the council's founding and earliest times.

Brad's first several chapters recounting the development of various activities, Native and non-Native, for the benefit of Indian communities brought to my mind the wonderful deep voice of Chief Clinton Rickard of the Tuscarora Nation. From across the Rickard oak dining table, which easily sat a dozen people at any given time, I heard the retelling of adventures that he and son William were part of during the early years of the Indian Defense League of America. His *Fighting Tuscarora: The Autobiography of Chief Clinton Rickard*, edited by Barbara Graymont (1973), is a perfect backdrop for the early chapters of Brad's *Red Power Rising*.

In the early 1960s, I was enrolled at the University of Omaha, Nebraska, taking Anthropology 101, when I saw an article in the *Omaha World-Herald* about the upcoming American Indian Chicago Conference. I later met Wayne Gilpin, chair of the Omaha Tribe, at a powwow, and he encouraged me to attend, saying that he would be there too. By the time the June 1961 AICC convened, I found myself at the University of Massachusetts with just enough money to buy a plane ticket to Chicago.

Although I did not participate in or even know about the student workshops that Brad describes, I now know more about the preparation my peers had prior to the AICC and wish that I had had a like opportunity. That said, it was one of those miracles that we students found each other at the AICC and discovered that we shared a common devotion to the betterment of our people. Voilà! The birth of the National Indian Youth Council!

There is one more matter of importance to me with regard to the fine product that Brad has put before us, and that is his recognition of the key role played by women throughout NIYC's history. This contrasts with many, perhaps most, of the student movements in the civil rights surge. Looking through the books about NIYC at Amazon.com, which lists more 150 items, I would challenge you to find more than a few of the volumes that include the names of women who were integral to NIYC's efforts. You will see Mel, Clyde, Herb, Hank, and so on in virtually all of them, but rarely the names of the women. So I will give you some here for whom I have great respect and affection: Karen, Joan, Bernie, Florine, LaNada, Harriett, Tillie, Fran, KRC, Angela, Janet, Ramona, Diana, Belma, Mary, Christine, Agnes, Sandy, Anita, Vivian.

Shirley Hill Witt
Akwesasne Mohawk

ACKNOWLEDGMENTS

I want to begin by thanking my editor at the University of Oklahoma Press, Alessandra Jacobi Tamulevich. Over the last few years she has been encouraging, patient, and supportive. I could not have wished for a better guide through the publication process. I would also like to thank series editors Colin Calloway and Tsianina Lomawaima, along with the anonymous reviewers, for their insightful comments, which ultimately helped make this book much better. A big thanks goes to Alice Stanton for her patience and perserverance in shepherding the manuscript through its final stages.

Red Power Rising would have been impossible without the assistance of numerous librarians, archivists, and interviewees. The personnel at the NAES College library and the Newberry Library in Chicago, Stanford University Special Collections, the New Mexico State Archives, and the Center for Southwest Research at the University of New Mexico's Zimmerman Library proved particularly helpful. Norman Ration, Cecelia Belone, and the Board of Directors of the National Indian Youth Council were kind enough to welcome me to their meetings and to share a treasure of stories, as well as their expertise in current Indian affairs. Their dedication as they continue to fight for Native people is an inspiration. A special thanks to Sam English, Karen Rickard Jacobson, James Nez, Gerald Brown, Charlie Cambridge, Viola Hatch, James Zion, Della Warrior, and Dan Edwards, who took time out their schedules to talk with me and offer their memories of the NIYC. Sam English also contributed the artwork that appears on the back jacket of the book, for which I am much obliged. And I am eternally indebted to Shirley Hill Witt, who shared so many great stories. Her vignettes and keen insight have greatly enriched this book from top to bottom. Dr. Witt remains one of the most important Native leaders in recent history, and her tenure with the NIYC stands as just one facet of her overall body of work.

I would like to thank all of my colleagues and friends in Tsaile and Albuquerque for their support and camaraderie. To my former adviser at the University of New Mexico, Professor Margaret Connell-Szasz, I owe the deepest of gratitude. If not for her insights and editorial eye, I would probably still be hunting for a publisher. Chris Vigil, Joe Lenti, Paul Gilon, Joe Sperry, and the late Emmanuel Agbolosoo deserve a big thanks for being such great friends. I would like to thank my parents, Janet Kay Buehler Shreve and Richard the Lionhearted, for all of their love and support. They have always been there for me; one could not wish for a finer set of parents. Finally, a special thanks to Amanda Sutton, the mother of our son, Winter.

And it is that beautiful boy, Winter Sequoyah Shreve, to whom this book is dedicated.

ABBREVIATIONS

AAIA	Association on American Indian Affairs
ABC	*Americans Before Columbus*
ACLU	American Civil Liberties Union
AICC	American Indian Chicago Conference
AID	American Indian Development, Inc.
AIDA	American Indian Defense Association
AIF	American Indian Federation
AIM	American Indian Movement
AMERIND	American Indian Movement for Equal Rights in Indian-Native Development
ARROW	Americans for the Restitution and Rightings of Old Wrongs
BIA	Bureau of Indian Affairs, or Indian Bureau
BYU	Brigham Young University
CETA	Comprehensive Employment and Training Act
CORE	Congress of Racial Equality
FLN	Front de Libération Nationale
ICC	Indian Claims Commission
IRA	Indian Reorganization Act
KU	University of Kansas
NAACP	National Association for the Advancement of Colored People
NCAI	National Congress of American Indians
NIYC	National Indian Youth Council

NMAIA	New Mexico Association on Indian Affairs
OEO	Office of Economic Opportunity
OU	University of Oklahoma
RIYC	Regional Indian Youth Council
SAI	Society of American Indians
SAIA	Survival of American Indians Association
SCLC	Southern Christian Leadership Conference
SDS	Students for a Democratic Society
SLID	Student League for Industrial Democracy
SNCC	Student Nonviolent Coordinating Committee
TVA	Tennessee Valley Authority
UN	United Nations
UNA	United Native Americans
UNM	University of New Mexico
USS	United Scholarship Service

Red Power Rising

INTRODUCTION

For decades, we have heard how the Red Power movement commenced when urban-based American Indians took over Alcatraz Island in November of 1969. Historians, journalists, and the activists themselves have told of the men who started the American Indian Movement and their great protests of the 1970s, including the occupation of the Bureau of Indian Affairs building in Washington, D.C., the siege at Wounded Knee, and the shootout on the Oglala Sioux reservation that resulted in the arrest and incarceration of Leonard Peltier. The purpose of this book is not to contest that these events were major milestones in Native American history. Nor is it to challenge the media attention they caught or the historiography they produced. Rather, this book seeks to illustrate how these episodes, and their main actors, followed in the footsteps of an earlier generation. In the summer of 1961, Indian students from throughout the United States congregated in Gallup, New Mexico, where they hoped to form a new intertribal organization. After two days of discussion and debate, they founded the National Indian Youth Council (NIYC) and launched the Red Power movement.[1]

The students who established the NIYC had a firm conviction to uphold tradition and the ideals of their elders. They believed in the cornerstone principles of tribal sovereignty, treaty rights, self-determination, and cultural preservation that had guided intertribal politics since the founding of the National Congress of American Indians (NCAI) in 1944. This continuity with the past

The dawn of Red Power. Mel Thom *(left)* and Clyde Warrior *(cowboy hat)* of the National Indian Youth Council were the first to articulate and use the words "Red Power." (Courtesy of Department of Special Collections and University Archives, Stanford University Libraries)

distinguished the Native student activists of the 1960s from their contemporaries in the Student Nonviolent Coordinating Committee (SNCC) or even in Students for a Democratic Society (SDS), who ultimately challenged the fundamental ideals and assumptions of their elders.

The NIYC also followed their elders' example in that both men *and* women shaped and led the organization. Like their forebears in the Society of American Indians, the American Indian Federation, and the NCAI, women played a pivotal role in the council—the organization's initial first and second vice presidents were women, as were five of the ten founding members. Moreover, sexism in the organization, according to at least four of the council's early leaders, was virtually nonexistent. Shirley Hill Witt (Mohawk), Karen Rickard (Tuscarora), Viola Hatch (Arapaho), and Della Warrior (Otoe-Missouria) all steadfastly maintain that not once did they feel marginalized or ignored because they were women. When posed with the question of whether sexism played any role in the NIYC, Witt answered point blank: "I would insist that the answer is no, and emphatically no. . . . It would have served no purpose and only lessened everyone's contribution to the overall mission." Karen Rickard theorized that perhaps the lack of sexism was due to the strong matrilineal traditions of many Native peoples, which led to a respect for women not found in non-Native organizations. Indeed, women in SNCC and SDS frequently complained of sexism, a blight that eventually contributed to each organization's downfall.[2]

Despite these differences, the Native student activists were also very much a product of their time. Like their white, African American, and Hispanic counterparts, the Native youth who came of age during the Cold War were, to borrow the words of Maurice Isserman and Michael Kazin, part of a "superheated ideological atmosphere," which painted a black-and-white political landscape of good versus evil. Viewing the world through such a lens created a sense of superidealism and spurred these young women and men to challenge actively the injustices they saw in the society around them and—as one NIYC founder put it—"not be swayed from our mission as we saw it." Hence, the Native student activists of the 1960s never broke ideologically from the past, but they did have the same sense of urgency as others of their generation, using the same militant tactics and rhetoric as SNCC and SDS.[3]

Also like their contemporaries, the NIYC in the 1960s was a small, tightly knit group. Historians who have chronicled NIYC's white counterpart, SDS, have referred to that organization as "a very small and somewhat incestuous community," or, in the words of Terry Anderson, "a movement family." SNCC, too, has been described as a family or, as one book title avowed, "a circle of trust." Similar portrayals have been used when referring to the NIYC leadership. Gerald Brown (Flathead) described the council as "a think tank," while Sam English (Ojibwe) called it "a community of intellectuals" whose members cared deeply for one another and forged lasting bonds in their mutual quest "for a greater Indian America." Although the NIYC claimed a few hundred members in the 1960s, only a core group of ten to fifteen individuals shaped the organization and steered it through that tumultuous decade.[4]

A distinct majority of those leaders came from reservations or rural tribal communities. Karen Rickard, Melvin Thom (Paiute), Clyde Warrior (Ponca), Joan Noble (Ute), Herbert Blatchford (Navajo), and others took pride in their traditional upbringing and had their background in mind when they leapt into action during the 1960s. Such demographics change the story of Indian activism, as well as that of movement politics of the 1960s broadly construed. Until recently, academics have maintained that Indian activism sprang from the inner cities of San Francisco, Los Angeles, and Minneapolis. They have asserted that, like the young black activists who launched SNCC following the Greensboro sit-ins or the white radicals who founded SDS in Ann Arbor, the Indians who initiated the Red Power movement were urban based. Such a rendering simply ignores the facts. The young Native leaders who first articulated Red Power as an ideology and took direct action to advocate that ideology came primarily from reservations and rural areas.

So what is "Red Power" anyway? Over the years, the words have been used in myriad ways. Some scholars, such as Alvin M. Josephy, Jr., defined the slogan in the broadest, most abstract of ways. In *Red Power: The American Indians' Fight for Freedom* (1971), Josephy compiled numerous documents that supposedly exemplified Red Power. His examples embodied a whole host of perspectives, attitudes, and angles. There was the militant, like the Indians of All Tribes' oration "We Must Hold On to the Old Ways," and the moderate, such as the American Indian Task Force's address "We Speak as Indians." The only common denominator was that each selection stood under the umbrella of the greater Indian struggle. At the other end of the spectrum, Troy Johnson, Joane Nagel, and Duane Champagne defined the Red Power movement in their edited volume, *American Indian Activism* (1997), as "a series of collective actions" that commenced with the 1969 takeover of Alcatraz and ended with the Longest Walk in 1978. More confusion abounded in 1999 when

Mel Thom raises his fist in defiance before being arrested during a protest in Washington, D.C., 1968. Thom grew up on the Walker River Paiute Reservation in western Nevada. (Photograph by Diana Jo Davies; courtesy of the Ralph Rinzler Folklife Archives and Collections, Smithsonian Institution)

Johnson and Nagel teamed up with Josephy to update *Red Power: The American Indian's Fight for Freedom*. This second edition took an even looser view of Red Power than Josephy's original tome, adding a statement from the American Indian Policy Review Commission, a report on Indian education by the U.S. Senate Committee on Labor and Public Welfare, and even a speech from Richard Nixon![5]

With all of the misunderstanding surrounding this slogan, perhaps it is best just to listen to the Native activists and lobbyists of the 1960s and 1970s and abide by their own definitions of Red Power. Simply put, those who used the slogan remain proponents of Red Power, and those who did not can be excluded from the movement. So the NCAI, which disavowed all direct action and protest in favor of lobbying and litigating, is freed from the confines of Red Power, while the activists who stormed the shores of Alcatraz and the American Indian Movement militants who sacked the Bureau of Indian Affairs (BIA) building remain a part of it. Under such a rubric we must also include the first group of students to use the slogan—the National Indian Youth Council—who employed both lobbying tactics and protest actions. The NIYC often posted banners proclaiming "Red Power" at parades and other public events and also used the slogan in their newspapers and newsletters to rail against the establishment.[6]

When we define Red Power this way, the published literature has just begun to touch upon the early movement, for the takeovers and occupations of the 1970s have long been the primary focus of scholarly discourse on the movement. The first book to engage the NIYC was Stan Steiner's *The New Indians* (1968). Although it is a contemporary journalistic account that excludes citations or a comprehensive list of references, Steiner's work is valuable for its firsthand nature. In the mid- to late sixties the journalist traveled around Indian country in search of a story about the rising Indian militancy. Steiner befriended and interviewed important early activists and NIYC founders like Shirley Hill Witt, Clyde Warrior, Mel Thom, and Herb Blatchford. His book highlights the rhetoric, ideology, and general nature of Red Power in its formative years.[7]

Charles Wilkinson's *Blood Struggle: The Rise of Modern Indian Nations* (2005) is the most thorough chronicle of the postwar Native American sovereignty movement. Wilkinson, who worked as a lawyer for the Native American Rights Fund in the 1970s, proposes that the sovereignty struggle that unfolded in the years after the adoption of the termination policy was immensely successful and drastically changed the face of Indian country. The author singles out key Native American leaders, including NIYC activists such as Hank Adams (Assiniboine), and credits them with using the American legal and political system to the advantage of all Indians. The author deftly pulls together disparate components of the sovereignty movement and shows how each contributed to upsetting the termination policy. Still, for all the book's fine points, the history of the NIYC and the origins of Red Power remain largely untold.

Daniel Cobb's *Native Activism in Cold War America: The Struggle for Sovereignty* (2008), does more than any other work since Steiner's *The New Indians* to illustrate the NIYC's importance in shaping intertribal politics during the 1960s. Cobb redefines political activism to include those seeking reformative goals through lobbying and litigating. He shows how certain NIYC activists, such as Mel Thom and Clyde Warrior, worked alongside the NCAI and other tribal leaders to bring about change in federal Indian policy. Much of the book focuses on how Native activists used President Lyndon B. Johnson's Great Society programs to bring about a greater degree of sovereignty for Indian nations. The author claims that the War on Poverty shaped intertribal politics in the mid- to late 1960s, but more importantly Cobb refutes the notion that Alcatraz served as the impetus for Native activism, pushing the story back to the early 1950s.[8]

Cobb and Loretta Fowler's edited volume, *Beyond Red Power: American Indian Politics and Activism since 1900,* further expands the discussion on Native activism. This collection of essays, published by the School for Advanced Research, brings together some of the giants in American Indian history, such as Donald Fixico, Clara Sue Kidwell, Sherry Smith, and Frederick E. Hoxie, with other leading scholars, newcomers, and former activist Della Warrior. Each writer contributes to Cobb and Fowler's overall thesis that the history of American Indian activism has been a diverse, long-standing, and ongoing tradition stemming from an overarching drive for self-determination. The volume broadens our perspective by expanding the discussion on Native activism beyond the American Indian Movement or Alcatraz. Cobb, Warrior, and Smith's respective essays touch upon the history of the National Indian Youth Council, but the book lacks a chapter on the NIYC—the second oldest intertribal organization in existence and the organization responsible for launching the Red Power movement.

The present addition to the growing literature on Native activism stands as the first comprehensive study of the National Indian Youth Council and the origins of the Red Power movement. Heretofore the history of the NIYC has remained condensed in a variety of manuscript collections and in the memories of those who founded and led the organization. Many of the council's great leaders have passed on or have remained silent. But others, such as Shirley Hill Witt, Karen Rickard Jacobson, Gerald Brown, Charlie Cambridge

(Diné), Della Warrior, Sam English, and Viola Hatch have come forward and recounted those days, so long ago, when they stood up to the powers that be and made change.

To understand this movement, we must acknowledge that the NIYC was built on a long tradition of pan-Indian organization extending back to the early twentieth century. In chapter 1, I begin the story during America's so-called progressive era, when Carlos Montezuma, M.D. (Yavapai), Gertrude Bonnin (Sioux), Charles Eastman, M.D. (Sioux), and their colleagues, who helped found the Society of American Indians (SAI) in 1911, advocated racial uplift by calling for citizenship rights and self-determination. These early reformers also firmly believed in the assimilation and acculturation of Native people. If Indians were going to survive, Montezuma and other SAI members reasoned, they had to adopt the ways of the outside white world, thus shedding their traditional culture and identity. Their platform remained dominant in the public sphere until the 1930s and the advent of the Indian New Deal.[9]

As economic depression gripped the nation and the greater global community, President Franklin D. Roosevelt adopted a program to tackle the crisis. The president surrounded himself with a cadre of innovative minds who devised radical new solutions to age-old problems. As his commissioner of Indian Affairs, FDR nominated John Collier, a social reformer who had worked with immigrant communities in New York City before founding the American Indian Defense Association in 1923. Collier's program for Indian reorganization sought to overturn the government's long-standing policy of assimilation. The commissioner hoped to preserve Native cultures and traditions by protecting the tribal land base, upholding treaty rights, and extending a greater degree of self-determination to Indian communities. His "Indian New Deal" led to a backlash among Native people who subscribed to the SAI's goals of acculturation. Such opposition coalesced under the banner of the American Indian Federation (AIF), which fought throughout the 1930s to overturn the Indian Reorganization Act.[10]

Although the AIF failed in its quest, its platform of assimilation and of abolition of the BIA remained a flash point in Indian policy during the 1940s and 1950s, when the federal government set a new agenda to eliminate "the Indian problem" once and for all. This impulse emerged out of the civic nationalism of the postwar sociopolitical milieu. According to adherents of this doctrine, all people—regardless of ethnicity, creed, or color—should be incorporated into American society. Such integration, however, was contingent upon abiding by white America's culture and values. In the case of Native peoples, Congress created the Indian Claims Commission (ICC) to pay off tribes for past injustices, sever the federal government's trust responsibilities, and force Native people into the American mainstream. The approach was flawed from the start, as ICC officials gave tribes just five years to file and prove their claims. The subsequent policy of termination, which called for the dismantlement of the reservation system and an end to the federal government's trust responsibilities, turned out to be an even more pressing issue. Proponents of termination eventually forced through House Concurrent Resolution 108, a measure that ultimately threatened to eliminate Native American political and territorial sovereignty.[11]

To confront this changing landscape, former Native bureau employees D'Arcy McNickle (Flathead), Archie Phinney (Nez Perce), Ruth Muskrat Bronson (Cherokee), Charles Heacock (Sioux), and others founded the National Congress of American Indians to fight to preserve the legacy of the Indian New Deal. Beginning in 1944, the NCAI lobbied lawmakers and litigated in the courts for self-determination, tribal sovereignty, treaty rights, and territorial integrity. The birth of the NCAI marked a distinct shift in the focus of intertribal political organization, which abandoned the assimilationist doctrine of the SAI and the AIF for a program of Native cultural preservation.[12]

As the federal government's new termination policy gained momentum in the mid-1950s, Native leaders and their non-Native allies sought to confront this perceived threat to the future of Indian nations through two major student-oriented organizing initiatives. First—and the focus of chapter 2—was the Regional Indian Youth Council (RIYC). These annual gatherings, held throughout the Southwest, taught Native students the essentials of organization building and parliamentary process. Mel Thom, Joan Noble, Clyde

Warrior, Herb Blatchford, Bernadine Eschief (Shoshone-Bannock), Gerald Brown, and other future NIYC leaders ran in council elections, debated major issues facing Native America, and planned future gatherings. Although the councils never produced a uniform ideology, the RIYC stands as the first project aimed at creating an intertribal student organization, and it served as the organizational forebear to the NIYC.[13]

Just as students met in regional councils, University of Chicago professor Sol Tax, along with NCAI leaders such as D'Arcy Mc-Nickle and Helen Peterson (Sioux), hoped to encourage young Native people to question and challenge the government's agenda of assimilation and acculturation. They believed that if Indians were to survive as a distinct people, the younger generation needed to embrace the cornerstone principles of self-determination, sovereignty, cultural preservation, and protection of treaty rights. Throughout the 1950s and into the 1960s, they brought Native students together for the Workshop on American Indian Affairs, the subject of chapter 3. At these workshops, the organizers presented their philosophy during six intensive weeks of coursework. By the end of the decade a new generation of future leaders had the ideological and organizational tools to build the Red Power movement of the 1960s.[14]

All these young people needed was a spark to ignite the movement. In 1961, students from the workshops and the RIYC met in Chicago for the largest intertribal gathering in modern history, the American Indian Chicago Conference. They participated in group discussions with Native people of all generations and drafted the preamble to "The Declaration of Indian Purpose," a document that McNickle and the NCAI conceived to reaffirm the principles of self-determination, sovereignty, treaty rights, and cultural preservation. The Chicago Conference inspired the student participants to form a new, independent, national intertribal organization—the National Indian Youth Council. The founding of the NIYC serves as the main topic of discussion in chapter 4.[15]

Although these students embraced the ideals of their elders when forming the NIYC, they were children of a different era. As part of the sixties generation, which saw the world in dualistic terms of right and wrong, the NIYC founders adopted an entirely new set of tactics and body of rhetoric to fight for the principles they had inherited from their elders. In early 1964 the NIYC began publication of the first militant Red Power newspaper, *Americans Before Columbus*, which pulled few punches in its forceful commentary. Thom, Witt, Warrior, and others articulated a new ideology that was at once traditional, new, and even militant.

For the first few years of the decade, however, the NIYC failed to find a useful way to turn its words into action. Then, in 1964, the council found an issue that demanded action. In Washington State, game wardens began arresting Native fishers for fishing out of season, despite a series of nineteenth-century federal treaties that guaranteed the Puyallups, Nisquallys, and Muckleshoots the right to fish at "all usual and accustomed places." In response, NIYC activists launched a series of "fish-ins," which they modeled after the sit-ins that black students had employed in the South. The subject of chapter 5, the story of the fish-ins illuminates how council members risked arrest and bodily harm when they purposely violated state conservation laws by fishing out of season. Like civil rights activists, or perhaps even the yippies who burst onto the scene just a few years later, NIYC members recognized that they could use the media as a tool to propagate the issue of treaty rights and bring it to the fore of public conscience. The NIYC deftly secured the support of movie star Marlon Brando and contacted a host of media outlets to give the demonstrations and the issue of treaty rights the widest possible publicity. The fish-ins stood as the first instance of intertribal direct action in the modern era, making the NIYC the foremost Native activist organization in operation.[16]

The NIYC's sense of purpose only grew through the decade, as detailed in chapters 6 and 7. By 1966, SNCC activists called for "Black Power" and even began questioning the tactics and goals of their elders. Similarly, the NIYC adopted the slogan "Red Power," shocking the Indian establishment. The Red Power and Black Power movements, however, differed significantly. The militants in SNCC broke away from and challenged the ideological assumptions and goals of the larger African American civil rights movement. They refuted the ethos of integration and called for separation, so that black people could maintain their own institutions and nurture their own distinct culture. The Red Power warriors, alternatively, continued to support fully their elders' goals, albeit in a more militant manner. At times they criticized the NCAI, even referring to the organization's leaders as "Uncle Tomahawks," but at the end of the day, they stood on the same sideline. As Herb Blatchford told journalist Stan Steiner in 1967, "It started with the old people. . . . The youth, when they get together now, always meet on Indian land, always with the old tribal people."[17]

Besides direct action, NIYC activists believed that the best way to propagate the high ideals of their elders was through Native control over Indian education. With the development of LBJ's Great Society and the passage of the Economic Opportunity Act in 1964, new possibilities and sources of funding opened up for Indians seeking to improve education. The NIYC backed scholarships earmarked for Native students, financed sweeping studies of Indian schools, and launched new educational endeavors that fostered traditional Native culture. At the same time, activists within the organization became increasingly militant, attacking the Indian Bureau, the Office of Economic Opportunity, and even the NCAI. By the late 1960s the NIYC leadership's attempt to define the organization as both a respectable educational agency and a militant Red Power front proved increasingly difficult. In the end, the balancing act failed and tore the council apart.[18]

But that was not the end of the NIYC. As SDS and SNCC disintegrated in the late 1960s and early 1970s, the NIYC somehow managed to patch itself together and pull itself up. Hence, *Red Power Rising* concludes with the revival and expansion of the organization, which can be largely attributed to the efforts of Gerald Wilkinson (Cherokee) who served as executive director from 1969 until his death in 1989. Wilkinson recognized that if the council hoped to survive, it must cut ineffective programs while initiating new, more imaginative ones. Wilkinson grew the organization's membership, opened new offices, and secured multiple sources of funding. He guided the council through the 1970s and 1980s, cementing the NIYC's legacy as the second-oldest intertribal organization in operation.

Within the following pages, I hope to contribute to our growing knowledge of American Indian activism by uncovering the roots of

Red Power and intertribal student activism. I strive to show how a small yet totally dedicated group of Native students fought for the betterment of all tribal peoples. Not always successful and often encountering immense obstacles, these leaders nevertheless threw themselves into what they saw as a great battle for the very survival of American Indian nations. Theirs is a story of triumph and failure, tragedy and hope, determination and adversity. And it is a story that is long overdue.

CHAPTER 1

"Freedom for Our People"

Foundations of a Movement

Clyde Warrior always had a great deal of respect for tradition. He learned the Ponca language from his grandparents, memorized traditional ceremonies and songs, and became a highly respected fancy dancer. Warrior also had only admiration for those elders who had fought for Native people throughout history. When the National Indian Youth Council set about establishing a scholarship for college-bound Native youth, Warrior suggested they name it the Geronimo Scholarship, in honor of "a true Indian patriot." Clyde Warrior was not alone in this regard. When he and other students gathered in Gallup, New Mexico, to draw up the NIYC's articles of incorporation, they recognized "the inherent strength of the American Indian heritage" and paid tribute to the ancestors who had come before them in their quest to build a brighter future for all Native peoples.[1]

Indeed, movements for social change do not emerge in a vacuum. They are built upon precedent, they incorporate and borrow ideas from the past, and they may find inspiration from contemporaries. This certainly proves true for the NIYC and the origins of the Red Power movement. To be sure, those young people who founded the council in 1961 started something new and different. They laid out a militant pan-Indian ideology and incorporated direct action methods into the Native struggle for sovereignty, self-determination, treaty rights, and cultural preservation. Still, their movement can be characterized as an evolution in intertribalism.

They followed on the heels of earlier generations, even while they blazed a new trail.

Intertribalism or pan-Indianism—that is, Native peoples from different backgrounds and parts of Indian country coming together in common purpose—is nothing new. Various tribes have united for mutual benefit throughout history. Some of the most common examples include the Haudenosaunees, or Iroquois League of Six Nations, which brought many of the Iroquoian-speaking peoples along the Atlantic seaboard into confederacy. The Senecas, the Oneidas, the Cayugas, the Onondagas, the Mohawks, and late, the Tuscaroras found it expedient for defensive purposes and regional stability to develop a political alliance. Similarly, just to the west, Algonquian tribes such as the Shawnees, the Ottawas, the Delawares, the Potawatomies, and the Miamis, among others, united to challenge, first, the powerful Iroquois League and, later, European invaders. Under the great Ottawa chief Pontiac, Algonquian tribes came together in the early 1760s to deal the British Army a series of devastating blows west of the Appalachian Mountains. A few decades later, many tribes in the region coalesced under the leadership of the Shawnee leader Blue Jacket and the Miami chieftain Little Turtle to defend their lands against the newly independent United States.[2]

Such intertribalism also found form west of the Mississippi. In the Spanish colony of New Mexico, the various pueblos of the Rio Grande valley overcame linguistic differences and united in 1680, driving their colonizers out of the region. The Pueblo Revolt stands as one of the most resounding Indian victories since the European invasion—it took twelve years and an invitation to return before the Spanish made their way back into New Mexico. Out on the Great Plains, Siouan-speaking tribes forged alliances and staked out a massive inland empire. As white Americans moved west, they ran up against the Ihanktunwans, Tetonwans, and Isanti Sioux, as well as the Northern Cheyennes. The United States suffered some crushing defeats before overcoming the alliance and assuming control of the region.[3]

Back in those days, language, common culture, and region proved to be the greatest factors in the development of intertribalism. The alliance the Shawnee chief Tecumseh forged remains the one great exception. Television documentaries and popular history books have portrayed Tecumseh as a great military leader—a warrior whose prowess, bravery, and fighting skills made him the stuff of legend. No doubt Tecumseh was a force to be reckoned with on the battlefield, but even more significant was his political savvy. He recognized that all Native people—not just those in his Ohio River valley homeland—must join forces and work together in confronting the onslaught of white expansion. Tecumseh therefore looked beyond language, culture, and region, traveling south to forge friendships with different tribes. Tecumseh only partially succeeded in realizing his vision. He did develop a wide alliance, but the War of 1812 broke out before he could solidify his power. The great Indian leader died at the Battle of Thames River toward the end of the war, and his dream of a great intertribal alliance that brought all Native people together in common purpose was put on hold.[4]

Nearly one hundred years later, in October 1911, Professor Fayette A. McKenzie of the Ohio State University's Sociology Department called together the best-known college educated Indians in America with the purpose of establishing the first Indian-controlled intertribal organization. Like the predominantly white Indian rights groups of the period, such as the Women's National Indian Association or the Indian Rights Association, this new entity was very much a product of America's "progressive era," a time of reform and change. The laissez-faire capitalism and great industrial growth of the late nineteenth century created fissures in the social fabric of the nation, thus prompting a vast array of new organizations and special interest groups that sought social justice, greater governmental oversight of business, and widened political rights. White progressive reformers lambasted the treatment of Native people and insisted that with proper training and new policies that encouraged acculturation, American Indians would become "productive" U.S. citizens. The Native leaders who met in Columbus during the autumn of 1911 shared this nominally progressive approach to Indian affairs. Calling themselves the Society of American Indians (SAI), the founding members believed that Native people needed to move away from the past, reject tradition and custom, and embrace currents of "modern civilization."[5]

Carlos Montezuma, Charles Eastman, Sherman Coolidge (Arapahoe), Thomas Sloan (Omaha), Henry Roe Cloud (Winnebago), Elizabeth Roe Cloud (Ojibwe), Arthur C. Parker (Seneca), Charles Daganett (Peoria), and Gertrude Bonnin were among the founding members who played pivotal roles in the SAI. Their initial platform centered around three themes: assimilation, self-help, and social justice. SAI members aligned themselves with the prohibition movement and other progressive causes of the day. They rejected notions of racial superiority or inferiority but believed that "natural laws of social evolution" placed Native people below Europeans. Only through hard work, individual initiative, citizenship, and perseverance could the Indian advance up the hierarchical ladder. Moreover, the government could make strides toward social justice by breaking up the reservations and continuing its policy of allotment.[6]

No one in the SAI voiced this platform of assimilation and self-help as forcefully as Dr. Carlos Montezuma. Born in Yavapai country in southern Arizona and adopted by whites at a young age, Montezuma attended the University of Illinois before earning his medical degree in 1889 at the Chicago Medical School. Montezuma eventually developed a close friendship with Richard Henry Pratt while serving as a physician at the Carlisle Indian School. As head of Carlisle, Pratt maintained that Indian identity and culture needed to be wiped away. He developed an ethnocentric curriculum that more or less forced students to shed their tribal backgrounds and adopt white customs and habits. It was Pratt who coined the famous slogan "Kill the Indian, and save the man." Mirroring Pratt, Montezuma believed that traditional Indian culture held Native Americans back. In order to overcome this handicap, Indians, especially children, should be thrust into the mainstream of American society, rather than secluded and isolated on reservations. In a speech delivered before the University of Illinois's Illini Club, Montezuma declared, "Away with your excuses to keep the Indian children from enjoying the Christian homes of our eastern states! It is not climate or civilization that kills my people. It is bondage to the

tribe, and ignorance of the advantages of civilized life that kills."
He concluded that Indians "must be surrounded with that which is
highest and best in order to rise above the inherited bad tendencies
of the race."[7]

Montezuma's call for complete assimilation eventually led him to
target the Office of Indian Affairs for perpetuating the reservation
system and slowing the process of acculturation. He insisted the
SAI stand firm—without dissent—against the government agency
and adopt a resolution calling for its abolition. The society, however,
refused to pass any sweeping condemnation of the federal government, as many members believed they could reform the system
from within. So in 1915, at the SAI annual meeting in Lawrence,
Kansas, Montezuma went on the offensive, delivering his famous
speech "Let My People Go." He ridiculed the society for its hesitancy in condemning government oversight and launched into a
tirade against federal policies. "We are wards, we are not free!" he
exclaimed. "There is only one object for this Society of Indians to
work for, namely—'Freedom for our people.'" The Indian agency's
"blood stained paws" held Native people down by encouraging
"beggary, gambling, pauperism, and ruin," while reservations only
encouraged that "Indians remain as Indians."[8]

Although Montezuma influenced many of the SAI's rank-and-
file members, he remained at odds with the organization's leadership. A year after his fiery speech in Lawrence, he founded the
newsletter *Wassaja*, which he funded and distributed himself. Montezuma used the column "Arrow Points" to press his militant, un-
compromising stance on the Indian Bureau and to attack society
members who failed to fall in line with his thinking. He disparaged
SAI officers Arthur Parker and Sherman Coolidge for their efforts
to create a national American Indian Day to highlight Indian history and development. Indians needed to forget their past, Montezuma claimed; even the slightest hint of celebrating the traditional
culture of Native people was unacceptable.[9]

If Montezuma's broadsides against society members who failed
to fall in line with his rigid ideology were not enough, the controversy over the ritual use of peyote led to further fissures within the
SAI. Some influential members, such as Thomas Sloan, staunchly

supported peyoteism and the right of its adherents to conduct ceremonies as they saw fit. Others, such as the society's secretary, Gertrude Bonnin, felt differently. Bonnin, also known as Zitkala-Ša, joined Montezuma as one of the SAI's most outspoken members. An ex-Carlisle teacher, she was engaged to marry the physician before the two clashed over Pratt's curriculum at Carlisle. Zitkala-Ša argued that Indians should attend college or university rather than pursue outmoded industrial education. But more than anything, it was the emergence of peyoteism that bothered Bonnin; she believed that the hallucinations or visions that resulted from the ingestion of peyote corrupted Native people and inhibited their progress. She insisted that the SAI adopt a platform condemning the use of peyote and backing legislation to outlaw possession of the cactus.[10]

The society's internal struggles over peyote seemed minimal when compared with the profound ideological differences between the SAI and the only other intertribal organization of the era, the Brotherhood of North American Indians. Founded in Washington, D.C., just months after the SAI, the brotherhood adopted a platform that stood in stark contrast to the positions that Montezuma and Bonnin had staked out. Richard C. Adams (Delaware), founder and chief spokesman for the brotherhood, called for cultural retention, treaty rights, compensation from the federal government for lost lands, and the preservation of the reservation system. Due to its radical agenda that challenged the basic assumptions of the SAI and other progressive organizations of the day, the brotherhood never garnered the publicity or support that propelled the society. Moreover, severe criticism from both SAI leaders and the Indian Office led to the brotherhood's downfall just two years after its founding.[11]

The society, in contrast, lasted as a viable organization until 1923, when Carlos Montezuma died. That same year the SAI held its final conference. Montezuma's death undoubtedly contributed to the society's demise, as did America's changing social and political climate. In 1924, Congress passed the Indian Citizenship Act, which conferred all the rights and privileges of American citizenship on Native people. The act seemed to negate much of the SAI's purpose, leading to waning interest in the organization. Moreover, the

progressive impulse of the twentieth century's first two decades
had come to an end.

Many SAI leaders abandoned Indian affairs, but others continued
to involve themselves in some capacity. Charles Eastman served
as the head chief of the Teepee Order of America, an urban-based,
fraternal Indian organization. Toward the end of his life, however,
the onetime assimilationist dropped out of the mainstream and
returned to his Sioux tribal roots in the remote reaches of Minnesota. In 1926, Gertrude Bonnin pieced together remnants of the SAI
and founded the National Council of American Indians, an intertribal outfit geared toward organizing the Native vote. Although
Bonnin's organization claimed members from fifty-one tribes, it
never achieved the widespread appeal or prominence of the SAI.
By the 1940s, her council had faded into obscurity.[12]

If Eastman and Bonnin held together some semblance of intertribal organization—no matter how tenuous—Henry Roe Cloud
proved to be the one SAI leader who would most deeply affect the
course of federal Indian policy. The Brookings Institution drafted
the Yale graduate and educator to join a government-sponsored
research group commissioned to conduct a full-scale study of Indian policy and tribal conditions. The secretary of the interior at
the time, Hubert Work, had come under immense pressure from
reformers critical of the Indian Office and its way of doing things.
The result was the 1928 publication of *The Problem of Indian Administration*, better known as the Meriam Report.[13]

This massive indictment declared the federal government's policies of assimilation and allotment complete failures. Indians lived
in poverty, destitution, and misery, with little hope of progress, the
report asserted. The Indian Office's education of Native children
needed revision; the vocational training taught in many Indian
schools was antiquated, while boarding schools stunted growth
by tearing young children away from their home communities. To
amend the horrendous situation, Roe Cloud, Lewis Meriam, and the
report's other primary authors detailed necessary reforms in health
care, education, economic development, family and community life,
and policy formulation in general. The 872-page survey was the first
of its kind and ultimately set a new course in federal Indian policy.[14]

It took a new president, however, to bring about change. In 1932, in the midst of the nation's worst economic depression, the American people elected Franklin D. Roosevelt to the presidency. Roosevelt promptly appointed a cadre of visionaries and intellectuals known as the Brain Trust to steer the country in a new direction. Harold Ickes landed the job as secretary of the interior and in turn nominated John Collier as the new commissioner of Indian Affairs. Collier would prove to be the most influential commissioner in the agency's history, laying down a radical new direction in Indian policy.[15]

For years, Collier, like Carlos Montezuma, had been one of the agency's greatest critics. He also shared Montezuma's refusal to compromise, his zealotry, and his rigid thinking. But unlike Montezuma, Collier lauded Native culture and embraced an agenda of cultural retention and preservation. In 1923, the same year the SAI disbanded, he established the American Indian Defense Association (AIDA), which emerged as the foremost defender of the Indian land base and Native control over natural resources on tribally owned land. The AIDA also took issue with continued efforts to assimilate Native people. Collier infuriated missionaries and other Christian reformers when he argued that religious proselytizing exploited and degraded Indians. He defended the Indians' rights to their cultural traditions, acknowledging the value in Native religion, art, and customs. Just because these practices seemed foreign to whites did not mean that Native cultures were devoid of value. Collier even went a step further, asserting that Euro-American culture had much to learn from American Indians, who stood as the "possessors and users of the fundamental secret of human life." Their communalism, sense of shared identity, and spirituality could very well redeem the United States.[16]

To put it mildly, Collier and his organization rocked the boat in Indian Affairs, challenging the very foundations that had been in place for nearly fifty years. He even angered Gertrude Bonnin and her National Council of American Indians, the only remaining intertribal political association of the period. Initially, the two organizations worked together, but Bonnin believed that the AIDA and, more specifically, Collier were inflammatory in their rhetoric.

She accused Collier of being as "oppressive as the Indian Bureau" in his zealous crusade against assimilation. Zitkala-Ša maintained that the Indians whom Collier was politicizing "know little or nothing about" bureau policies. Collier shot back that Native people had "plenty of sense to understand" the issues. He reprimanded Bonnin, stating, "You do not own the Indians in the United States, and . . . if you did own the Indians it would be a sad situation for the Indians."[17]

Collier and the AIDA remained at odds with Bonnin and many other Indian reform organizations. The publication of the Meriam Report, however, elevated Collier and gave his philosophical stance credence. After all, he had been clamoring for years about the issues raised in the report. His newfound stature and the growing respect for the AIDA's work earned him the job of commissioner of Indian Affairs. Once in office, Collier launched an ambitious new platform to promulgate his vision of tribalism, self-determination, cultural retention, sovereignty, treaty rights, and economic development for Native peoples. He backed New Deal projects that would benefit Native people, such as an Indian branch of the Civilian Conservation Corps and $15 million in appropriations for Works Progress Administration and National Youth Administration projects. He secured funds to build new health care facilities and roads on reservations. He assumed responsibility for executive orders that reeled in the missionaries and their efforts to spread Christianity in Indian schools through compulsory church attendance. He instituted a Native-preference hiring policy within the bureau. In stark contrast to past federal policy, he called for an affirmation of Indians' right to practice freely their traditional Native religions.[18]

At the same time, there was a dark side to Collier's new Indian policy. So zealous in his crusade, the new commissioner often overlooked the views of the very people he sought to help. Nowhere was this clearer than in his dealings with the Navajo Nation. In an effort to preserve grazing land and arrest soil erosion on the Navajo reservation, the commissioner authorized a program of massive livestock reduction. Diné families watched helplessly as government agents set about killing large portions of their herds. In theory, individuals would receive compensation for their losses, but too often the government failed to live up to this promise. From a Navajo perspective, Collier's program seemed like pointless slaughter and yet another example of American aggression. To this day, many of the Diné remember the Indian New Deal not as a time of progress and positive reform but as a dark age of oppression and Biligáana (outsider, or white) duplicity.[19]

With obvious exceptions, many of Collier's programs helped rejuvenate Indian culture and curb widespread unemployment on the reservations. The commissioner's greatest feat proved to be the Indian Reorganization Act (IRA), or the Wheeler-Howard Act, named after its sponsors, Senator Burton K. Wheeler of Montana and Representative Edgar Howard of Nebraska. The act completely transformed the Office of Indian Affairs. The initial bill bolstered self-determination through the creation of new tribal governments that would eventually assume the duties held by the Department of the Interior. The IRA also sought the preservation of Indian culture through an educational program that rejected the assimilative notions of the past and encouraged children to embrace their Native heritage. Another section would restore a large portion of allotted Indian land that the federal government had held as surplus.

Many tribal leaders remained skeptical of Collier's IRA proposal. The commissioner therefore scheduled regional meetings across Indian country in which he and his Indian backers—including Henry Roe Cloud—explained and gained support for the bill. The meetings also gave Collier and his allies the opportunity to press the commissioner's new vision of sovereignty, self-determination, tribalism, and cultural renewal. Most Indians concurred with Collier, believing his program promised an improvement upon the ill-conceived policies of the past. In all, 178 tribes and bands approved reorganization.[20]

Still, 78 tribes voted against the IRA. The eastern Iroquois of New York and Pennsylvania, for example, overwhelmingly rejected Collier's plan. These tribes adhered to a notion of sovereignty that rejected any and all federal initiatives, no matter how enlightened or revolutionary. Many Haudenosaunees reserved their loyalty solely for their own tribe. As one tribal leader stated, "We are not citizens of the United States. . . . We must insist on our rights as a separate

territory not responsible to any other government. We must rule
ourselves." The eastern Iroquois were by no means the only Indians
to reject Collier's platform. Besides many tribes in California and
the Yakama Nation of Washington State, the Navajo Nation could
never forget the commissioner's policy of livestock reduction. The
Diné, the largest tribe in the United States, therefore rejected Collier
and his IRA.[21]

The reorientation in Indian policy also drew the ire of other Native people. While Collier had strong Indian supporters within the
bureau, a minority of Indians continued to fight his reorganization
plan, lobbying for the IRA's immediate revocation. This faction,
which fundamentally disagreed with Collier's vision, adhered to
the Montezuman philosophy of assimilation, allotment, citizenship, and anti-bureauism. They hated the Office of Indian Affairs
and its wardship over Indians. Even more, they hated John Collier, his stance on cultural relativism, and his "back to the blanket"
policies. The men and women of this faction revered Carlos Montezuma and held him up as their figurehead. They joined together
to fight Collier and established the most significant intertribal organization since the SAI. They called themselves the American Indian
Federation.

When the AIF held its first national meeting in Gallup, New
Mexico, August 27–28, 1934, delegates from California, Oklahoma,
Arizona, and New Mexico attended. Many of its founding members came from the Indian National Confederacy of Oklahoma, an
assimilation-minded organization that advocated progress through
self-help. Other federation members, such as Thomas Sloan, had
been leaders in the Society of American Indians. In a sense, the AIF
was the logical extension of the SAI; the AIF's platform called for
the assimilation of Native people into mainstream white America.
For this to happen, the Indian Office would have to be abolished,
the IRA overturned, and John Collier removed as commissioner of
Indian Affairs.[22]

The mastermind behind the impetus of the AIF was O. K. Chandler, a mixed-blood Cherokee from Oklahoma, whom Interior Department officials would later describe as angry and vindictive.
"When he talks of his self-made enemies his voice shakes, his eyes

gleam and his hands tremble," wrote Collier's field representative Floyd LaRoche. Chandler had always been politically conservative, identifying with the Republican Party. In the 1920s and early 1930s, however, he maintained cordial relations with advocates of Indian reform—John Collier included. Indeed, Chandler subscribed to the AIDA's publication, which, he told Collier, he read "with great interest." Up until 1934, his anti-bureauism was either publicly muted or nonexistent. Corresponding with Collier on a semiregular basis, in June of 1933 Chandler sent the newly appointed commissioner his recommendations for Oklahoma Indians who would be qualified Indian Office employees. Given this background, why did he form the AIF? Evidence suggests it was because Chandler himself sought a position in the government, which was ultimately rejected.[23]

If Chandler emerged as the AIF's mastermind, Joseph Bruner (Creek), elected as the organization's first president, served as its figurehead. A wealthy beneficiary of the Dawes Act from eastern Oklahoma, Bruner had his hand in many pots, amassing a fortune through oil speculation, real estate, farming, and insurance. Like Chandler, he had enjoyed cordial relations with Collier and the Indian Office. The future AIF president invited the commissioner to Oklahoma to meet with Native leaders, whom Collier "received with great pleasure." Described as "good natured and not too intelligent," Bruner, according to fellow Creek A. R. Perryman, was "easily misled and kept active in the cause by being elected president of the organization from year to year." His good nature, however, was questionable. Bruner ascribed to old southern racial prejudices and was outraged when the Indian Office appointed an African American nurse to a position in the Sequoyah Training School in Tahlequah, Oklahoma. The AIF president wrote to Secretary Ickes, declaring that he was "formally protesting against the appointment of negroes in any capacity in the Indian Service of the United States Government." Bruner contended that bureau officials should remove the nurse and replace her with a white woman.[24]

Bruner's racism seemed almost quaint in comparison with the far-right affiliations of Seneca activist Alice Jemison. She had befriended American fascist leader James True, whom she described as a "fine, sincere, Christian gentleman." The future AIF secretary also contributed articles to the *Defender* and the *Christian Free Press*, two extreme right-wing publications. As with Chandler and Bruner, Jemison's politics became known only when Collier launched the IRA. Earlier, Jemison had worked for the Erie County Women's Democratic Party and had been involved in local tribal politics. Though she feared big government and overbearing federal authority, she staunchly advocated Indian civil rights. In 1933, as Ickes and Roosevelt shopped for a new commissioner of Indian Affairs, Jemison backed Joseph Latimer, Montezuma's faithful attorney. Concurring with her Yavapai Apache hero that Indians needed to shed their past and assimilate into American society, she saw Collier's appointment as an outrage and a step away from progress.[25]

Chandler, Bruner, and Jemison thus emerged as the most vociferous members of the AIF. They maintained that the federation stood as the only remaining intertribal organization (Gertrude Bonnin's National Council of American Indians had since faded into obscurity) and therefore best represented the interests of Native peoples. Initially, the AIF founders posited that the IRA and Collier's bureau undermined the Indians' bid for full American citizenship. In one of their first statements, they petitioned President Roosevelt to strike down the commissioner's misguided policies. The Citizenship Act of 1924 had given Indians hope that at last they would be free from government wardship and possess all the benefits and rights guaranteed under the Constitution. By reorganizing the tribes, Collier had "maliciously and flagrantly ignored the rights given the Indian by virtue of the greatest gift the American Government can bestow—citizenship."[26]

The AIF also presented its case for citizenship, assimilation, and the abolition of the Office of Indian Affairs through articles appearing in national publications. In early 1935, Bruner penned an essay for the right-wing magazine *National Republic*, entitled "The Indian Demands Justice." Claiming to speak for all Native people, Bruner asserted that they "revere the American flag" and "shall ever be loyal to it." The American Indian merely sought equal rights, as guaranteed under the Constitution. "The Indian today," Bruner wrote, "is more sorely disappointed with his treatment, or mistreatment, by the present heads of the Indian Bureau, more restless

and more uneasy than at any time during his Bureau enslavement."
In order to appeal to his conservative audience, the AIF president
painted Collier's agency as a "gigantic octopus" that created "federal jobs for thousands of political employees" and wasted tax-
payers' money.[27]

The AIF's initial strategy of arguing its case for assimilation and
citizenship through petitions and articles had little effect on federal Indian policy. In 1935, Congress debated the Thomas-Rogers
Bill, which sought to extend the provisions of the IRA to Indians in
Oklahoma. Changing strategies, the AIF began accusing the Indian
Office of being under the influence of the Soviet Union and argued
that the bill was a "communistic scheme" devised by the commissioner and the American Civil Liberties Union (ACLU). Bruner
challenged Collier to come to Oklahoma to talk about his policy
and his connection with the ACLU. "[Collier] has been an associate and admirer of radicals, liberals, free thinkers, and communists
for the past twenty years or more," Bruner contended. His association with the ACLU, an organization the federation believed to
be a Stalinist front, was offered as evidence of the commissioner's
duplicity.[28]

The passage of the Oklahoma Indian Welfare Act, which extended the provisions of the IRA to tribes in Oklahoma, pushed
the AIF to adopt even more inflammatory, quasi-religious rhetoric. At their 1936 conference in Salt Lake City, federation members
proclaimed the United States "a Christian nation, colonized and
established by Christians with a Government founded upon Christian principles and teachings." It was the organization's "sacred
duty to the Cross and the Flag" to fight atheism, communism, and
John Collier: "[We] solemnly pledge our lives, our property, our resources, everything which we do possess to loyal, patriotic service
to America, our homeland, and the preservation of Christianity and
our American form of Christian Government."[29]

The AIF's drift to the extreme right provided an opportunity for
Collier to investigate the organization and gather evidence of its
fascist affiliations. The commissioner linked Bruner with the ex-
tremist William Dudley Pelley and the Silver Shirts of America,
while associating Jemison with the Militant Christian Patriots and

the James True Associates. Collier also identified AIF member Earl
Towner as a Nazi sympathizer and a member of the German American Bund. A Hoopa from California, Towner once proclaimed that
Adolf Hitler had the spirit of an Indian prophet. He depicted Franklin Roosevelt, on the other hand, as a "dirty, stinking Jew" whose
real name was "Rosenfelt." According to Towner, FDR's "Jew Deal"
was a communist conspiracy responsible for holding Native people
in reservation concentration camps. The evidence Collier obtained
proved damning. He went on the offensive and presented his
case, accusing the AIF of being a subversive, un-American, fascist
organization.[30]

In response to Collier and to similar allegations made by the
ACLU, Chandler wrote the pamphlet *Now Who's Un-American?*—a
sweeping indictment that linked the Indian Office, the Department of
the Interior, and the ACLU with the Soviet Union. Chandler declared
that "red radical forces" had infiltrated the federal government, undermined America's Christian heritage, and imposed a state of communism on Indian tribes. He accused Collier of segregating Native
people on reservations and teaching them to be Indians rather than
American citizens. Moreover, he asserted that the government's Indian schools replaced Christian education with the instruction of
Indian languages, music, and art that harmed Native pupils and perpetuated antiquated traditions. The IRA and the Oklahoma Indian
Welfare Act were clearly "patterned after Soviet Russia," while reservations stood as the Indian Office's counterpart to the sovkhozes,
or state farms, found in the USSR. "THIS IS COMMUNISM," boomed
Chandler, and the present administration had to go.[31]

The struggle between Collier and the AIF climaxed when they
met before the House Committee on Un-American Propaganda
and Activities in 1938 and the House Committee on Indian Affairs
two years later. In round one, the two sides exchanged barbs over
supposedly unpatriotic leanings. Collier accused the AIF of Nazism
and pointed to the members' association with "fifth column" organizations. For their part, the AIF hammered home the communist
tendencies of Collier and Secretary of the Interior Ickes.[32]

By the second round, internal clashes over the Settlement Bill, a
proposal that called for the complete resolution of all Indian claims

against the U.S. government, had weakened the AIF. Specifically, the bill stated that Congress would pay three thousand dollars to "each enrolled, recognized, or allotted individual Indian, or his or her heirs who have agreed to accept the full responsibilities of American citizenship." This would constitute the "full, final, and complete settlement" between Native people and the federal government. Bruner strongly supported the measure, as did many Oklahoma Indians who favored assimilation. Jemison, however, believed the bill broke with the AIF's original aims of no compromise with the government—no matter what the issue. Jemison felt that Bruner was only self-interested and had reneged on his original commitment to destroy the Indian Office. Hence, when Jemison and Chandler appeared before the House Committee on Indian Affairs to testify on behalf of Senate Bill 2103, which had exempted certain tribes from the IRA, their federation stood on its last leg.[33]

Chandler and Jemison found common cause in their support for S. 2103, but it would prove to be their last stand. During the congressional hearings, the two leaders were on the defensive. Collier again presented evidence of their fascist affiliations, showcasing Towner's Nazi sympathies and Jemison's far-right publications. For her part, the Seneca activist spent most of the hearing rebutting Collier's accusations. She toned down her extreme anticommunist rhetoric and insisted that the AIF remained a loyal, patriotic organization that disdained Collier's policies but supported the American government. Jemison tried to discredit the commissioner by attacking his administrative assistant, D'Arcy McNickle, who had criticized Christian missionary activity on Indian reservations. Her attack, however, fell flat, as the committee seemed more interested in her political leanings. The hearings went on for ten days, and at their conclusion Jemison and Chandler limped away, failing in their effort to convince key legislators that they should revoke the IRA. By 1940 the AIF's membership had dropped off precipitously. Bruner and Jemison went their separate ways and faded from the national political scene, leaving Chandler to direct AIF activities during the organization's twilight years.[34]

Collier resigned as commissioner of Indian Affairs in 1945. Before leaving the bureau, however, he recognized the mounting threat to tribalism and the Indian land base among lawmakers in the House and Senate. Directly after the war they began to advocate for the termination of federal trust responsibilities and the establishment of an Indian Claims Commission, essentially a revised settlement bill, minus the payments of three thousand dollars. The new ICC would settle the score with Native people by paying off tribes for lost land and resources. In the minds of its architects, the ICC would get the federal government out of Indian business once and for all.[35]

This new platform reflected the emergent civic nationalism that arrived in the wake of World War II. As historian Gary Gerstle explains, the global conflagration had made clear the dangers of fascism and racial nationalism, leading Americans to open the nation's doors to minority groups whom they had previously shut out. For civic nationalists, however, cultural pluralism failed to show up on the radar. Integration into the body politic and the greater American nation meant doing away with difference, including separate tribal affiliations. Collier and like-minded Indians employed in the bureau recognized the threat that this new civic nationalist milieu posed to tribal sovereignty, cultural preservation, treaty rights, and territorial integrity. Even before the war ended, as the tide of civic nationalism grew, D'Arcy McNickle, Archie Phinney, Ruth Muskrat Bronson, Charles Heacock, and other Indian Office employees took steps to establish an organization that would combat federal efforts to dismantle the spirit of the IRA and would help tribes receive just settlements from the Indian Claims Commission.[36]

In May 1944 this core group of women and men met in Chicago, where they organized themselves into a steering committee. Whether or not they knew of Gertrude Bonnin's earlier association is unclear, but McNickle, Phinney, Bronson, Heacock, and the others serving on the steering committee chose the provisional name "National Council of American Indians." They agreed that only Indians should be members and that in order to prevent any conflict of interest, the new organization should maintain its independence, avoiding alignment with other minority groups. The founding members also drafted their council's constitution and bylaws. Based on the constitution for the Federal Employees Union, the document called for an executive committee consisting of a president, two vice presidents, and seven committee members, all of whom delegates would elect at the organization's annual national convention. The constitution further outlined the committee's powers and duties, which included appointing an executive secretary and a treasurer.[37]

The steering committee's next order of business was bringing together Native leaders from throughout Indian country and choosing a location for the inaugural conference. Though it had the largest Native population, they rejected Oklahoma, which was the birthplace of the AIF, as a "particularly bad place to organize Indians." Instead, the founders decided on Denver, which they favored for its central location and proximity to many western reservations. Enlisting participants proved more difficult. Using the Indian Office's field organization as their model, the steering committee divided Indian country into nine regions. From there committee members contacted tribal governments and called on them to hold regional meetings to select delegates for the council's first national convention.[38]

Conscious of the lingering sentiment against government oversight in Indian country, the founders downplayed the organization's association with the federal agency. For his part, Collier chose to forgo the national meeting in Denver in order to avoid accusations that the Indian Office had organized and supported the council. Although the commissioner offered his undivided support, he warned the steering committee, "Not since the treacherous days of some twenty years ago has there been in Congress, and in some segments of public opinion, such danger to Indians, to their property, and to their wholeness of being." Extolling the merits of forming a united intertribal association, he asserted, "It can only be through competent and inspired group organization that the greater problems facing the whole Indian people will ever satisfactorily be dealt with."[39]

When the convention opened on November 15 at the Cosmopolitan Hotel in Denver, the steering committee registered eighty-one delegates from twenty-seven states and fifty tribes, making the meeting the largest and most diverse intertribal conference to date. An aura of excitement inundated the gathering. Heacock presided, but he allowed for an open forum where all delegates could voice

their views on issues facing Native America. After Sioux leader
Basil Two Bears gave an invocation that ended with a stirring war
whoop, the delegates got down to business, calling for the election
of the council's first slate of officers. A strong antibureau drive was
soon mounted to exclude Indian Office employees from holding office. But Ben Dwight, a former Choctaw chief who gave the keynote
address, sought to polish the image of Indians who worked in the
agency, lauding them for their courage and determination. One del-
egate from Oklahoma, also argued for their inclusion, proclaiming,
"Their hearts and souls are vested in the Indians—Indians first."
The delegates finally rejected the petition to exclude bureau employees. Showing their desire to establish as broad a base as possible, convention participants elected former AIF member Napoleon
Johnson (Cherokee) as the first president, while choosing government employee Ruth Bronson as executive secretary.[40]

Once they had elected officers, conference delegates hammered
out several resolutions. They decided to change the organization's
name to the National Congress of American Indians (NCAI) to
avoid any confusion with Bonnin's council. They created a legal
aid bureau that would represent tribes in need of counsel in land
claim cases. And they determined to lobby Congress on key social,
economic, and political problems facing Indians, including voting
rights, land claims, and job discrimination. This latter point was of
particular interest, as the council's founders believed the federal
government needed to offer Indians more opportunities to serve
in the National Park Service, the Border Patrol, the Fish and Wild-
life Service, and, most importantly, the Indian Office. Rather than
calling for the agency's abolition, the NCAI again broke with the
traditional stance against government oversight held by past intertribal organizations and argued for greater Indian participation in
the agency and the selection of a Native as commissioner of Indian
Affairs. Working within the system, many believed, offered the best
way to facilitate change.[41]

The architects of the NCAI had their share of detractors, especially when it came to their connection to the Indian Office. Tuscarora chief Clinton Rickard spoke for many of the Six Nations of
the Iroquois Confederacy when it came to tribal sovereignty and

treaty rights. Rickard believed that tribes remained independent nations outside of the U.S. government's control. In 1926 he had been instrumental in the formation of the Indian Defense League of America, which would eventually petition the United Nations to protest against attempts by Canada and the United States to assimilate them. Rickard even argued for UN membership for the Iroquois Confederacy. He maintained that the Indian Office—and NCAI by association—could not be trusted. Rickard's son, William, carried on this father's fight. Even though the Rickards and the NCAI leaders agreed on many issues, such as cultural preservation and treaty rights, the disparate camps would clash on more than one occasion.[42]

When the inaugural convention adjourned on November 17, 1944, McNickle, Phinney, and Heacock had triumphed, establishing what would turn out to be the sturdiest, most resilient organization in the history of intertribalism. Moreover, they completely transformed the nature of pan-Indian politics. Where assimilation and acculturation had been bedrocks of the SAI and the AIF, the new intertribalism embraced cultural preservation, treaty rights, and tribal sovereignty. Nearly all pan-Indian organizations or movements that came in the wake of the NCAI adhered to these basic ideals.

Through the remainder of the 1940s the NCAI concentrated on civil rights and Indian claims. The organization helped overturn discriminatory laws in Arizona and New Mexico that had barred Native people from the polls, arguing successfully that such laws violated the Citizenship Act of 1924. On the claims front, the organization supported tribal councils in their bid to secure their traditional land bases. The creation of the Indian Claims Commission had appeared to be a grand victory for tribes that had lost territory, but the ICC's backers in Congress turned out to be more concerned with severing the government's trust responsibilities than in serving justice to American Indians. The NCAI therefore wrangled with the ICC and often failed in its efforts to extract just compensation for many of the tribes the organization represented.[43]

By decade's end, government officials and media pundits called for the dismantlement of the reservation system. U.S. senator O. K. Armstrong and journalist Oswald Garrison Villard wrote pieces

for *Reader's Digest* and the *Christian Century*, respectively, arguing that the reservation system stood as the foremost obstacle to
the economic and social progress of the American Indian. Politicians on both sides of the political spectrum embraced Armstrong
and Villard's words, resulting in the passage of House Concurrent
Resolution 108. The measure, which officially called for the termination of the federal government's trust responsibilities, proved to
be an even greater threat to tribal sovereignty, treaty rights, Indian
identity, and the protection of Native people's land base. When the
federal government effectively terminated the Menominees of Wisconsin, the Klamaths of Oregon, and the Alabama-Coushattas of
Texas in 1954, NCAI executive secretary Helen Peterson leapt into
action. Under Peterson's leadership, the organization drew up the
"Declaration of Indian Rights," which rejected forced termination
and proclaimed the organization's support of federal guardianship
and the reservation system.[44]

The NCAI fought forced termination through the 1950s and well
into the 1960s. Many members of the organization, however, believed termination inevitable, maintaining that the best way to deal
with the government's policy was to prepare tribes for the future.
McNickle founded American Indian Development, Inc. (AID), to
help tribes attain self-sufficiency through economic progress. AID's
first annual report stated it was of "critical importance" that Indians develop management skills and assume control over tribal
resources. The organization later elaborated, noting that health
and education deficiencies, a lack of hospitals, underdeveloped resources, and rampant poverty remained serious problems facing
Indian country. Native people must "organize and manage industrial and business enterprises utilizing [their] own resources." Relying on funding from a host of philanthropic foundations, McNickle
held exploratory workshops in Brigham City, Utah; Tahlequah,
Oklahoma; and Phoenix, Arizona. For the workshops, he called for
participants with "leadership potentialities" who would eventually
help their respective tribes in development.[45]

AID eventually turned its attention to preparing Indian youth
for leadership roles. McNickle and other AID members realized
that the young people would have to wrangle with the great issues

facing Indian country, especially termination. How would future leaders manage their respective tribes' economic development? Would a lack of federal funds and government oversight result in outside corporate entities assuming control of tribal resources? Would the next generation share, respect, and uphold the values of their elders? Through annual summer workshops in Colorado, McNickle and his cohorts hoped to teach students the NCAI's vision for a brighter Indian future. Tribal sovereignty, treaty rights, cultural preservation, and self-determination remained the most salient issues facing Indian country; these stood as the ideals the next generation had to protect.[46]

As AID organized student workshops in Colorado, the New Mexico Association on Indian Affairs and college Indian clubs sponsored regional youth councils in the Southwest and beyond. Like AID members, the organizers of the regional councils harbored great concerns over the government's new policy of termination and its implications for tribes all over the United States. They too hoped to prepare future leaders to deal with such a policy. At the councils, Native students learned about organization building and parliamentary process. They discussed major issues confronting Indian country, including but not limited to termination. These regional councils, along with the workshops, paved the way for a new intertribal political movement.

Looking back, we can see that the leaders of the Native student movement that began taking shape in the 1950s took their cues from those who came before them. They embraced the ideals that informed the Indian New Deal and served as the bedrock principles of the National Congress of American Indians. Sovereignty, self-determination, treaty rights, and cultural preservation remained their foremost concerns. On the surface, it may appear that the founders of the Red Power movement had little in common with earlier pan-Indian organizations such as the Society of American Indians or the American Indian Federation. Ideologically speaking, this is true in regards to tribal sovereignty, treaty rights, and cultural preservation, which the SAI and the AIF steadfastly refuted in favor of assimilation and acculturation. But like those two forebears, the Red Power warriors of the National Indian Youth Council pulled few punches in their efforts to achieve their goals. One cannot help but notice similarities in the fiery rhetoric of Carlos Montezuma and that of NIYC leader Clyde Warrior. Most significantly, all believed that Native people must determine their own future. For the Native students who came of age under the long shadow of the federal government's termination policy, that future seemed especially precarious and uncertain. Let us now turn our attention to the Regional Indian Youth Council—the first effort to organize and prepare young people for the termination era.

CHAPTER 2

"We Are Born at a Time When the Indian People Need Us"

The Regional Indian Youth Council

On May 22, 1958, Charles Minton, the executive secretary of the New Mexico Association on Indian Affairs, boarded a plane in Albuquerque destined for Salt Lake City. After a choppy flight over the windswept canyons and high mountain peaks of the great Southwest, Minton proceeded by bus to Brigham Young University in Provo, Utah, where he met with university officials, as well as representatives of the Indian student club, Tribe of Many Feathers. Melvin Thom (Paiute), a sophomore engineering student, served as the club's president and acted as Minton's main liaison. Thom hoped to convince the NMAIA representative that BYU would be an ideal place for the following year's Regional Indian Youth Council. Minton expected hundreds of Indian students to attend the gathering and wanted to make sure that the campus and the university's facilities were adequate. In his log, he noted that the university prohibited smoking and offered neither coffee nor tea in vending machines or cafeterias. Disappointed, Minton lamented, "The beverage consumed on campus is milk."[1]

Such shortcomings aside, the NMAIA executive secretary believed that BYU would be a good location for the upcoming council because of its central western location. Indians from the Southwest, California, the Great Basin, and the Northwest could all attend, making the third annual RIYC the largest and most diverse inter-tribal youth gathering to date. Over the previous four years, the councils had grown tremendously. They began in 1955 when the

NMAIA, along with the University of New Mexico's Indian student organization, the Kiva Club, jointly sponsored the Santa Fe Indian youth council. The meeting's success gave rise to subsequent councils held annually. Initially, only Indians from New Mexico attended the meetings, but in 1957 the sponsors broadened the councils' scope and invited Native youth from all over the Southwest to participate.[2]

By the end of the 1950s, the Regional Indian Youth Council, as it came to be known, brought together hundreds of young women and men who, in intertribal fellowship, discussed and debated pertinent issues of the day. Though the NMAIA provided the funding and assumed responsibility for much of the groundwork, the students themselves ran the RIYC—they elected officers, organized workgroups, and determined where they would hold subsequent meetings. It was the first sustained effort at intertribal youth organization. The RIYC failed to articulate a uniform ideological statement or embrace fully the ideals of tribal sovereignty, self-determination, treaty rights and cultural preservation, but it did serve as a sounding board for varying opinions on Indian policy and the future of Native America. Students discussed the same issues that the National Congress of American Indians and American Indian Development, Inc., wrestled with, including termination, the Indian Claims Commission, and Indian education. Most significantly, however, former RIYC participants adopted the organizational framework and parliamentary process employed at the regional council when, years later, they went on to form their own, independent student organization—the National Indian Youth Council.

Not so long ago, historians generally characterized the 1950s as a time of relative peace and consensus. This holds true in the United States to an extent, but internationally the decade proved to be a time of conflict and resistance. For hundreds of years, European powers had extended their colonial control, whether directly or indirectly, over most of Africa and Asia. They did so by drawing political lines, creating new nation-states modeled after those in Europe, and establishing economic structures designed for their own benefit. After the international economic depression of the 1930s and the subsequent world war, indigenous peoples throughout the colonized world began revolting in full force against their European overlords.[3]

Weakened by World War II, France began losing its grip on many of its colonial possessions. Vietnamese fighters dealt the first blow. Coalescing under the leadership of the charismatic Marxist leader Ho Chi Minh, rebels hit the better-financed and better-equipped French army from all directions in a protracted guerrilla war. Ho's peasant army suffered high casualties, but they refused to give up their quest for full political sovereignty. The Viet Minh eventually outlasted the colonizers, ending the First Indochina War and creating the new state of North Vietnam. Halfway around the world in Algeria, rebels formed the Front de Libération Nationale (FLN), which launched a protracted bombing campaign in the capital city, Algiers. The conflict quickly descended into savagery, as the French army tortured suspected rebels and carried out a series of extralegal executions. For its part, the FLN targeted and murdered French civilians in the name of self-determination.[4]

Great Britain also had its share of colonial problems. In South Asia the Indian National Congress under the direction of Mohandas Gandhi employed passive resistance to secure self-determination. Even in the face of British atrocities, Gandhi insisted that violence was never justified and that the people of India must use reason to confront their oppressors. After struggling for decades, India and Pakistan eventually achieved independence shortly after World War II. The Mau Mau uprising in Kenya stood in stark contrast to India's predominantly nonviolent path. The Gikuyu people organized cells to attack government officials and civilians. In response, Great Britain unleashed its military might, killing thousands and detaining tens of thousands more in makeshift concentration camps. British actions proved to be both economically unviable and a public relations disaster, ultimately paving the way for Kenyan independence.[5]

The decolonization process in Africa and Asia remained part of a larger global trend of subaltern peoples seeking empowerment. In the United States, a nation built on colonialism and racial hierarchy, people of color challenged the status quo and vied for greater liberty and equality. In their struggles, however, they never took on the radicalism, militancy, or violence of their African or Asian counterparts, as postwar civic nationalists' calls for integration tempered movements for social change in 1950s America. African Americans broke down racial barriers by embracing the nonviolence of Gandhi's movement in India. In 1955 the mainstream of the civil rights movement commenced in Montgomery, Alabama, when black people peacefully refused to ride the city's racially segregated buses. Over the next several years, African Americans throughout the South employed protest marches, sit-downs, and other forms of civil disobedience in their attempt to overthrow the South's racial caste system of segregation and disenfranchisement.[6]

American Indians also rode the wave of decolonization. As Paul Rosier has contended, Native activists "sharpened their identities" and threw themselves into the fight against the federal government's attempts to undermine their sovereignty. The Iroquois League of Six Nations in New York State and Pennsylvania launched a major campaign to protect their sovereignty and halt government attempts to seize their land for massive public works projects. Many Haudenosaunee tribal leaders rejected American citizenship altogether and insisted the United States respect their status as a sovereign and independent people. Thus, when the Army Corps of Engineers unveiled its plan to dam the Allegheny River and flood Seneca land, Tuscarora leader Wallace "Mad Bear" Anderson organized sit-downs and other acts of civil disobedience in opposition. He also traveled to Cuba with a delegation of Miccosukee Indians from Florida to meet with Fidel Castro in hopes of gaining recognition of the political independence and full sovereignty of the First Nations located within the borders of the United States. Anderson went on to meet with North Vietnamese leaders on seven separate occasions.[7]

"Mad Bear" may have put up a good fight, but the most influential Native organization, the NCAI, chose to utilize more acceptable channels to bring about greater self-determination and sovereignty for American Indians. Litigating in the courts and lobbying in Congress, the NCAI fought the government's policy of forced termination after observing its devastating consequences among the

Klamath of Oregon and the Menominee of Wisconsin. The congress also continued its bid to secure compensation for tribes throughout the United States by presenting evidence before the Indian Claims Commission. Predominantly White-controlled Indian rights organizations, such as the New Mexico Association on Indian Affairs, followed the NCAI lead.[8]

If not as influential as the NCAI, the NMAIA had a much longer track record. In the early 1920s, the organization fought alongside John Collier's American Indian Defense Association and the All-Pueblo Council in their bid to protect Pueblo lands from Anglo and Hispanic land grabs. In succeeding years, the NMAIA continued fighting for the Pueblo Indians' territorial integrity and water rights. After World War II and the new impetus toward civic nationalism that came in its wake, working for a Native America that remained part of the greater United States became a key feature of the NMAIA. Along with sovereignty and treaty rights, it deemed citizenship and education as essential for the future of American Indians. By the 1950s, expanding educational opportunities for Indian children became the primary focus of the organization. NMAIA representatives visited and assessed Indian schools, while also sponsoring several scholarships and grants for Apache, Navajo, and Pueblo students. Its education committee emerged as the association's largest and best-endowed enterprise.[9]

Increasingly, the NMAIA earmarked funds for higher education, as universities provided more nuanced training for a new generation of leaders who would have to cope with the realities of termination. The association thus forged a partnership with the University of New Mexico's Kiva Club. Founded in 1952, the club acted as a support base for Native students attending UNM. The club also raised money for scholarships by holding annual Nizhoni Indian Dances, which brought in performers from local New Mexico tribes, including the pueblos of Zuni and Taos. Students set the admission rate at one dollar, and their profits enabled them to fund six scholarships.[10]

The Kiva Club could not claim to be the first university-based Indian student organization. In 1914, Native youth at the University of Oklahoma founded an organization they called the Oklushe

Degataga, Cherokee for "standing together." They eventually took the name "Sequoyah Indian Club" to honor the creator of the Cherokee syllabary. The founding members sought to promote interest in Indian lore and history. In subsequent years, the club fully embraced Native cultural heritage and intertribalism. The Sequoyah Club's updated 1936 constitution asserted that its purpose remained "perpetuating our tribal traditions and ceremonies, establishing brotherly friendship among ourselves . . . and adopting any policy that may advance our race in these United States." Officer titles included principal chief, medicine man, keeper of the wampum, and keeper of the tom-tom, while members had to claim at least 1/32 Indian blood.[11]

Beginning in the 1930s, the Sequoyah Club joined with other student associations in Oklahoma to hold the annual Ittanaha Conference, a predecessor of the Indian youth councils. The Ittanaha—Choctaw for "red man"—served as an umbrella organization for all of the college Indian clubs in Oklahoma. Adopting the motto "In the Indian youth is the hope of the Indian race," participants resolved to hold an annual meeting every April at a college or university in Oklahoma. Article 3 of the Ittanaha's constitution stated that all chapters had to secure the approval of school authorities and, like the Sequoyah Club, reserved membership to students with at least 1/32 Native blood quantum.[12]

The passage of the GI Bill in 1944 and the subsequent rise in Native student enrollment led to a proliferation of on-campus Indian organizations that followed the lead of the Sequoyah Club. In addition to the Tribe of Many Feathers at Brigham Young University, Native students established the Shalako Club at Fort Lewis College, and students at Arizona State University founded the Dawa Chindi Indian Club. Indian clubs also cropped up at other universities that boasted a substantial Native population. Numbers varied depending on the school, but nearly all served the same purpose—"to encourage Indians to look out for each other and . . . prevent dropouts as much as possible, so they can complete work for their degrees," as NMAIA executive secretary Charles Minton put it.[13]

In June of 1954 the NMAIA invited leaders of UNM's Kiva Club to the New Mexico Conference of Social Welfare in Albuquerque, where the state's Apache, Navajo, and Pueblo peoples convened to discuss common problems. They addressed issues of law and order, Indian health and education, preservation of tribal resources, irrigation, and federal-state-tribal relations. Oliver La Farge of the Association on American Indian Affairs moderated the gathering, while Minton served as chairman. Shortly after the conference, Kiva Club members and representatives of the NMAIA discussed the possibility of holding a youth council modeled after the Conference of Social Welfare. Such a gathering, they hoped, would initiate dialogue between Indian high school and college students in New Mexico.[14]

Their vision translated into reality in January 1955, when Native students congregated in the St. Francis Auditorium in Santa Fe for the first Indian youth council. Just as D'Arcy McNickle and American Indian Development, Inc., were holding workshops to prepare Native people for the effects of termination, the students who gathered below the towering Sangre de Cristo Mountains likewise focused on the federal government's new Indian policy. Besides termination, they discussed a myriad of other issues, including education, assimilation, language retention, and religion. Opinions varied considerably. Unlike the platform the NCAI had hammered out in 1944, there appeared to be little consensus among the students at the Indian youth council—even in the debate over the costs and benefits of termination. About the only thing the students agreed on was that Native youth needed to stay in school and graduate. Part of the reason for the lack of any uniform ideology lay in the hands-off approach of the organizers.[15]

Nevertheless, the NMAIA and the Kiva Club hoped to achieve three objectives through the Indian youth councils. Foremost, they sought to promote higher education and prepare the next generation for tribal leadership. The NMAIA and the Kiva Club shared a concern about the high dropout rates among Native students in both high school and college. They believed the councils could motivate young people to stay in school and graduate. A learned and skilled generation of college graduates could do much to help their fellow tribal members deal with the changing outside world. Minton summed up the NMAIA's philosophy behind the youth councils, asserting, "If there is a solution to the Indian problem, it lies in educated youth aware of Indian problems, desirous of solving them, and dedicated to this task. There is no better use of our funds, and we should not hold back on expenditures for youth meetings and for scholarship aid."[16]

Related to this first objective, the NMAIA and the Kiva Club hoped to prepare Indian youth for "the New Age" of federal Indian policy. Like many observers, they saw the termination of the federal government's trust responsibilities and the eventual abolition of the Bureau of Indian Affairs as foregone conclusions. In ten to twenty years, the NMAIA maintained, the "crisis in Indian affairs in the Southwest will have reached its terrifying peak." Rather than follow the NCAI's strategy of combating forced termination in the courts and halls of Congress, the NMAIA and the Kiva Club expected the Indian youth councils to teach future leaders about parliamentary process, political organization, and self-determination. The young people must be able to solve problems effectively and sort through issues as an independent unified body. Eventually, they even adopted Robert's Rules of Order to guide council proceedings. "By the time the Bureau is abolished," Minton emphasized, "if we can prepare a substantial number of Indian youth for withdrawal of federal services, perhaps the result of withdrawal will not be as disastrous as so many fear. . . . We should do all we can to help them prepare to meet the blow when it comes."[17]

Finally, the organizers of the Indian youth councils hoped to give Native students a platform for speaking their minds on issues facing their home communities. On the insistence of the Kiva Club, the NMAIA invited tribal elders to listen to the young women and men and to give their ideas on the great issues of the day. Hence, they designed the councils to allow *anyone* to speak on *any* issue she or he desired. The open forum allowed for a provocative exchange of ideas, but the myriad of voices and opinions hindered the formulation of a coherent pan-Indian ideology based on the principles of tribal sovereignty, treaty rights, and cultural preservation. Students engaged such principles in their sessions but never established a platform, a position paper, or a consensus of any sort. Furthermore, the NMAIA never attempted to intervene and force its vision on the council participants. Dialogue and discussion, not indoctrination, remained the goal of the RIYC's architects.[18]

The first three Indian youth councils met in Santa Fe as one-day gatherings. A huge success, the NMAIA reported a "capacity crowd" at St. Francis Auditorium by the second year, in 1956. Kiva Club members and students from the Santa Fe Indian School made up the bulk of the attendees. The organizers also invited the governors from the Pueblos of the Rio Grande valley, along with other prominent tribal leaders. Most youth participants had little public speaking experience and often echoed what other students before them had said. Minton described these speeches as "stilted and not too original," while a former participant recalled that students "leapt on each other's ideas."[19]

One student, however, stood out as a visionary. Born in Fort Defiance, Arizona, and raised in the Navajo Nation, Herbert Blatchford had descended from a family of sheepherders and traced his lineage back to the great nineteenth-century Diné leader Manuelito. Once Blatchford reached school age, he attended a Methodist mission school on the reservation and excelled academically. Fellow Navajo and future colleague Charlie Cambridge described him as "the strong, silent type Navajo [who was] extremely intelligent." Blatchford served in the Air Force before enrolling at the University of New Mexico in the early 1950s, where he joined about seventeen or eighteen other Native students. There he helped found the Kiva Club, serving as its president in 1954. At the first youth council in 1955, Blatchford questioned the American educational system. The Indian youth had been told repeatedly that education was of the utmost importance. Such proclamations, he thought, often implied the supremacy of White cultural values and ignored the United States' long history of aggression. For Blatchford, there remained great value in Native culture, which the young people should work to preserve.[20]

In January 1957, after the third annual youth council in Santa Fe, the NMAIA and the Kiva Club decided to expand by organizing what they called the First Regional Indian Youth Council. The RIYC would be much larger in scope than the previous councils and would bring in hundreds of Indian students from all over the Southwest to

The Kiva Club of the University of New Mexico, along with the New Mexico Association on Indian Affairs, organized the Regional Indian Youth Councils of the 1950s, which gave rise to Native leaders such as Beryl Blue Spruce (*front row, left*) and Herbert Blatchford (*front row, second left*). (Mirage Yearbook, 1956, Center for Southwest Research, University Libraries, University of New Mexico)

the University of New Mexico's campus in Albuquerque for three days of discussion and debate. Organizers hoped that broadening the councils would enable them to further press their message on the benefits of higher education and provide Indian youth with further intertribal experience. Ultimately, the NMAIA envisioned Indian students themselves taking complete control over the RIYC. "Our objective," Minton later reflected, "was to work ourselves out of a job as soon as feasible." For the time being, however, the RIYC effectively became the centerpiece of the NMAIA's efforts at youth organization and educational development. Indeed, beginning in 1957, the association devoted the bulk of its funds and resources to the youth councils.[21]

Students who participated in the RIYC came primarily from colleges and universities in the Four Corners region, even though organizers attempted to recruit Indian students from all over the United States. In order to broaden and diversify the council, the Kiva Club and the NMAIA resolved to rotate annual meetings among different college campuses. After the initial regional council at UNM, they held subsequent gatherings at Arizona State College in Flagstaff, Brigham Young University in Utah, and the University of Oklahoma. Their strategy worked: at the 1958 meeting, students from seven states and more than thirty tribes, bands, and pueblos attended. The 1959 RIYC built upon the diversity, attracting participants from fifty-four tribes and seventeen states. At the fourth RIYC in 1960, students from Hawaii and East Africa joined the 350 Native students representing fifty-seven tribes, bands, and pueblos.[22]

The growth of the Indian youth councils required a great deal of organization and planning. With more than a thousand people on the RIYC mailing list, the Kiva Club and NMAIA representatives concentrated on Indian clubs, faculty advisers, and university and college administrators for recruiting. They had to plan transportation, review applications for scholarship aid, and work out details for accommodations, housing, and conference space with the host institution. Although Minton hoped the students eventually would take over these planning duties, the NMAIA executive secretary was chiefly responsible for organizing the RIYC during its formative years.[23]

Minton's dominant role in the council's preparation partly reflected his own paternalism and his belief that Indian students simply could not yet organize a large interuniversity gathering. Describing his duties, he wrote, "My job is to require them to do for themselves everything they can, tell them what needs to be done to insure the success of the meeting, turn over to them what they agree to be responsible for, and be ready to move in quickly and help if necessary." Minton was especially concerned with what he saw as the students' complete ignorance of parliamentary procedure. "Although I sit alongside the presiding officer, I let them flounder along as best they can, intervening only when things are hopelessly messed up," he reported.[24]

Recalling the organization of the RIYC, Vine Deloria, Jr., characterized NMAIA representatives as overly domineering and patronizing. In his trademark cantankerous style, Deloria asserted that the RIYC "featured whites who had power anointing various well-behaved Indians as 'future leaders' and acting as their sponsors." But Deloria's hindsight did not necessarily represent the beliefs of those Native students who actually participated in the councils. Minton and the NMAIA had the trust and respect of many Indian students, including Kiva Club president and future scholar and activist Alfonso Ortiz (San Juan Pueblo). In a letter to the executive secretary, Ortiz thanked Minton for his help, noting, "I do not know what I could have done in situations such as this without your ever-available help. Most important to me, however, have been your advice and counsel." Another RIYC participant, Gerald Brown (Flathead), took the middle road in his assessment: "Minton was a nice old guy. He wanted things to go his way, [but] his heart was in the right place. He wanted Indian people to succeed." The executive secretary of the NMAIA may have been paternalistic, but his skills in organization and planning proved vital to the initial success of the RIYC.[25]

Still, the host Indian club played an important role in preparing for the RIYC. The members chose themes for the conference, registered attendees, conducted campus guides, and aided in making local arrangements for room and board. Host clubs helped determine the council's format and structure, which typically followed

Like the Kiva Club, the Tribe of Many Feathers at Brigham Young University brought Native students from diverse backgrounds together. The club also hosted and organized the Regional Indian Youth Council of 1959. Mel Thom *(front row, second from right)* served as president of both the Tribe of Many Feathers and the RIYC. (Courtesy of L. Tom Perry Special Collections, Harold B. Lee Library, Brigham Young University)

the same general pattern as in previous years. Conference organizers scheduled Thursdays for Native high school students to discuss
and debate a variety of topics without interference from their college counterparts. Education, of course, continued to be a central
theme, as moderators stressed the importance of finishing school
and obtaining a high school diploma. Younger students also discussed other pressing problems facing Indian country, including
juvenile delinquency, alcoholism, and early or underage marriage.
Although the high school sessions were not the central focus of the
RIYC, they were nevertheless well attended by students, teachers,
and administrators alike.[26]

Fridays and Saturdays remained the heart of the RIYC, as college
student attendees from throughout the Southwest convened for intertribal dialogue. Friday councils usually opened with singing and
drumming. During and after the day's sessions, students interested
in holding office in the RIYC or hosting the following year's council
electioneered to gain support for their candidacies. Indeed, choosing the location of the RIYC and the election of officers absorbed a
great deal of the students' energy; they created handbills, posters,
and banners and canvassed the attendees for support. During the
Friday evening banquet, RIYC participants voted for president, vice
president, secretary, and even a treasurer—despite the absence of a
treasury—and decided which Indian student club would play host
to the next council. The officers' chief function was to preside over
Saturday's sessions and the opening day of the following year's
RIYC. The point of the elections, then, was not to vest any degree of
power in council officers but to teach students about parliamentary
procedure and the details of political organization. Both women
and men served as officers, and many eventually became leaders
of the early Red Power movement, including future NIYC officers
Mel Thom, Gerald Brown, Joan Noble, and Clyde Warrior.[27]

Once the elections concluded, students could devote all their energies to Saturday's sessions. A combination of small workshops
and mass assemblies, the sessions focused on various topics the
NMAIA and the host Indian club had earmarked for discussion.
Though topics varied year to year, students typically engaged the
most pertinent problems facing Indian country. At the 1959 council

at BYU, for example, they tackled the issues of segregated versus integrated education, relocation, tribal resource development, "the liquor problem," health and sanitation on reservations, tribal traditions and customs, community development, and law and order. The students divided into smaller groups of twenty to thirty, and moderators assigned each group one of the specific topics, which they would discuss and debate. Groups nominated a chairperson to head the committee and report findings back to the main assembly. The small workshops gave the more introverted students an opportunity to voice their opinions, while the main assemblies enabled attendees to pull together all of their various ideas.[28]

As with the early Santa Fe Indian youth councils, opinions expressed at the RIYC diverged considerably. No uniform ideology or consensus emerged, as the minutes from the 1959 meeting clearly illustrate. The argument over assimilation and cultural preservation proved to be the greatest source of disagreement. Many came down firmly on the side of cultural preservation. At this third annual RIYC, Bob Pacheco (Laguna Pueblo) headed the workshop on traditions and customs and concluded that Indians needed to celebrate their heritage. Too often Whites derided and criticized Native culture—some Indians failed to embrace their background and practice traditional religion because they feared outsiders might ridicule them. For Pacheco, this was unacceptable. To overcome this widespread prejudice, he argued that Native people should educate whites and teach them about Indian customs.[29]

Other students believed adamantly in assimilation and acculturation. Clarence Weahkee (Cochiti Pueblo) stated that Indians' problems paled when viewed in the global context of the Cold War and atomic warfare. Native people should concern themselves more with the hydrogen bomb and radioactive fallout than with preserving traditional culture. Weahkee even questioned the value of Native culture. Change was inevitable, he argued, and Indians needed to better prepare themselves for the modern world. Another student wondered whether Native people were equal to whites. He declared that Indians occupied a "below par" status and were equal only in God's eyes, concluding that the "whole [council] meeting is founded on that basis."[30]

Future NIYC founder Bernadine Eschief attempted to carve out a middle ground between assimilation and cultural preservation. In her speech, "A Belief in Ourselves and Our God," she championed education as a means of improving the Indians' situation. Eschief saw the RIYC as a vehicle for Indian youth to "become more aware" of their cultural background and to overcome "the feeling of inferiority." Though Native people should retain the best of their traditions, they also needed to combine those positive elements with the culture of mainstream America. For Eschief, integration should stand as Native people's primary goal.[31]

In the debate over House Concurrent Resolution 108, the federal government's measure that codified forced termination, opinions again varied. Eschief pointed out that the Klamath Indians of Oregon had great troubles due to the government's ill-conceived policy. Frank Enos (Paiute) took a harder line, describing termination as "all wrong" and those who favored the policy as misguided souls "trying to throw away the culture" of Native people. Tom Swaney, a Flathead from Montana, added that Indians were better off as wards of the government, noting the benefits of federally funded health care and education. However, another student, to the applause of the audience, compared the terminated tribe to a person who left home and went out into the world to make something of himself. By contrast, he described the nonterminated Indian as an infant sitting at home "waiting to be fed with a spoon." Joe Jimenez (Nambe Pueblo) concurred, proclaiming that government programs fostered idleness in Indians.[32]

Such self-help rhetoric characterized much of the discussion and debate at the youth councils. From the initial gatherings in Santa Fe, Native youth stressed the tenets of individualism, self-discipline, a strong work ethic, and civic nationalism so fundamental to postwar America. At the first annual RIYC, Beryl Blue Spruce of Laguna and San Juan pueblos reflected this spirit when he delivered what would prove to be one of the most enduring and influential speeches in the council's history, entitled "We Are Born at a Time When the Indian People Need Us." In his speech, Blue Spruce maintained that Indians had many problems: "We have problems with our cultural environment, problems with our physical environment. . . .

Things don't happen the way we want them to happen," he noted, but Indians themselves must solve such tribulations. Blue Spruce opined that Native peoples' attitude, unfortunately, hindered them from moving forward:

> We're lazy. We're lazy and we're proud that we're little babies sitting in a mud puddle, sitting there and wishing that someone else would come and pull us out. We're saying to ourselves, "I'm just a poor little Indian. I'm ignorant. If I go to school, I won't make it. I just know I won't make it!" . . . You're sitting there in that mud puddle watching the world go by. . . . The man who gets anywhere in this world is the man who gets out and works. I don't think we're even nearly the proud Indian that used to live long ago. I don't think we even have a right to be proud that we are their descendents. . . . They had courage. They had pride and they had self-discipline. Those are things we seriously lack today. We don't have them any more. We're cowards. We can't face the world.[33]

Blue Spruce continued his broadside, blaming Native people themselves for the high dropout and poverty rates that plagued their communities. He asserted that Indian students needed to educate themselves and return to the reservations with their newly acquired skills. It was up to his generation to lift themselves out of that "little mud puddle" and bring progress to the Indian people.[34]

Blue Spruce's call to action resonated with the students in attendance and with the NMAIA. Council organizers reproduced and distributed the speech throughout Indian country and beyond. They sent three hundred copies alone to South Dakota and another thousand to those on the RIYC mailing list. Even missionaries in Southern Rhodesia received copies. At future councils, students echoed Blue Spruce's rhetoric and even plagiarized the speech. Minton attributed NMAIA's increase in membership to the address. The Laguna–San Juan speaker became the association's shining star, as he received special scholarships and repeat invitations to the RIYC.[35]

The widespread distribution and influence of Blue Spruce's speech stood as a testament to the growth of the youth councils.

Indeed, the NMAIA expected that the RIYC would eventually reach to all corners of Indian country. Minton envisioned regional student gatherings in the Pacific Northwest, the Midwest, the Great Basin, the Great Plains, and Oklahoma. Once each region had established its own RIYC, the executive secretary believed these disparate councils would create a national intertribal organization. Minton reported to association members and Indian youth alike, "Our aim has been to have a national Indian youth council eventually."[36]

Minton and the NMAIA continued to believe that the students themselves would take complete control of the regional councils, as well as the future national organization. Ideally, tribal councils would sponsor the meetings, assuming all of the duties and expenses that followed. Still, the organization balked at handing over control to the students. Despite its proclamations, the NMAIA remained dominant in all aspects of planning and organizing the councils. This could have been due to a fear that "professional Indians," including the NCAI, would appropriate the RIYC. "It is likely that ARROW, Inc., will take over the national youth council," Minton worried. "Meanwhile, if the regional groups can gradually develop to the point where a national group naturally results, it will be a healthy development. The publicity seekers and the limelight grabbers will jump on the band wagon, of course, but I am counting on the maturity of the kids in the Southwest to hold them steady."[37]

In 1957, Native students from the Great Plains took a step toward realizing the NMAIA's vision of a national network of regional councils when they congregated at the Standing Rock Sioux Reservation in Fort Yates, North Dakota, for the first Tri-State Youth Council. Carroll Mickey, chair of the Sociology Department at the University of South Dakota, organized the gathering. As with the RIYC, the organizers intended to encourage Indian youth to remain in school and "improve their attitude and outlook." The Tri-State council also followed a similar schedule, though it ran midweek rather than on the weekend. The council met in the local high school auditorium since the area lacked a university or college. During the sessions, registered attendees and adult observers discussed pertinent issues facing Indian country. They concluded on a Thursday evening with traditional dancing and music.[38]

Charles Minton attended the second Tri-State gathering and reported on the affair to the NMAIA. The executive secretary was unimpressed. The discussions, he stated, "were the typical high school or even elementary school kind," and the council itself seemed to be more of a platform for adults to talk than for the students. "They just sat and said nothing," Minton complained. He further criticized the immaturity of the students and what he perceived to be their lack of dignity, noting they wore "duck-tail haircuts and droopy trousers." Minton was appalled that the students drank heavily, lacked initiative, and "smoke[d] like furnaces." In his typical paternal fashion, he attributed this "depressing" situation to Sioux culture and the buffalo hunt: "When they needed any of these [buffalo], they went out and got them, but there was no need to store up a supply, so they either fished and hunted or just loafed."[39]

Despite its perceived shortcomings, the Tri-State Youth Council marked the first stride in expanding the regional councils. Others followed. Native students from Alaska, Idaho, Montana, Oregon, Utah, Washington, and Wyoming met in mid-May 1961 for the Northwest Youth Council. That same year two hundred Menominees, Sioux, Ojibwes, and other Indians from the Midwest met at Wisconsin State College in Eau Claire for that region's first intertribal youth gathering. Even the Ittanaha Conference—the umbrella organization for Oklahoma's college Indian clubs—adopted the structure of the RIYC and renamed itself the Ittanaha Youth Council. This proliferation of youth councils fulfilled Minton's dream, but at the same time it also led to fragmentation of the RIYC, as students in Oklahoma and New Mexico found that their own councils attracted fewer participants and less tribal diversity.[40]

The RIYC (which by this time had adopted the name "Southwestern Regional Indian Youth Council") further transformed at the fifth annual council in Norman, Oklahoma. Due to the distance, organizers feared that students from California, the Pacific Northwest, and the Great Basin would be unable to attend. "[They] had better start saving for next April," Minton warned. To be sure, the meeting failed to draw large numbers of students from those regions, but hundreds of students from Oklahoma and Kansas, as well as devoted past participants such as Mel Thom and Herb Blatchford, attended. Hosted by the University of Oklahoma's Sequoyah Club, the conference followed the same general pattern as previous councils but grew in scope. RIYC president Alfonso Ortiz secured recorders, a public address system, food service, and four hundred chairs to seat what he believed would be the best-attended council to date.[41]

The 1961 council in Norman indeed proved the largest yet, but another development was even more significant than the council's size. At the annual election, a new leader emerged—a leader who, more than anyone else, could claim responsibility for the development of Red Power. His name was Clyde Warrior. Born into poverty in rural Oklahoma, Warrior was a full-blood Ponca whose maternal grandparents had steeped him in their tribe's traditions and customs. Warrior not only spoke his ancestors' tongue but also had become an excellent fancy dancer, winning top honors at powwows all over Indian country. Remembering him as "the most graceful, dedicated Native dancer" she had ever seen, Shirley Hill Witt added, "It seemed as though his moccasins only grazed the earth as he floated through dreamlike ancient motions. He was mesmerizing." So talented was the young Ponca, he worked at Disneyland for a spell in the late 1950s and early 1960s.[42]

Besides excelling in fancy dancing, Warrior commanded a towering intellect. He attended Cameron Junior College in Lawton, Oklahoma, and had been named "outstanding Indian Student" by the school. He later studied at the University of Oklahoma and eventually graduated from Northeastern State College in Tahlequah, Oklahoma, with a bachelor's degree in education. When Karen Rickard first met Warrior in 1961, she stood "awestruck" at his insightful and deep knowledge of Indian affairs, as well as his assertiveness. "Clyde said it as he saw it and did not mince words," Rickard recalled. Warrior's future wife, Della Hopper, was equally captivated by the Ponca. "When I heard him talk—I was just so glad that he had the guts to say what he said. I was in awe." On another note, Warrior also gained notoriety for his ability to consume legendary amounts of tequila or whiskey

This postcard from the late 1950s features Clyde Warrior *(left)*, who won top honors for fancy dancing at powwows throughout Indian country. At the 1961 Regional Indian Youth Council in Norman, Oklahoma, he emerged as one of the most important and outspoken Native political leaders of the twentieth century. (*Braves in Full Dress*, photograph by Harvey Caplin, 1914–1984; permission by Abbie Caplin, www.abbiecaplinsfrontiers.com, 928-205-9119.)

before passing out. His proficiency in drinking, however, would eventually lead to trouble.[43]

Warrior announced his candidacy for council president, facing off against Gerald Brown in the election. Born on the Flathead Reservation in Montana, Brown would also emerge as a young leader in his own right. When he was in high school, his family had moved to California's Bay Area as part of the government's relocation program. Brown's parents, Thomas William and Dorothy Morigeau, were vocal critics of federal Indian policy, and they became active members of the Intertribal Friendship House in Oakland. Thomas and Dorothy encouraged Gerald to take pride in his cultural heritage, never to forget his reservation roots, and to work on behalf of all Native people. After graduating from Mission High School in San Francisco, he enrolled in classes at San Francisco State University and became a regular attendee of the RIYC, traveling to the councils held at BYU, UNM, and the University of Oklahoma (OU).[44]

At the 1960 RIYC at UNM, Brown had been elected treasurer but was disheartened to learn that his position was more of a title than a real office. Therefore, the following year at OU, Brown jockeyed for the RIYC presidency by presenting himself as a moderate and reasoned candidate in comparison with his more confrontational and traditional opponent, Clyde Warrior. In his campaign speech, Brown discussed in detail the problems with the government's termination policy and relocation program, stressing how Natives who moved to urban areas were often cut off from the Indian Health Service. Warrior, alternatively, chose to contrast his dark skin and full-blood ancestry with the light skin and mixed blood of Brown. Although just two sentences in length, Warrior's speech and the way he delivered it would become the stuff of legend. Warrior jumped up on the stage and strolled across to the podium. He tipped back his cowboy hat, rolled up his sleeve, pointed to his arm, and simply stated: "This is all I have to offer. The sewage of Europe does not flow through these veins." In the ensuing plebiscite, Warrior defeated Brown in a landslide.[45]

Warrior's resounding victory indicated a shift in thinking among RIYC participants. Perhaps it reflected a degree of politicization among Oklahoma Indians largely absent in the far Southwest.

Alternatively, the shift may have been due to the broader, changing political and social milieu of the United States. The previous year, African American students had launched the sit-in movement and shortly thereafter formed the Student Nonviolent Coordinating Committee, an organization that quickly emerged as the militant vanguard of the civil rights movement. Then, just two months before the Norman council, demonstrators in Rock Hill, South Carolina, flooded the jails in an attempt to desegregate the city. Racist whites responded violently to this swell in activism and protest, bludgeoning bodies and cracking heads. Americans all over the nation watched the brutal struggle on their television screens—and Indian country was no exception.[46]

Certainly, such events influenced Warrior and the other council participants. But Warrior's militancy, his swagger, and his ability to identify and pointedly articulate a growing frustration and sense of urgency among many young Native people made the Ponca an exceptional leader and intellectual force. Like Stokely Carmichael, who assumed control of the Student Nonviolent Coordinating Committee five years later, Clyde Warrior in 1961 stood as a new brand of charismatic leadership. A militant before militancy had spread widely among the youth of the 1960s, he captured the imaginations of people and forged a new direction in intertribal politics.

Weeks after his election victory, Warrior and many of the other young men and women who had traveled to Oklahoma for the fifth annual RIYC attended what would prove to be the largest and most diverse intertribal gathering held in modern times—the American Indian Chicago Conference (AICC). Organized by University of Chicago anthropologist Sol Tax in conjunction with the NCAI, the AICC served as a grand workshop where Indians learned about the BIA, federal policy, and the ideological vision of the conference's coordinators. Warrior, Thom, Noble, Blatchford, and other youth participants observed the proceedings, formed their own caucus, and resolved to establish a new national Indian youth council that backed the principles of treaty rights, tribal sovereignty, and cultural preservation. Blatchford remarked that "a need for freer movement, for whatever sparks enthusiasm and interest," became apparent after the AICC. Years later, Vine Deloria, Jr., recalled that the Chicago Conference was a watershed; there students broke free from the RIYC's white sponsorship and embarked on a course of self-determination.[47]

Minton sensed the change. Despite his prior proclamations in favor of an autonomous national council, he seemed distraught over the students' newfound independence. The youth involvement in the AICC particularly incensed the executive secretary. Quick to criticize, he assumed that Sol Tax and the conference organizers sought "to exploit the Indians." In one of his association reports, Minton dubbed the organizers' attempt to draft a statement on Indian recommendations for federal policy "a waste of time." He argued that Native people's ideas were "already known." His suspicions led him to assert that Tax and the NCAI had organized the conference to provide "the Indian politicians and phonys [sic]" with an opportunity to claim to be the voice of Native America. Exasperated, Minton asserted that the conference would only "inflate the egos of Sol Tax and the professional Indians, but nothing new will be learned." He added, "This is the sort of thing the foundations love to grant funds for, and it is one of the reasons it is so hard to get money for worthwhile projects."[48]

Although Minton harbored reservations toward the Chicago Conference, he still attended the gathering. After sitting through a week's worth of sessions, he returned to New Mexico disenchanted, even angered. "They took their war bonnets with them, so people would know they claimed to be Indians," he remarked. "Nothing new was said, nothing new developed." He blasted Sol Tax, whom he nicknamed "Chief Guzzle Muzzle," and declared that the RIYC remained "more realistic and constructive."[49]

Minton's hostility may have been rooted in his strained relationship with his employer. The Southwestern Association on Indian Affairs (formerly the NMAIA) had fallen on hard times in 1959, when a lack of finances nearly led to the association's dissolution. During that year, several board members resigned, and a "sterile search" failed to find replacements. The organization nevertheless resolved to stay afloat by limiting its activities to the RIYC and Indian education. Matters only worsened in 1961, when Oliver La Farge's group, the Association on American Indian Affairs, cut off all affiliation with its southwestern counterpart. Justifying the action, La Farge stated that the relationship had not "proven fruitful" and that the "cooperation we had hoped for has not been forthcoming." The divorce proved costly for Minton and the Southwestern Association. La Farge and his outfit had contributed $1,500 annually to help defray the cost of scholarships and travel expenses for the RIYC, a substantial sum in the early 1960s for an organization working on a shoestring budget. The Southwestern Association's board blamed Minton for the calamities and claimed that the association could no longer pay an executive secretary, leading to his eventual ouster in January 1962.[50]

Despite Minton's firing, the RIYC lingered on. Clyde Warrior served as president for the 1962 gathering, again held at BYU. The association continued to fund the council, but Minton's departure left Warrior and the other officers floundering over organizational matters. The RIYC president wrote to Blatchford, a longtime council participant, querying about the workshops, general meetings, elections, and guest speakers. Blatchford contributed what he could, but he was not able to give the hands-on support that student organizers needed. This breakdown in organization also led to communication problems with the various Indian clubs. Just weeks before the scheduled meeting at BYU, a confused Gerald One Feather, president of the Sequoyah Club, wrote to the Southwestern Association wondering when the RIYC would be held.[51]

By this time, however, a new organization had already eclipsed the regional council, marking an end to white oversight and sponsorship and the beginning of a newfound assertiveness among Native students. Thom, Warrior, Noble, and Blatchford, along with other former RIYC participants, took matters into their own hands and founded the National Indian Youth Council in the summer of 1961. Their previous experiences proved essential, as NIYC's founders employed the regional councils' organizational structure and parliamentary process when they built their new national council.

In founding the Regional Indian Youth Council, the NMAIA and the University of New Mexico's Kiva Club succeeded in bringing together Native students from the Southwest and beyond to discuss

and debate the federal government's new policy of termination
along with other major problems facing Indian country. Students
learned the essentials of organization building and policy making.
The experiment stands as the first example of intertribal Native student political organization. Council participants, however, never
established a uniform agenda or position on the pressing issues of
the day. Even the policy of termination was hotly debated. Looking back on the legacy of the RIYC, Gerald Brown summed it up
by noting, "People talked about what they wanted, [but] the RIYC
brought a lot of kids together. That was incredible."[52]

Hence, the RIYC encouraged intertribal fellowship and gave participants a greater understanding of organization building and par-
liamentary process. Students learned, as future NIYC leader Viola
Hatch put it, "how to be self-sufficient and how to run their own
organizations." But the students who would go on to found the
NIYC and launch the Red Power movement took their ideological
aim from another source. As the RIYC convened through the 1950s,
Indian youth simultaneously met in Colorado for the Workshop on
American Indian Affairs—the catalyst for what would become Red
Power.[53]

CHAPTER 3

"NATIONALISM IS A JOURNEY, A JOURNEY FROM FEAR INTO HOPE"

The Workshop on American Indian Affairs

D'Arcy McNickle always kept up a steady correspondence with his old friend John Collier. Although the onetime commissioner of Indian Affairs had left the bureau in 1945, McNickle continued to write to him on a regular basis, elaborating on new projects and developments with the National Congress of American Indians (NCAI) or American Indian Development, Inc. (AID). On January 12, 1963, McNickle gave Collier an assessment of the AID-sponsored Workshop on American Indian Affairs. He reported that the student participants had gained a new sense of Indian identity and a better understanding of their place in American society. There was even a hint of militancy among the Native youth. "Some of them get so excited they want to go right out and start a war against all the teachers and administrators they have ever known who all along were telling them that as Indians they were dead," McNickle affirmed. Though the NCAI founder disavowed any attempt to foment rebellion among the participants, he seemed quite pleased with the outcome of the workshop.[1]

The Workshop on American Indian Affairs began during the summer of 1956, when anthropologists from the University of Chicago brought together Native students from all over Indian country with the intention of sharpening their ideological aim. McNickle's AID took control of the workshops in 1960, but the new sponsors retained the same structure and format. Like the Regional Indian Youth Council, the workshops encouraged intertribal discussion and the participation of both young women and men. Unlike the RIYC, however, this endeavor rejected the open forum concept of the councils and instead focused on instilling the principles of tribalism, cultural renewal, treaty rights, self-determination, and sovereignty, which the NCAI and AID championed. For six weeks, Native college students read the writings of John Collier, D'Arcy McNickle, and Felix Cohen, as well as the work of such prominent cultural anthropologists as Ruth Benedict, Edward Sapir, and Robert Redfield. In lectures, workshop instructors hammered home the concepts of colonialism, racism, cultural relativism, and nationalism and gave participants a better understanding of federal Indian policy. Clyde Warrior, Mel Thom, Joan Noble, Herb Blatchford, Karen Rickard, Bruce Wilkie (Makah), Della Hopper, Charlie Cambridge, Robert Dumont (Assiniboine-Sioux), Bernadine Eschief, Gerald Brown, Browning Pipestem (Otoe), and many more who participated in these intensive gatherings returned to their tribal communities with the ideological tools that would guide a new youth movement.

And initiate a movement they did. In 1961, workshop students, joined by others who had participated in the 1961 RIYC at the University of Oklahoma, traveled to Illinois to take part in the American Indian Chicago Conference, the largest intertribal gathering in modern history. At this conference, the student attendees formed a youth caucus to press for more immediate change in federal Indian policy. These youths would draft their own statement and forcefully present their perspective to their elders. This Chicago Conference Youth Council, as the students called their caucus, would serve as the springboard for a new national Native student organization that would ultimately inaugurate the Red Power movement.

More than any other decade in the twentieth century, the 1960s signaled a time when young people questioned and challenged the political, social, and moral direction of the United States. They took to the streets in their crusade: they protested, marched, occupied, sat-in, fished-in, broke in, blew up, and burned down. They railed against the structures, symbols, and processes they believed to be evil. The Cold War and the black-and-white world it spawned served as the greatest catalyst in this process. But young Americans, regardless of their race or ethnicity, also took a cue from their elders. Securing any sort of political legacy requires a degree of mentoring; the vigilant must always take care to pass the torch to the future generation.

African American civil rights leaders carefully cultivated a philosophy of equality, integration, and nonviolence among young black students. Like the National Indian Youth Council, the Student Nonviolent Coordinating Committee grew out of earlier organizational efforts by established civil rights leaders. In the mid-1950s, activists within the National Association for the Advancement of Colored People, such as Floyd McKissick, set up NAACP youth councils throughout the South. Students not only learned the philosophy of their elders but also became acquainted with direct action tactics that their elders had employed years before the famed Greensboro sit-ins. Indeed, such organizational efforts spawned SNCC itself. Ella Baker, a longtime activist within the NAACP and the executive director of the Southern Christian Leadership Conference during the late 1950s, called together black students from throughout the South with the intention of creating a new "coordinating committee" that would bring unity and greater direction to the sit-in movement.[2]

White leftist leaders also recognized the importance of training future leaders to carry on their agenda. Hence, the Socialist Party formed the Young People's Socialist League, the Communist Party founded the Labor Youth League, the Committee for Non-Violent Action established the Student Peace Union, and the League for Industrial Democracy created the Student League for Industrial Democracy (SLID). The tidal wave of anticommunism that came crashing down during the 1950s destroyed or seriously impeded leftist leaders' efforts at youth organization. With the help of its parent organization, however, SLID weathered the storm and even found new life as college enrollment grew in the latter half of the decade. In 1960, SLID leaders such as Al Haber adopted a more activist approach and renamed their outfit Students for a Democratic Society.[3]

Like the leadership of the NAACP youth councils and SLID, older proponents of Native rights organized the Workshop on American Indian Affairs to propagate a set ideological agenda and develop a new generation of leaders. The project was the brain-child of Sol Tax. Born in Chicago and raised in Milwaukee, Tax attended the University of Wisconsin as an undergraduate and later completed his Ph.D. in cultural anthropology under the direction of A. R. Radcliffe-Brown at the University of Chicago. In 1944, Tax landed a job in the Department of Anthropology at Chicago, where he pursued his interest in American Indian communities and focused especially on the Indians of the eastern plains. During this time, Tax developed the doctrine of "action anthropology." According to this new ethos, the anthropologist should shed the cloak of amorality and intervene where necessary to improve the condition of the people she or he studied.[4]

Tax and his students first devised and employed action anthropology in the late 1940s, while studying the Meskwaki, or Fox, Indians in nearby Iowa. The poverty and lack of opportunity that plagued the Foxes, along with the Indian Bureau's postwar emphasis on assimilation, alarmed the Chicago anthropologists. Many began wondering if it were possible for the Foxes to retain their culture and traditions, while advancing economically and improving their quality of life. On behalf of the Indians, Tax and his team requested federal funds for a new school and health clinic, which the Foxes themselves would operate. Tax and his colleagues also helped launch a scholarship program for the youth of the tribe. To encourage greater economic independence, the action anthropologists advised the Foxes on how to get their goods to market. The tribe eventually established a garden project, a grocery store, and business ventures to sell their arts and crafts. All the while, Tax maintained that the Meskwaki tribe must make its own decisions.[5]

Although Tax purposely avoided making any mention of his personal philosophical underpinnings, beneath his detached exterior the anthropologist adhered to the same set of beliefs as the NCAI. Tax abhorred the federal government's postwar policy of forced termination, which he believed would fail. If Native people had their ties to the tribe and traditional culture cut, they would "get lost in the general population." Rather, the government had a "moral obligation" to live up to its trust responsibilities and provide the necessary services to Indian nations. He concurred with

McNickle, Phinney, Heacock, Bronson, and the other NCAI leaders on the issue of self-determination, declaring, "Just as farmers who receive large subsidies from the federal government are permitted to run their farms and make their own mistakes, so could it be with Indian communities."[6]

To be sure, Tax qualified his statements, adding, "It is not for any white man, or Congress, or the Indian Bureau to demand that Indians either remain Indians or stop being Indians." The tenets of action anthropology prohibited him from making a strong ideological stand. Still, it proved difficult, if not impossible, to mask his true leanings. Like John Collier, Tax believed that Indian cultures had something of great value that must be preserved and propagated. In an address delivered to the Foundation of North American Indian Culture, he lauded Native people and their cultures, contrasting them favorably with Europeans: "They built; they did not destroy. They combined nature, man, and God into a harmonious whole." Echoing Collier's belief that Native people possessed sagacious insights long lost by modern industrial society, Tax maintained,

> American Indian communities need to be sustained . . . not only or even mainly because of the beauty of their artifacts, and charm and excitement of their dance and their song, and the grandeur of their thought and ritual, but because they are a living example of another way of life. We need the model of that way of life not because we ourselves can turn back history and become again like tribal peoples, but because while they exist there is a chance to learn from them some of the basic values of life which (like matter) we have ourselves transmuted into energy. To the degree that we can regain these basic values we may learn to live with ourselves again.
>
> . . . [Indian culture] will contribute in ways that we cannot now even imagine, to the beauty and integrity of the lives of all of us in North America. We may find that if American Indian cultures are preserved in this genuine creative way, they will show us how our technical civilization can preserve also our own humanity.[7]

Hence, although Tax founded action anthropology as a legitimate means of social scientific research, he operated under a distinct ideological rubric. Tax may have tried to keep his philosophy to himself when at work, but action anthropology ultimately was a soft science, not a hard one, resulting in a less-than-detached practice.[8]

Nowhere was this more obvious than with his new project—the Workshop on American Indian Affairs. The idea of bringing Indian students of different tribal backgrounds together for a month-long workshop came about in 1955 during a conversation between Tax, his graduate student Fred Gearing, and Galen Weaver of the American Missionary Association of the Congregational Church. They secured over eleven thousand dollars for the pilot project and were able to enlist Colorado College in Colorado Springs as the host institution. In order to make the workshops more appealing to college students, those who attended would earn credit toward their respective degrees.[9]

The workshop architects believed that conventional education had failed to fulfill American Indian students' needs. Like the organizers of the RIYC, they were greatly concerned with the high dropout rates among Native youth, and they believed the workshops might curtail this disturbing trend. But there was more to it than that. Tax and Gearing hoped to give workshop participants experience with issues that directly affected their home communities. As Rosalie Wax, an instructor for the workshops later reported, one of the foremost goals was "to develop wise Indian leadership." Of course, for Wax and the other workshop organizers, "wise" leaders were those who opposed termination and believed in cultural preservation, treaty rights, and tribal sovereignty. She went on to elaborate that the future generation should have a better understanding of the political, legal, and social relationship between their respective tribes and the United States at large. Workshop leaders recognized this relationship as one between colonizer and colonized. In his book *Native Activism in Cold War America*, Daniel Cobb makes this point clear by showing how Tax viewed the obstacles that Native nations faced as "domestic 'colonial' problems."[10]

D'Arcy McNickle's AID, which took control over the workshops in 1960, adhered to these same principles. The NCAI founder continued to employ Tax's students from the University of Chicago as instructors and retained the same general structure and curriculum. From the beginning, the workshops resembled AID's earlier efforts, most notably the Crownpoint Project, where McNickle and his staff had held intensive leadership training sessions to instill a sense of self-determination among the Diné. Although the Crownpoint Project fulfilled his desire to work closely with Indian communities, McNickle became discouraged with the younger participants' disrespect for their elders. Their lack of knowledge of the Navajo language, tribal values, and traditional culture only compounded his frustration. Tax's workshops were the ideal solution. Shortly after their inception, the AID leader became keenly interested in the program. He traveled to Colorado Springs twice during the first workshop in 1956 to deliver guest lectures and observe the proceedings. Shortly after AID assumed sponsorship, the summer workshops became the organization's most important and heavily funded endeavor.[11]

Whether under Tax's or AID's lead, the Workshop on American Indian Affairs remained another action anthropology project—helping Indian students to help themselves. Both Tax and McNickle, as Daniel Cobb has argued, drew parallels between Native nations in North America and developing countries around the globe, recognizing that Native peoples must turn back the tide of colonialism that continued to engulf them. To accomplish this, the organizers devised a curriculum that critiqued assimilation and acculturation, while embracing self-determination and cultural preservation. In a report drafted shortly after the first workshop in 1956, Gearing forcefully argued, "Until every Indian community has the freedom to make mistakes, the 'Indian problem' will continue and will not basically change." Native people needed to have sovereignty over their affairs, and tribal governments should make the decisions on how best to use federal subsidies. Congress and the BIA ought to reassess their strategies and responsibilities. Moreover, Gearing stated that one of the primary goals of the instructors must be fostering a sense of cultural pride among their Native students. "They should develop greater competence and assurance in interpreting themselves as Indians," he argued. McNickle built upon this assumption, advising Tax that "the design of the project should be to provide the young people with a sound working philosophy," which they would use to "benefit their people" and defend against "erroneous ideas."[12]

Yet year after year organizers dealt with "detribalized" students who, they believed, were ashamed of their Indian ancestry. Wax noted that she and other staff members disapproved of these "Indian haters" and their "credulous bigotry and self hatred." She emphasized that workshop instructors were "shocked at the students' rejections of their native communities and their past" and that some seemed to be "Indian only in name." Having little experience with Indian people, Wax employed social theory to understand Native youth. She posited that they suffered from a sense of "marginality," noting, "They are unable to see themselves as either Indians or as white people."[13]

Although workshop organizers avowed their adherence to the principles of action anthropology, they harbored distinct ideas on how best to remedy the "Indian problem." Tax himself made this clear in an address he gave to the participants of the 1957 workshop. He began by declaring that the workshops had only one major tenet—give Native youth the ability to make their own decisions. Neither he nor the workshop instructors opposed assimilation if Indians themselves sought this path. Tax's neutral facade, however, was transparent: "If the Indians assimilate of their own accord, and disappear from the face of the earth, who are we to stop them?" he queried. He proceeded to assert that Native people would never achieve true self-determination without knowing about their past. "One of the main impediments to this freedom is that you know little about being an Indian," he informed his Indian audience. The workshops merely intended to relate "knowledge about culture and the wisdom to appreciate that cultural heritage."[14]

To carry out this agenda, Tax recruited his graduate students to serve as instructors for the workshops, including Gearing, Robert Rietz, Albert Wahrhaftig, and Robert K. Thomas. Over much of the workshops' life, Thomas served as the chief ideologue and proved to be the most influential member of the staff. Born in Mount Sterling, Kentucky, in 1925 to parents of Cherokee descent, he served in the Pacific theater during World War II. He went on to earn his master's degree in anthropology from the University of Arizona, before moving to Chicago to study under Tax. With his folksy style, Thomas had an ability to connect with his students. McNickle described his demeanor as "positive, warm, colorful," characteristics complementing informal classes that drew upon his "personal wisdom" and experiences in Indian country. Thomas further gained his pupils' trust and affection by joining them in their social activities, including evenings of dancing, storytelling, and drinking that often extended late into the night. Workshop student Gerald Brown remembered Thomas as "a cool guy," while Karen Rickard recalled, "He had such a quiet nature that touched our Indian souls. He awakened ideas in me about being an Indian. . . . A truly awesome teacher."[15]

Thomas was a staunch traditionalist when it came to American Indians and Native culture. He fully rejected the notion of assimilation and attacked it full force in his lectures, consciously seeking to undermine what he perceived as his students' negative attitudes about their cultures and background while also encouraging them to view modern Native America through a colonialist and nationalist framework. In one of his lectures, Thomas argued, "Nationalism is a journey, a journey from fear into hope." Indians remained sovereign peoples who over centuries had been inundated with negative stereotypes of war-whooping and feathered headdresses. Such ideas grounded Thomas's lectures, and they never failed to instigate confrontation. Thomas's words disturbed or even angered some workshop participants. More often than not, however, his downhome manner, coupled with his penchant for direct communication, left his audience spellbound, captivating and even changing people. Vine Deloria, Jr., maintained that workshop participants and future National Indian Youth Council leaders Melvin Thom and Herbert Blatchford co-opted the Cherokee's philosophy and more or less reiterated what he told them. Another student asserted in a postworkshop questionnaire that Thomas "shook a few foundations" and planted new ideas in the participants' heads. "No strained baby food," he stated. "You fed us rare steak to be chewed."[16]

If Thomas served as role model and ideologue during the workshops' critical formative years, Rosalie Wax acted as the chief planner. She and her husband, Murray Wax, had worked as assistant professors of anthropology and sociology, respectively, at the University of Miami in Florida. Rosalie had limited experience with Native people, working only briefly as a discussion leader at the American Indian Center in Chicago. Her commitment to the project and its aims, however, proved unquestionable. She concurred with Tax's and Thomas's quest to instill cultural pride and a sense of intertribalism in Native youth. Rosalie Wax excelled as an organizer, doing everything necessary for the workshops to run smoothly. A heavy smoker, she had a resolute yet gritty character that rubbed many of her colleagues the wrong way. McNickle thought Wax dressed "sloppily" and exhibited manners that were "crass," "offensive," and "in poor taste." He expressed dismay at her inappropriateness, complete lack of social grace, and persistence in calling him "papa." Despite such criticisms, Wax got the job done, successfully planning and carrying out a project that would have been an organizational nightmare for the less determined.[17]

Indeed, workshop organizers had to secure funding and university facilities, recruit students, and deal with myriad problems. Religious organizations, tribal councils, private donors, and philanthropic foundations, such as the Emil Schwartzhaupt Foundation, contributed generous sums, but the overall expense of the projects required further sources of revenue. Participants paid what must have seemed like exorbitant rates for the time—in 1961, six hundred dollars covered tuition, travel expenses, and all other miscellaneous fees. After McNickle and AID took over operations, they promised that students who were unable to secure outside funding could apply for special scholarships earmarked for the workshops. Organizers adopted the philosophy that "no student otherwise qualified will be turned down on account of lack of funds."[18]

Sol Tax and his graduate students had initially chosen Colorado College as the best site for the workshops. The campus was intimate, and Colorado Springs was the ideal central location. They decided to forgo holding their gathering on a reservation, choosing not to "descend on [a] community" and leave a "cloud of dust." By 1958, however, McNickle and the directors of AID had moved the workshop to the University of Colorado in Boulder. They believed the institution was better suited for their program due to its large library and its extensive social science and Indian affairs collections. Moreover, because AID itself was based out of Boulder, the location allowed for greater oversight and control in planning.[19]

The Native youth who attended the workshops came from throughout Indian country, creating a truly intertribal program. The geographic distribution of participants mirrored that of Native America—most came from the Southwest, with the Dakotas and Oklahoma contributing heavily as well. Some came as far away as Alaska, Canada, and Iroquoia, on the East Coast. One attendee, Della Hopper Warrior, described her trip to Boulder as "a life changing experience," remembering it as her first opportunity "to meet Indian students from places like Alaska, the East Coast, the Northern Plains, and the Southwest." Besides geographical diversity, participants were overwhelmingly university students or recent graduates between the ages of twenty-one and twenty-five. Of the 340 students who attended the workshops between 1956 and 1970, there were slightly more women than men. Subsequent studies and testimonies indicated that most were from reservations or rural tribal communities; few came from cities.[20]

Karen Rickard in many ways embodied the typical workshop student. Born in 1938 on the Tuscarora reservation in New York, she grew up in a traditional home on a fifty-acre farm where her parents raised and canned their own vegetables. Her father was the famous Chief Clinton Rickard, who achieved international recognition in the 1940s and 1950s for his strong stance on the sovereignty rights of the Six Nations of the Iroquois League. Recalling her childhood, Karen provided this story:

> As a small child growing up on the Tuscarora Indian reservation, I used to listen to my father . . . tell us many stories. The huge oak table with its big clawed feet was always filled with many visitors. Some guests were local, some from faraway tribes, such as the Hopi, and some from foreign lands. All were fascinated with the many tales that Dad recounted to all listeners. He had a keen mind and memory. One story that always intrigued me was how the Tuscarora left their home in the Carolinas. Dad stated that as the colonists encroached [on] our lands

down there, our Tuscarora ancestors decided to head north. They gathered by the Roanoke River to begin their arduous journey. . . . [White
settlers] opened fire on our ancestors traveling down the river. Some
were killed and some escaped with the rushing waters. Some went into
the hills. Those lucky enough to make it through the waters eventually
made the long trek north, where they were eventually taken in by the
Iroquois, being the last tribe to be admitted under their wing.[21]

Such stories shaped Karen's worldview, instilled a sense of tradition, and spurred her to take action on behalf of her people. While
attending the State University of New York at Buffalo, she learned
of the workshops and immediately enrolled, making the long trip
to Boulder during the summer of 1961.[22]

Not all students were as proactive as Karen Rickard was. Organizers had difficulty finding and selecting participants for the
project. During the first four years, few students applied. Rosalie
Wax wondered if the limited applicant pool was due to skewed per-
ceptions of the workshops; she feared they had a reputation as "a
kind of Mormon wiener bake." A much more likely reason for the
lagging applications may have been that lines of communication
between organizers and Native youth were shaky at best. Workshop staff relied heavily on tribal officials to disseminate information on their program, but they also posted notices at universities
and colleges with relatively large Indian student bodies. Despite
such efforts, most participants reported hearing about the workshops through friends or relatives who had attended the previous
summer. Charlie Cambridge remembered that former participants
served as a "network that would get people to go to [the] workshops." Wax estimated that former attendees enlisted about five
students per year, which led her to recommend using them as a
formal recruiting force. She also advocated bringing back students
who had participated in prior workshops. These veterans would
serve as "an incalculable benefit to the younger students" and have
a firmer grasp on the workshop program, allowing them to help in
the "dissemination of a fairly complex philosophy."[23]

Such a complex philosophy was rooted in tribalism, sovereignty, self-determination, treaty rights, and cultural preservation.

Described as "a joint enterprise of student and instructor," the format for disseminating these ideals consisted of lectures in the mornings followed by afternoon discussion groups, which addressed the day's assigned readings. Although the curriculum changed from year to year, the first week of classes focused on social scientific theory and the history of Native people in the Americas. The lessons in subsequent weeks varied, but often dealt with Indian-white relations and problems in modern Native America. Instructors devoted the final week to examinations or special projects. In 1956, participants broke into groups and compiled reports on recent federal policy that affected Native communities. An editorial committee pooled the findings and drafted a final report, which they hoped to distribute to Indian schools, tribal councils, and government officials. Alternatively, the 1959 workshop participants played anthropologist, as they observed and interviewed white people and reported their findings at the end of the week.[24]

Organizers' lecture topics and reading selections followed a set ideological agenda. As Rosalie Wax later recalled, the students "might justly have accused us of being unfair to the assimilationists." The instructors all rejected the evolutionary scheme of earlier anthropologists such as Lewis Morgan and instead embraced the tenets of cultural relativism. They hammered home this point in lectures on the variation among white ethnic groups in the United States. Bob Thomas, for example, discussed how Mexicans, Scots-Irish, New Englanders, and Scandinavian midwesterners differed and had their own distinct traditions just as the Navajos, Sioux, or Cherokees had. In another lecture, Murray Wax discussed the differences between the Pawnees' and Western society's conception of science, giving equal time and due respect to each tradition. For many students it was their first encounter with such relativism.[25]

Instructors never failed to stress the concept of self-determination and the need for reform in federal policy. From the first workshop in 1956, students learned about legislation that threatened the sovereignty of Indian nations. Fred Gearing warned it was up to them to remind their tribal councils and the public at large "that until your community has the freedom to make mistakes, it has no freedom and indeed cannot be a community." He further avowed that

At the Workshop on American Indian Affairs, Native students learned about federal Indian policy, Native history, and social theory. Their experience served as the ideological foundation of the Red Power movement. (Edward E. Ayer Collection, the Newberry Library, Ayer Modern MS Mc-Nickle, box 33, folder 278)

"the unilateral and coercive nature" of termination threatened to destroy Native people, as they would "lose their status as historical political entities with reciprocal rights and duties with the U.S." According to Gearing, the federal government should abandon termination and continue to live up to its trust responsibilities, which meant providing Native communities with special services and giving Native people complete administrative control over the allocation of such resources and monies.[26]

Assigned readings reinforced the staff's lectures and steeped students in the pan-Indian philosophy of the workshop organizers. Though syllabi changed each year, certain books and articles served as mainstays. John Collier's 1947 tome, *The Indians of the Americas*, drew parallels between the various indigenous peoples of the Western Hemisphere. The former commissioner traced the atrocities inflicted on Native people since European contact, giving special attention to the history of BIA policy. He reiterated his earlier writings by underscoring the accomplishments and contributions of the First Nations. To its own detriment, the United States had failed to recognize the greatness of Native culture, which could prove to be humankind's saving grace.[27]

Harold Fey and D'Arcy McNickle's *Indians and Other Americans* staked out a similar position and presented Indian history from an Indian perspective. Accordingly, the Native experience emerged as a story of success rather than failure, as indigenous people had risen up and persevered in the face of adverse conditions. Indians had retained their own set of values and institutions, which differed from those of Europeans. "The laws of the nation, including the Bill of Rights, are the white man's laws, born of the white man's heritage," they argued. Like Collier, Fey and McNickle traced the course of federal Indian policy. They maintained that with the exception of Collier's administration, the BIA had failed Native people. Termination, the most recent manifestation of that failure, threatened to destroy the future of an entire race of people.[28]

Workshop instructors also used Felix Cohen's essays on colonialism to shed light on Native peoples' condition. Cohen, who had served in the Indian Bureau under Collier, maintained that colonizing nations, regardless of their rhetoric, cared solely for profit and power rather than the welfare of their colonial subjects. They would stop at nothing to achieve their goals, using liquor, bribes, and physical coercion and fomenting internal rebellion to maintain control. In his essay "Colonialism: A Realistic Approach," Cohen stumped for self-determination, which he avowed stood as "the highest political good." "No people is so deficient in human capacity as to be devoid of the means of self-government," he affirmed. He went on to argue for cultural relativity, declaring, "There is no such thing as general superiority among cultures." Rather, all societies had something to contribute to the greater human good.[29]

Organizers assigned numerous sociological and anthropological studies to supplement the more political works of Cohen, Fey and McNickle, and Collier. Alfred Schuetz's "The Stranger" and Robert Redfield's "The Folk Society" gave workshop participants a social scientific framework through which to view their condition and respective cultures. Instructors used Schuetz's essay to illustrate how Native people who did not share the basic assumptions of the dominant group were "strangers" in mainstream American society. They experienced feelings of marginality and sought to make sense of their world either through adapting or carving out a separate niche for themselves. Redfield's article assessed tribal peoples' basic values. A favorite of Robert Thomas, Redfield asserted that the group remained the central unit in a folk society, with social relations typically extending from the family. Such cultures based their economy on status rather than market forces. Moreover, behavior tended to be less rigidly structured than in modern society—there was no formal legislation or codified law as found in the Western world. Instead, elders, whose life experience was the primary source of knowledge, maintained the culture's unwritten rules. Redfield contended that most, if not all, folk societies shared these "generalized traits."[30]

Ruth Benedict's classic treatise, *Patterns of Culture*, also remained a top choice of workshop organizers for its insistence that all cultures had to be viewed on an equal plane. Benedict compared the Zunis of New Mexico, the Kwakiutls of Vancouver Island, and the Dobus of Melanesia. Each had its own distinct cultural traits that another society simply could not judge. The cultural anthropologist concluded, "Social thinking at the present time has no more

important task before it than that of taking adequate account of
cultural relativity." She envisioned an ideal future where the "social faith" of diversity would create acceptance of "coexisting and
equally valid patterns of life." Benedict reserved caustic words for
those who believed Western culture superior, avowing that such a
stance created intolerance and even mental illness: "There can be
no reasonable doubt that one of the most effective ways in which
to deal with the staggering burden of psychopathic tragedies in
America at the present time is by means of an educational program
which fosters tolerance in society."[31]

Benedict's book—along with the other readings—captivated
many students who had previously believed assimilation and acculturation the only option. Throughout the course of the workshops,
organizers brought in a slew of guest speakers to further propagate
their vision of pan-Indianism and the future of Native America.
Many of those who addressed the participants were noted NCAI
members or officers. McNickle, Helen Peterson, Ruth Muskrat
Bronson, John Rainer (Taos Pueblo), Georgeanne Robinson (Osage),
Clarence Wesley (San Carlos Apache), and Joseph Garry (Coeur
d'Alene) spoke of their organization's platform and espoused the
cornerstone principles of sovereignty, tribalism, treaty rights, and
self-determination. Other professionals, such as Arthur Lazarus of
the Association on American Indian Affairs and William Brophy—
Collier's successor at the BIA—spoke on the redirection of federal
Indian policy.[32]

Lectures, discussions, readings, and guest speakers gave students a lot to digest in a relatively short block of time. To unwind,
many students convened in the evenings for what they called Forty-
niners—after-hour parties held in a remote location away from the
campus where students sang songs, danced, and drank beer. The
Forty-niners also acted as an informal arena where students could
talk about what they were learning. Quite often the parties got
rowdy and went on into the wee hours of the morning, but Wax,
Thomas, and other staff members never tried to break them up. Such
gatherings seemed to be an integral social activity and a means for
students to forge friendships. As long as students attended class,
organizers turned a blind eye toward the Forty-niners.[33]

Some students refused to attend the late-night parties and even complained about the drinking, believing alcohol to be a destructive vice. But differing takes on the Forty-niners seemed minor when compared with the ideological gap that existed between some students. Those who arrived in Colorado for the six-week session held diverse opinions on the course of Indian affairs and varied considerably on how best to navigate problems facing their home communities. Many had little or no knowledge of the social sciences and failed to recognize the connection between Indian issues and those of other minorities and colonial peoples.[34]

Rolland Wright, a workshop instructor during the 1960s, later identified three main types among the participants, which he termed strivers, traditionalists, and generalized Indians. The former category encompassed those who had co-opted mainstream America's negative perception of Native people. Often they attempted to disassociate themselves from Indian culture and the rampant poverty on reservations, arguing that Native people needed to integrate and look to whites for direction. Strivers identified themselves as American citizens first and as members of their ancestral tribe second. Traditionalists tended to place the home tribal community above a greater American identity. They embraced their respective tribe's indigenous language and favored cultural preservation and self-determination. Finally, generalized Indians identified themselves as Native and favored a traditionalist or conservative platform, but had less knowledge of their ancestral culture due to prolonged contact with the larger society.[35]

Wright may have gone overboard in his attempt to pigeonhole students into various types, but major ideological differences did exist between students. Debate and even heated argument between integrationists and traditionalists occurred regularly. Classrooms served as battlegrounds, and instructors as referees, albeit partisan ones. According to Thomas, who made his prejudices and sympathies clear from the beginning, some assimilation-minded students "found it hard to be tolerant" of his position, becoming "threatened and more extreme" in their posture. Traditionalists likewise took the high ground and on one occasion questioned whether the workshops and education in general were tools of white society and hence "a threat to their identity as Indians."[36]

The debate carried over into lunch periods, social events, and even volleyball games. Rosalie Wax noted that hostility became more prevalent outside the classroom: "Staff-sponsored outings were grim affairs, resembling half-blood/full-blood conflicts in miniature." The occasional "generalized Indian" student suffered identity problems amidst the conflict. One Bannock student raised by a white family sought to identify as a traditionalist but had little knowledge of his ancestral culture. Wax reported that the youth became "miserable and upset" as he attempted to negotiate his philosophy, which was "based equally on the Reader's Digest, the Book of Mormon, and reputable archaeological and ethnographic works."[37]

Regardless of a student's position, organizers found that initial opinions "tended to be emotional, very general, ill-defined, and burdened with contradictions." Their job therefore centered on bringing some sort of structure to the students' thinking. Wright claimed that, over the course of the six weeks, most workshop participants developed a greater Indian consciousness, a better understanding of how social theory applied to Native people, and an interest in intertribal activity. Similarly, Wax indicated that a "spirit of pan-Indianism" arose during the 1960 workshop and that students acquired "knowledge that they are not the last lone specimen of a good-for-nothing people who are sort of vanishing." One indicator of the workshop's effect was the number of students who reported comprehension of their indigenous language. Wax observed in 1960 that, in the first week of class, just two students admitted to being able to speak or understand their Native tongue; weeks later, seven reported proficiency.[38]

Perhaps the best way to assess the impact of the workshop, however, is to listen to the participants themselves. Charlie Cambridge described a transformation that took place among the students:

There was a pattern of behavior displayed by the Indian students. The first week was absorbing information, forcing rural and reservation students to reflect on that. So there was a lot of questioning of many things that made up your personality. Toward the second or third week there was this discovery—something you really didn't understand—a glimmer of awareness that would become a flood. Then the students would want to learn more. . . . People [would] get really really ticked off that they don't control their own destiny. It's all a product of colonialism. The idea is how do you deal with this and basically, how do you help your people.[39]

Responses to postworkshop questionnaires complement Cambridge's words and illustrate that students developed a newfound respect for Native culture and traditions. "Prior to the workshop . . . I was completely convinced that the best thing for Indians to do was to take up the ways of the white man and assimilate," Phyllis Bigpond (Euchea) confessed. "My values have been those of the white man." She continued, noting she had "become aware of [her] attitude" and recognized that cultural preservation was an option. Orville McKinley (Navajo) echoed Bigpond's remarks, affirming, "The Indian sees things very differently than does the white man. . . . I probably would never have looked at the problem this way or thought of it this way if I had not come to the workshop."[40]

The workshops not only stressed the uniqueness of Native culture, according to the students, but also instilled a sense of pride. "Proudness is the most important thing I have learned in these six weeks," remarked one student. "The Indian is more than a dirty, poor, underprivileged person allowing his life to be wasted away in idleness. The Indian for me has become a person rich in a way of life that is fast being swept away by others." Another reported becoming "proud of my existence" and "proud of what (really *who*) I am." Still others took the instructors' lessons on cultural relativism and readings on Native history to mean there was something inherently superior in the American Indian's past. Delaine Byington (Sioux) lauded Native people's accomplishments in the pre-Columbian era, concluding they "had a civilization that was far ahead of most of the civilizations in Europe at this time."[41]

Students reported being motivated to instigate change in federal policy and their tribal communities upon the conclusion of the workshops. Responding to a questionnaire, one participant planned on confronting Indian problems "instead of being idle and having to depend on others all the time." Others reiterated this position: "[The workshop] made me think of myself in a way that I would like to make use of myself. Before I came here, I had no ambition of ever doing anything or trying anything again." Karen Rickard remembered that the experience fostered a greater sense of intertribalism: "It opened my eyes . . . and I began to realize that the Indian problem spanned the whole country. The Iroquois were not alone." And Della Hopper Warrior added, "Finally I could start to understand why our people are the way they are—why we can't get jobs and why we have such poverty and drinking problems. . . . I just thought, well, there's something very wrong with this. This needs to change, and we can do this. I can do this."[42]

Further insight into student thinking can be gained by looking at examinations and written assignments from the workshops. Clyde Warrior, who would become president of the National Indian Youth Council, lashed out at those who would attempt to erase Native culture. When asked to assess his home community on an examination, he employed Robert Redfield's schema and divided his Ponca brethren into two camps, the progressives and the "folk-like" people. The former he classified as greedy assimilationists who were "out for themselves" and had a "what's mine is mine" attitude, whereas the traditionalists were community oriented and concerned about the well-being of their neighbors. On a separate quiz, Warrior expressed his anger at the discrimination against his people and pressures on the Poncas to assimilate. "This is very sickening to me, it's very threatening to me," he lamented. Warrior defended the tenets of Collier's program and the Indian Reorganization Act, refuting the argument that it was an attempt to "freeze" traditional culture. Rather, the IRA promoted self-government and gave Native people an opportunity "to decide for themselves in their own way."[43]

Future NIYC and NCAI leader Bruce Wilkie took a strong stance for self-determination in his course work. He complained that the BIA did not work for Indian people due to "the federal government's insistence on complete assimilation." Such policies from this "colonial agency" meant a "loss of identity" for Native people. Wilkie, however, stopped short of calling for the agency's abolition, positing that it needed to continue with its trust responsibilities, while "return[ing] power to the people." In another essay, he spoke of treaty rights and sovereignty, offering insight into his motivations when he helped launch the fish-ins in Washington State years later:

The Workshop on American Indian Affairs gave rise to future Red Power leaders and NIYC founders, including Bruce Wilkie (*top row, fourth from left*), Fran Poafpybitty (*top row, sixth from right*), Browning Pipestem (*top row, fourth from right*), Clyde Warrior (*top row, first from right*), Gerald Brown (*middle row, fifth from left*), Angela Russell (*middle row, second from right*), and Kathryn Red Corn (*front row, first from left*). Workshop instructor Robert K. Thomas (*top row, second from right*) influenced and even transformed many workshop participants. (Edward E. Ayer Collection, the Newberry Library, Ayer Modern MS McNickle, box 34, folder 289)

> Giving up his property is to the Indian giving up part of himself, his
> identity, and certainly his security. This is not an easy adjustment to
> make. . . . Indian land was secured by treaties of one sovereign nation
> with another. In order not to appear hypocritical in the international
> situation, Americans must look upon the abrogation of treaties in terms
> of aggressive acts, not as a beneficial sacrifice made by the Indians to
> better society.[44]

Wilkie went on to assert that Native people would not, must not,
give up their identity and land base. Their very survival, he argued,
depended on retaining both.[45]

H. Browning Pipestem, who reorganized the NIYC in the late
1960s and later became an attorney for the Native American Rights
Fund, also adhered to the philosophy behind Thomas's lectures
and Felix Cohen's writings. Pipestem argued that Native people
were living under a colonial administration, because they had no
control over their own resources, institutions, and business affairs.
Whites had "no respect for the Indians" and looked down upon
them. The only way to shed this colonial yoke was for Native people to assume control of their own destinies. While he lauded tribal
"folk peoples" for their community orientation, Pipestem critiqued
mainstream urban America as being "impersonal, marginal, seg-
mented, alienated."[46]

Beginning in 1960, participants propagated the ideals of the
workshop through a newsletter entitled *Indian Progress*—the first
intertribal student publication to circulate nationally. The newsletter began in earnest when Jerre Chitwood (Cherokee), Hattie
Thundercloud (Ho-Chunk), and Robert Dumont lobbied the staff
for a venue to articulate their thoughts. Chitwood, whom Wax labeled as a "slave driver," took control as editor, while Thundercloud, Dumont, and others assumed reporting duties. Chitwood's
total control over the venture led many students to censure him
and to exclude him from extracurricular activities. One student
who worked on the paper suffered a "nervous attack" and was
even hospitalized on account of Chitwood's harsh oversight. Despite his strong-arm tactics, Chitwood and his staff succeeded in
getting *Indian Progress* off the ground. In subsequent years, future

NIYC leaders Karen Rickard, Clyde Warrior, Bruce Wilkie, Bernadine Eschief, and Joan Noble assumed control of the bulletin.[47]

From its inception, *Indian Progress* reflected the politicization of
the workshop participants. Editorials from the newsletter's formative years railed against the assimilationist policies of the past. One
such article from 1961 criticized educated Indians who adopted
a white worldview and neglected to use their skills to help their
tribal communities. It was "important that college training develop
attitudes" that remained Indian in nature and encouraged students
to stay on the reservations. An editorial from the following year
echoed such sentiments, affirming, "It is the contention of young
Indian leaders today that they wish to preserve Indian identity."[48]

Other editorials attacked termination, relocation, and the government's failure to recognize treaty rights. One student editori-
alized, "With the coming of the white man up to the present the
American Indian has been in constant danger of losing his rights."
Ill-conceived Indian Bureau policies threatened the very existence
of Native peoples. The construction of the Kinzua Dam on Seneca
land without the tribe's consent, and Washington State's infringe-
ment on the fishing rights of the Muckleshoot, Nisqually, Puyallup, and Yakama tribes stood as just a few examples. The author
concluded that the best way to confront this problem was through
intertribalism: "The Pan-Indian movement which is active today is
designed to achieve and improve understanding of Indianism to
the dominant society. Indian people are beginning to realize that
together they will stand a better chance of protecting their rights."[49]

The articles and editorials found in *Indian Progress*, along with
evaluation and examination responses, testify to the influence the
workshops had on the student participants. Those who enrolled
in the workshops adopted—overwhelmingly—the principles of
self-determination, tribal sovereignty, treaty rights, and cultural
preservation. They also came to embrace intertribalism, recognizing that regardless of tribe, Native peoples faced many of the same
overarching problems—problems they could best confront through
a united effort. The generation of Native youth who partook in the
workshops thus formed a powder keg that needed only a spark to
explode into a movement.

The American Indian Chicago Conference (AICC) of 1961, planned for the late spring of that year, served just that purpose. D'Arcy Mc-Nickle and the officers of AID decided to invite the enrolled workshop participants to the largest intertribal gathering recorded in modern times. Workshop organizers declared that the AICC would be "an exceptional opportunity for learning and for participating in a major conference on Indian affairs." Thus, between June 13 and 20, workshop students joined some eight hundred Indians from over ninety bands and tribes in Chicago for the largest, most diverse intertribal gathering ever recorded up to that time.[50]

Like the Workshop on American Indian Affairs, the AICC was another action anthropology project originally conceived by Sol Tax. The conference gave Native people from all over the United States—especially Native youth—the opportunity to join one another in intertribal fellowship and discuss crucial issues facing Indian country. For a week they met in small discussion groups and mass assemblies to argue, advise, and debate termination, the Indian Claims Commission, treaty rights, tribal sovereignty, and self-determination. By the end of the conference, they produced "The Declaration of Indian Purpose," a fifty-page document that outlined Indian solutions to Indian problems and that they hoped to present to the new U.S. president, John F. Kennedy.[51]

Although many of the students who went to the AICC also attended the summer workshops, others had come from the Regional Indian Youth Council, and a few, such as Shirley Hill Witt, belonged to eastern tribes and had no connection to Indian students in the western half of the country. Born in Whittier, California, but raised in the East, Witt was a member of the Mohawk Nation's Wolf Clan. As a youngster, she excelled in school and received the Carnegie National Art Scholarship Award her sophomore year of high school. She went on to attend Bates College in Lewiston, Maine, and by 1961 had enrolled at the University of Michigan, where she studied anthropology. Witt would emerge as one of the foremost intellects and architects of the nascent Red Power movement. The Chicago Conference united eastern Indians such as Witt with the students from the workshops and regional councils.[52]

Following the first day's sessions, the student attendees met, became acquainted, and talked. And they continued talking all night and through the rest of the week. Brimming with enthusiasm and excitement, Herb Blatchford remembered being unable to sleep for four days. Ultimately, the students resolved to form a youth caucus to give the younger generation a voice in the conference proceedings. As the week progressed, many members of the youth caucus concluded that the conference was overly bureaucratic and "going out on a tangent," deviating from its original intention. Blatchford, Mel Thom, Clyde Warrior, and others thought the youth should come up with a separate statement of purpose to redirect the AICC's aims.[53] Looking back on the youth caucus, Witt recalled a sense of urgency among the students:

> As our youth caucuses felt more and more lifted up by our convictions and commonality of ideas, and as those ideas began to take shape on scraps of paper passed from group to group, we knew that we had something of value to contribute to the ponderous, atavistic deliberations taking place each afternoon in the general assembly. We rejected much of the "hang around the fort" Indian leadership—the Uncle Tomahawks— which we saw as dedicated to appeasing the Washington bureaucracy, be it the new Kennedy administration or the Department of the Interior and its BIA entrenched minions. It was diplomatic to avoid direct confrontation with the NCAI and others—we kept reminding ourselves that honoring our elders was an important cross-cultural value among all the tribes—still it was time to break the "youth does not speak" rule at this threshold in pan-Indian development, we were certain. Yes, there were many forward-thinking delegates, and we indeed sought them out as sounding boards and even sponsors of our position, but in the end we would not be swayed from our mission as we saw it.[54]

At a subsequent mass gathering, they spoke before the conference and presented their position.

Recollections of events surrounding the youth caucus and its role vary considerably. Years later, Thom, Warrior, and others remembered the conference as a springboard for Red Power militancy. Thom told journalist Stan Steiner that he and Warrior were discouraged with the "Uncle Tomahawks" who refused to take a strong stand and instead were "fumbling around, passing resolutions, and putting headdresses on people." As Steiner reported in his book *The New Indians*, "Neither the official Indians nor the university sponsors were aware of the youthful rebellion," even as students were scribbling angry epitaphs in their notebooks. Gerald Brown's recollections underscore Thom's assessment. The former RIYC treasurer remembered shouting matches between the older leaders who feared offending the white mainstream, and the students and younger tribal leaders who hoped the AICC would adopt a more militant position. Another attendee and affiliate of the Workshop on American Indian Affairs, Dorothy Davids (Stockbridge-Munsee), recalled an angry disenchanted youth caucus forcing its way to the podium, where students seized the microphone and presented their statement.[55]

Such a dramatic telling of events makes for a good story and, in the case of Stan Steiner, better book sales. But was the AICC really the key event that ushered in the Red Power movement? Were the students really the antiestablishment militants that some participants reminisced about? The evidence remains ambiguous at best. Just weeks after the conference, Shirley Hill Witt wrote to Blatchford, noting that the youth caucus had gained a "perspective on Indian affairs" and "learned their responsibilities as Indian citizens." Witt has further stated that the running narrative of students "seizing the microphone" is "not only untrue but denies the pervasive courtesy of the conference [organizers]." Similarly, Lurie wrote extensively on the conference yet never mentioned any surging student radicalism. Even the students who later attended the Workshop on American Indian Affairs reported on the AICC in a positive light. Their newsletter, which Clyde Warrior coedited in 1961, focused on how Indians stood in unity regarding their disdain for the policy of termination, and it elaborated that "a common interest, purpose, and feeling of good will" had prevailed at the conference. The newsletter further reported that the AICC benefited students in that it helped them better understand problems facing Native peoples.[56]

Regardless of whether students were angry or not, the AICC acted as a grand workshop of sorts. It brought Native students from all over Indian country together to learn about termination, sovereignty, self-determination, and the preservation of Indian heritage. The conference coordinators largely adopted the youth caucus's statement, or preamble. and printed it in the final version of "The Declaration of Indian Purpose." Reflecting the ideological underpinnings of the instructors at the Colorado workshops and the AID, the statement read:

> In order to give recognition to certain basic philosophies by which the Indian People live, we, the Indian People, must be governed by principles in a democratic manner with the right to choose our way of life. Since our Indian culture is threatened by presumption of being absorbed by the American society, we believe we have the responsibility of preserving our precious heritage. We believe that the Indians must provide the adjustment and thus freely advance with dignity to a better life. In order to accomplish the general objectives of the creed adopted at this conference, we the Indian People herein assembled adopt as official the report herewith attached.[57]

Those students who drafted the statement stood as a shining example of the future in intertribal leadership. They had brought a new energy and vivacity to the movement for sovereignty and self-determination, and many within the youth caucus felt that the AICC marked a turning point in Indian affairs. But, as Witt later recalled, the assembly's recognition of the students and their delivery of the statement of purpose proved to be more of a "performance" and not the "earth-shaking tidal change they were hoping they had brought about." It became clear to these young people that they themselves would have to do a lot more if they hoped to bring about change. They would need to break from the NCAI establishment and create their own movement.[58]

Although the students of the Workshop on American Indian Affairs eventually declared their independence by establishing a new organization and initiating a movement, they owed much to their mentors. Workshop participant Gerald Brown acknowledged, "D'Arcy [and other workshop organizers] were on the front lines since the 1930s, so we got the benefit of their knowledge. . . . We felt an obligation to learn the skills to help our tribe[s]." During their six weeks in Colorado, they gained a greater understanding of issues facing Native peoples, learned about the intricacies of federal Indian policy, and were spurred to take action. The students took these lessons on colonialism, racism, nationalism, and cultural relativism and constructed an activist, even militant, pan-Indian ideology. Such lessons were reinforced at the American Indian Chicago Conference, which brought workshop students into contact with those from the Regional Indian Youth Council. Together, along with students from eastern tribes, they resolved to take action.[59]

Shortly after the Chicago Conference, Warrior, Rickard, Bernadine Eschief, Mary White Eagle Natani (Winnebago), Ansel Carpenter, Jr. (Sioux), and sixteen others headed out to Boulder for the sixth annual Workshop on American Indian Affairs. Blatchford, Witt, Thom, and others who were a part of the Chicago youth caucus returned to their tribal communities to begin planning a national youth gathering later that summer. When the students finally assembled in Gallup, New Mexico, that August, they created an intertribal movement that combined the ideals of the summer workshops and the organizational structure of the Regional Indian Youth Council. They would call themselves the National Indian Youth Council.

CHAPTER 4

"We Believe in a Future with High Principles Derived from the Values and Beliefs of Our Ancestors"

The Founding of the National Indian Youth Council

In October 1963, National Indian Youth Council president Mel Thom launched his column, "For a Greater Indian America," in the inaugural issue of the organization's new publication, *Americans Before Columbus*. Thom refused to pull any punches, undoubtedly shocking the older generation with his combative rhetoric. "Today the Indian life is being threatened by poverty, assimilation, termination . . . And it is not likely that we can challenge the problems facing the Indian people with the 'wait and see, let the rest of the world go on' attitude," Thom maintained. With seething sarcasm, he went on to thank America for its "handouts and civilization," which Native Americans exchanged for their lands and rights. Thom quickly took a more serious tone: "We are tired of being pushed down and held down. We are tired of experts making decisions for us. . . . We just want to be Indians. . . . We want our rights as America's original inhabitants respected and our right to remain a people protected."[1]

Americans Before Columbus and, more specifically, "For a Greater Indian America" served as the voice of the NIYC, forcefully expressing the organization's core values of tribal sovereignty, self-determination, treaty rights, and cultural preservation. As the protest movements of the 1960s gained momentum, the publication became increasingly pointed in its rhetoric. Many of the young people who established the NIYC had grown frustrated with the federal government's plodding pace in making changes in Indian affairs—and they weren't scared to express their views. The found-ers of the council may have adhered to a set of values handed down to them by their elders, but they struck a much more assertive tone when vocalizing those ideals. There remained an immediacy in their message that was missing from the rhetoric of the National Congress of American Indians or AID.

Taking the organizational structure of the Regional Indian Youth Council and the ideals promulgated at the Workshop on Ameri-can Indian Affairs, Thom, Clyde Warrior, Shirley Hill Witt, Her-bert Blatchford, Karen Rickard, Joan Noble, and others broke with the white sponsorship and control of the past after the American Indian Chicago Conference. These young women and men—most of whom came from reservations or rural tribal communities—established the first independent Native youth organization. Their vigorous spirit sustained their project through the NIYC's critical formative years. By 1963 they had founded *Americans Before Colum-bus*, the first Red Power publication, to propagate their message. When the newspaper first appeared, the council had already begun to move in a new direction, embracing direct action as a means to resolve Indian problems.

When the 1960s began, most Americans forecast a bright and shin-ing future for their nation. In this time of widespread affluence and prosperity, the economy had expanded—the stock market soared and the gross national product increased from $282.3 billion in 1947 to a whopping $439.9 billion in 1960. Most Americans owned au-tomobiles and televisions, and the average American's income had almost doubled since World War II. Not all Americans, however, were content with the status quo. Many young African Americans, driven by the civic nationalist promise of inclusion, hoped to expe-dite the desegregation process in the South through vigorous new tactics. Although the Student Nonviolent Coordinating Commit-tee grew out of the greater civil rights movement, the organization gained its own reputation for direct action and civil disobedience.[2]

Challenging the region's Jim Crow laws through sit-ins and freedom rides, SNCC members risked serious bodily harm as rac-ist southerners reacted with a fury of hostility and aggression. The national media captured on film the activists' struggle and the ensuing police violence, making it available for the entire world to see. In 1961, SNCC launched a new voter registration drive throughout the Deep South in hopes of chipping away at the monolith of political disenfranchisement that had stood firm since the end of Reconstruction. Although the new project failed to gain the media exposure of the organization's earlier campaigns, SNCC achieved national recognition for its relentless approach to social change.[3]

The idea that young people could bring about change and make a difference resonated beyond ethnic or racial boundaries. The Students for a Democratic Society, an organization composed of mostly liberal white youths, joined with SNCC in confronting racism in the South. In 1962, as its membership expanded, SDS issued a fifty-page manifesto to articulate its political position. Known as "The Port Huron Statement," the document epitomized the high-minded idealism that had swept over many college-educated young people throughout the United States. The authors declared, "The bridge to political power . . . will be built through genuine cooperation, locally, nationally, and internationally, between a new left of young people, and an awakening community of allies." They vowed to "replace power rooted in possession, privilege, or circumstance by power and uniqueness rooted in love, reflectiveness, reason, and creativity." They criticized American racism, economic inequality, the arms race, and the entire Cold War culture that had permeated American society.[4]

The founding of the National Indian Youth Council was also a part of the growing politicization of young people in the United States. There were, however, some significant differences between the NIYC and its contemporaries. Women, for example, played a much greater role within the NIYC than they did in other student organizations. Joan Noble, Shirley Hill Witt, Karen Rickard, and others not only helped create the NIYC but also assumed positions of leadership. They often directed policy, planned meetings, edited the council's publications, and greatly contributed to the overall ideological evolution of the NIYC. Rickard has stated quite firmly, "In all of my dealings with NIYC, never once did I feel any sexism because I was a woman." Some observers may argue that a degree of institutional sexism existed within the council, as it was not until 1989 that a woman became executive director. But Viola Hatch, who has served on the board of directors for nearly forty years, insists, "Women were the backbone [of NIYC] and the men knew it. They were the most militant. They're the ones that forced them to get things done." Della Warrior corroborates Hatch's analysis, noting, "We just all had respect for one another and appreciation for our different roles and responsibilities." Regardless of one's final judgment, the NIYC had a much greater level of gender equality than did SNCC, SDS, and most other student organizations of the era.[5]

Another difference was that young people themselves independently founded and built the NIYC. African American students ran and led SNCC, but Ella Baker, executive director of the larger and older Southern Christian Leadership Conference, was primarily responsible for establishing the organization. Similarly, the SDS traced its roots back to an Old Left outfit called the League for Industrial Democracy, which created a student wing to propagate its ideals of peace and participatory politics on college campuses. Although the New Mexico Association on Indian Affairs had called for a national youth council to pull together people from the disparate regional councils, the organization never took solid steps to create such a body. Unlike the membership of SNCC or SDS, the students who formed the youth caucus at the Chicago Conference were solely responsible for the creation of the NIYC. They planned the charter conference and drew up articles of incorporation.

Independently establishing a national affiliation of Native women and men took considerable time and planning, not to mention the presence of someone with finely tuned organizational skills. Herb Blatchford was just the person for the job. A founding member of the Kiva Club and a veteran of both the Regional Indian Youth Council and the Workshop on American Indian Affairs, he eventually landed a job with the New Mexico State Department of Education after graduating from UNM and worked there during that fateful summer of 1961. Blatchford had a keen organizational mind and an eye for detail. Vine Deloria, Jr., observed that he "was very business-like and always wrote everything down." Moreover, he was older and more experienced than the other founders. "His

A graduate of the University of New Mexico, Herb Blatchford worked for the New Mexico State Department of Education before becoming the first executive director of the National Indian Youth Council. (Laura Gilpin, *Herbert Blatchford in the Field*, 1958, gelatin silver print, 4¹¹⁄₁₆ × 6¾ inches © 1979 Amon Carter Museum, Fort Worth, Texas, bequest of the artist, P1978.128.222)

leavening effect was important," Shirley Hill Witt recounted, adding, "I never once heard him [being] less than entirely reasonable."[6]

In the closing days of the Chicago Conference, Blatchford gathered the names and addresses of those who had participated in the youth caucus. Numerous people had expressed interest in calling an intertribal national gathering to continue the dialogue they had started in Chicago. "This unity would not be allowed to dissipate," the tenacious Blatchford vowed. Others, including Witt, felt the same way. Her enthusiasm for turning the Chicago Conference youth caucus into something meaningful matched that of Blatchford. A day after the conference, she sent her own list of contacts to Mel Thom—whom many saw as the de facto leader of the youth caucus—stressing that she and the others hoped to stay in touch and to hear from him.[7]

"Gregarious, honest, committed, and sincere," Mel Thom was born on the Walker River Paiute Reservation in Schurz, Nevada, on July 28, 1938. He shared the same tribal background as Wovoka, the famous spiritual leader and father of the late nineteenth-century Ghost Dance movement. Thom, however, reflected a much different era, having graduated from Lyon County High School in nearby Yerington before attending Brigham Young University to study civil engineering. Possessing a knack for leadership, he served as president of both the university's Indian student club, Tribe of Many Feathers, and the Regional Indian Youth Council. Dan Edwards (Yurok), a classmate of Thom's at BYU, remembered the Paiute as a "brilliant organizer" and a "very creative person." Edwards recalled how Thom was able to put together a float for BYU's 1959 homecoming the night before the parade. "We held a kegger and at 2 A.M. Mel put the float together. . . . He had every piece accounted for—every nail and everything. . . . He was that kind of brain." The next day, Thom, Edwards, and other members of the Tribe of Many Feathers slid into the parade and took second prize. After graduating from BYU, Thom landed a job in Los Angeles as assistant resident engineer for the Federal Aviation Administration. Thom took pride in his reservation roots and Paiute upbringing, noting that he had "subsisted on everything from fried jackrabbit and potatoes to chow mien."[8]

Recognizing that Thom had the ability to unify people, Blatchford wrote to him about calling a national Indian youth meeting. Blatchford posited that perhaps the meeting would lead to a new, national organization. Indian student clubs, youth councils, and workshops brought Native youth together, but they still lacked any sort of permanent vehicle for expressing the needs and political voice of young Indian people at the national level. "Where can he go to further his training before attempting to hold a leading position?" Blatchford asked. The answer was a new organization led and run by Indians. Blatchford continued to work out the details of his vision as he wrote. Perhaps at their national gathering, he mused, they could organize as a nonprofit corporation, adding, "All that is needed is a meeting of the charter members wherein they keep a careful record of the minutes." They could then draft

After graduating from the engineering school at Brigham Young University, Mel Thom helped establish the NIYC. He also served as the council's first president. (Used by permission of Fort Lewis College, Center of Southwest Studies, Theodore Hetzel Photograph Collection, P003 series A.5.g: 1959, 10:4)

articles of incorporation and submit them, along with an application to the state.[9]

Blatchford attempted to reassure Thom that enough people had expressed an interest to embark on such an endeavor. He suggested they hold the meeting in his hometown of Gallup between August 10 and 13 of 1961. By that time, the Colorado workshop would have concluded and students would still have a couple of weeks before the fall semester commenced. Moreover, the dates coincided with Gallup's Annual Inter-Tribal Indian Ceremonial, which would attract greater attention to their meeting. The ceremonial "could be used to gain public opinion on our ideas for an organization[,] thus giving us a set of guidelines along which to proceed," he noted. To facilitate discussion on such a conference, Blatchford offered to mimeograph the letters of Thom, Witt, and the others and send them out to all those who had been part of the Chicago youth caucus.[10]

Bursting with enthusiasm, Blatchford continued to build on his idea for a national, incorporated organization. In a letter to Witt, he wondered whether the new outfit could take over sponsorship of the regional youth councils. Perhaps the time had come for Indians themselves to assume control of their own destinies, rather than rely on non-Native sponsors. Though he believed that any future organization needed to be focused on and led by students, he maintained it should also pay respect to tribal elders, employing their advice and developing a working relationship with them. The organization should also allow for a "diversity of opinion" within its ranks, keeping the door open to all Indian youth who expressed interest in the future of Native America. Both Witt and Thom liked Blatchford's ideas, with the former vowing to make the Gallup meeting even if she had to travel by oxcart.[11]

After Blatchford laid the groundwork, Thom assumed command and sent out a blanket statement to the "Tentative Charter Membership" of what would become the NIYC. Thom emphasized the importance of breaking with the past, criticizing previous conferences and youth councils as being limited in their utility. Picking up on Blatchford's ruminations, he echoed the idea that non-Indian organizations had sponsored earlier endeavors. Native students, he asserted, "would prefer to have their own kind carry out their contentions." However, those interested in a new direction for Indian youth needed serious commitment rather than just "dedicated intentions without means to carry out their intentions." Thom mocked such impotence, commenting that past organizers always proclaimed "a new beginning" after each conference or council, only to remain idle until the next meeting the following year. He further reiterated Blatchford's ideas by noting that a new national council could act in a coordinating capacity by sponsoring regional youth councils and uniting the disparate college Indian clubs. The new council "should not become too far separated from the local youth groups," he affirmed. "We must maintain our position as a channel providing due recognition to the younger people."[12]

In a subsequent letter, Thom queried for ideas regarding the details in establishing a new organization. He wondered whether they should adopt a constitution and bylaws, appoint an executive director, elect officers and a board of directors, or even maintain a central mailing office. Should they hold an annual meeting, and if so, where was the ideal location? What kind of membership base did they need to establish to maintain a viable organization? Whom should the charter members tap for financial support? Thom quickly discovered the difficulties and intricacies of organization building.[13]

Thom's letters instigated further dialogue among the tentative charter members. John Winchester (Potawatomi) lent his voice to the discussion, asserting there was a need for a new intertribal association that could "contribute to carrying out new ideas for our senior Indian population." Joan Noble, another BYU student who had also participated in the Regional Indian Youth Council, suggested the new organization focus its energies "to help develop youth for leadership." She wondered if there would be any membership restrictions or if the new venture would be open to all. Blatchford continued the dialogue, contending that the only requirements for charter membership should be attendance at the Chicago Conference. Blatchford's list of conference attendees contained the names of twenty-four young people from across the United States, the majority of whom lived in rural tribal communities or on reservations.[14]

As the summer unfolded and the meeting in Gallup approached, Thom and Blatchford sorted out the last-minute details. The Paiute from Walker River resolved that the new organization should incorporate. He drew up a statement of incorporation and sent it out to the tentative membership for suggestions. He also registered his support for electing officers and creating a five-member executive board. Meanwhile, Blatchford made arrangements with the local BIA office in Gallup to secure one of the agency's school dormitories for the attendees. The Gallup Indian Community Center lent meeting space to Blatchford, despite the concurrent ceremonial, while the city's Chamber of Commerce donated miscellaneous convention materials. Blatchford and Thom would serve as a de facto taxi service, as they assumed responsibility for shuttling attendees about Gallup in their beat-up Chevrolets. Blatchford also devised an agenda for the gathering and asked that charter members develop answers to questions regarding the new organization's membership, purpose, duties, home base, and sponsorship.[15]

Only ten of the most devoted members from the original youth caucus—five women and five men—made their way through the high desert of New Mexico to attend the meeting in Gallup. They came by all modes of transport. Joan Noble roared into town in a bright red Karmann Ghia sports car, while others traveled cross continent via Greyhound bus. The stark realities of the reservation border town horrified some. Witt, for example, recalled: "Navajos were exploited for their crafts and then exploited for the little money they got back through pawn and crafts sales. Alcohol in the form of cheap red Thunderbird wine arrived in tank cars geared totally toward the Indian trade. The streets were littered by staggering, vomiting and passed-out Indians." Such exploitation, however, would only underscore the young peoples' sense of urgency and determination to bring about positive change for all Native people.[16]

Calling themselves the Chicago Conference Youth Council, the ten students held their first session on August 10. All in attendance dressed with what they perceived to be proper middle-class decorum: the women wearing skirts and heels and the men donning suits and ties in hopes of cultivating their image as responsible young people. Blatchford, with his penchant for parliamentary procedure, presided over the gathering and reiterated the main points of the agenda he had worked out, while Thom offered inspirational yet fiery opening remarks. Discussion initially centered on the organization's purpose. "What are we trying to do?" queried Clyde Warrior, the militant president of the Regional Indian Youth Council. Attendees questioned whether they were really establishing a viable organization or simply seeking status for themselves. Witt expressed concern about "political climbing" and creating an organization that was essentially a feeder for some other, larger outfit.[17]

The charter membership, however, overcame such fears, recognizing that it was high time for Native students to forge their own association. They also recognized that their youth and vigor would work to their advantage. Joan Noble put it best when she declared, "One thing about the young people is that they are more apt to go out and do what they think is right than the older group. They see the world as a place to explore." She contended it would be best if the new youth organization maintained its independence and avoided working for a sponsor. Others agreed, but questioned how they would relate to their elders. Should the Chicago Conference Youth Council turn their backs on the older generation or become their warriors?[18]

Mary Natani took the latter position, arguing they needed to leave leadership to the adults and the National Congress of American Indians. The youth would eventually grow and take their place, but it was improper to usurp the traditional order of things. "I think that if we are going to organize, let us not do it to fight the adults. . . . Maybe someday when I am older and I'm recognized as [having] some potential . . . I will get my chance to be a leader." Blatchford negotiated a "delicate balance," where youth leaders could strive for change through their own channels, while also respecting their elders and avoiding any "rapid change" that might come as a shock.[19]

Once they resolved their place in Indian country's organizational matrix, the charter members concluded the first session by turning their attention to membership criteria. Some asserted maximum age limits, while others believed the council should remain open to everyone. The majority argued that if they established an age limit, they would inevitably leave out a significant portion of those who showed genuine interest in their program. A more perplexing question was whether to devise a tier-system for memberships. Like the Society of American Indians some fifty years earlier, they grappled with the issue of whether non-Indians could become members. They settled on a two-tiered system. Native youth—whatever that meant—could hold full memberships, regardless of whether one were enrolled in a federally recognized tribe, while associate membership was reserved for their elders and non-Indians. Such a practical arrangement made sense. "After all," Warrior clarified, "we need the money, and theirs is as good as anyone else's."[20]

The second day's sessions began bright and early following breakfast at the Paramount Café, where Warrior had hollered to the waitress to "bring on the hot sauce" in hopes of adding a little fire to the morning. The attendees opened discussion with a rousing debate over what to call the new organization. Blatchford stuck with "National Indian Youth Council," the title the New Mexico Association on Indian Affairs had devised for its vision of an umbrella outfit to oversee the various regional youth councils. It seemed to make sense, but some members opposed the suggestion. Warrior, who remained silent during the initial conversation, eventually chimed in, declaring, "I don't like the ring of youth." He believed that observers might think "that I'm just a little young boy running around." Witt suggested they go with "National Indian Service Organization," while Noble recommended "National Indian Council." Warrior did not like either option. The first was "too energetic," while the second was "too powerful." Eventually, Thom convinced the irritated Ponca to go along with Blatchford's initial suggestion, and thus they became the National Indian Youth Council.[21]

The NIYC founders next discussed the hard truths of financing. Not only would they have to maintain a home office, but they also needed to fund an organizational newsletter, whose first issue would cost an estimated one hundred dollars. Once their publication got off the ground, it could potentially bring in some revenue. Moreover, a registration fee for the annual conference, as well as membership fees, could further offset operational costs. The founders therefore resolved to charge a flat membership rate of four dollars along with a registration fee that they would determine before the next meeting.[22]

When it came time to nominate the NIYC's first slate of officers, Warrior took charge as kingmaker. For president, he proclaimed his "good friend and colleague" Mel Thom as best suited for the job. Warrior proceeded to nominate Witt, "a young lady who has given valuable advice and worthy information," as first vice president and Noble as second vice president. Blatchford, an obvious choice, received the unanimous nomination for executive director. The initial board consisted of the remaining charter members, including Warrior, Bernadine Eschief, Howard McKinley, Jr., and Karen Rickard. John Winchester and Edison Real Bird would later replace Natani and Thomas Eschief, who withdrew their names.[23]

In closing, Warrior reminded those present that the NIYC's first year would be difficult. "I hope all of you will keep this fresh in your mind," he asserted. "This is going to be a tough year because we are building a foundation, and if we all get lax and let it go, then the whole organization will disintegrate." Thom agreed, adding that they might not accomplish much initially but eventually their efforts at this summer meeting in Gallup would pay off. He went on to note that young Indians needed guidance in navigating their way through white society and bridging the gap between tradition and progress. It was their responsibility to solve such problems and create a brighter future for all Native people. After these concluding words, Thom moved to adjourn.[24]

Following the sessions, the founders of the first independent Native youth organization rushed back to their dorms, where they traded their business suits and heels for jeans and moccasins. As the annual Gallup ceremonial coincided with the meeting, they took off for the city fairgrounds to take in the sights and sounds of the festivities. They navigated through the throngs of people as the smell of roasted corn and lanolin permeated the air. Later in the evening, they made their way out to McGaffey Lake near the Continental Divide for a grand Forty-niner. Blatchford and his wife, Christine, brought a pot of mutton stew and offered his coconspirators a taste of the local cuisine. Some found the concoction incredibly bland and opted to cook out over open fires. The fun lasted late into the night, as the founding members of the NIYC solidified their friendships and vowed to make their new organization last.[25]

As their time in Gallup concluded, Mel Thom, Shirley Hill Witt, Herb Blatchford, Joan Noble, Clyde Warrior, Karen Rickard, Howard McKinley, Mary Natani, and Thomas and Bernadine Eschief said their good-byes. They made their way back to their respective corners of Indian country with more concerns than they had time to address. Witt offered this memory:

The long ribbon of roadway and time allowed flashbacks to accompany me as I was swayed and jounced in the bus ride back to Massachusetts. I thought first about what we may have accomplished with this establishment of the National Indian Youth Council. Was it real? Definitive? Worth anything at all? Fragile? That last question bothered me the most: were we just noise signifying nothing? I thought about the reluctance to end that last afternoon's session. After voting to close, we sat there in silence for long minutes, reflecting, perhaps, on what we had come together to do and—most sobering of all—had we done it . . . and for what? . . . Mel and Joan had jobs to return to right away.

The time taken away for the American Indian Chicago Conference and now this, the week for building the National Indian Youth Council, put them in some jeopardy. Herb blessed us in his quiet, comforting way. We dispersed with more questions and far less zealotry than what we had brought to the meetings.[26]

Blatchford alone remained in Gallup, and within the following week he opened an account at the First State Bank there, depositing a meager sixteen dollars. Undaunted, he marched down to the McKinley County commissioners' office to file the NIYC's articles of incorporation. Over the course of the founding meeting, the charter members added articles on office holding, membership, and annual meetings but left Thom's initial statement more or less intact. The final version read:

We, the younger generation, at this time in the history of the American Indian, find it expedient to band together on a national scale in meeting the challenges facing the Indian people. In such banding for mutual assistance, we recognize the future of the Indian people will ultimately rest in the hands of the younger people, and Indian youth need be concerned with the position of the American Indian. We further recognize the inherent strength of the American Indian heritage that will be enhanced by a National Indian Youth Council. We, the undersigned believing in a greater Indian America, in order to form a non-profit corporation for the purposes hereinafter enumerated, do hereby certify as follows. . . .[27]

Unfortunately, as county employees informed the new executive director, the organization had to post an advance public notice in a local newspaper, announcing the dates and whereabouts of their meeting, which the charter members had failed to do. Blatchford therefore had to hold off until after the 1962 meeting to incorporate.[28]

As predicted, the National Indian Youth Council's first year of existence was shaky. Though the organization resolved to support the NCAI and its elders, the founding members also hoped to maintain their independence. For a group of young people, this proved difficult. Thom, who was an active voting member of the

NCAI, continued his activity within that organization and tapped executive director Helen Peterson for support. Peterson gave Thom permission to hold an NIYC board meeting at the NCAI annual gathering in Lewiston, Idaho. Blatchford believed the conference would be an excellent opportunity to plug for memberships and donations to lift their fledging outfit off the ground and finance the first edition of their newsletter, *Aborigine*. The NIYC might have disintegrated had the NCAI not given its financial support. Operating on a shoestring budget, the NIYC organizers happily received any contributions. When the United Traders Association donated funds, Blatchford celebrated, writing Witt, "It was a fine day for the Redskins when that $200 came in." Still, the charter members feared, as Thom put it, "a detrimental degree of dependence by relying too heavily on such assistance."[29]

For its part, the NIYC balked at sponsoring the 1962 Regional Indian Youth Council, which convened at Brigham Young University. Witt and Karen Rickard, however, organized a planning meeting in New York State to address the government's proposal to build a dam that would flood Seneca lands. After returning to the East Coast following the meeting in Gallup, the two women petitioned Karen's brother, William Rickard, for use of the Rickard family house as a gathering place for eastern Indian students and nonstudents concerned about the proposed dam. William had long been an advocate for full tribal sovereignty, believing the Iroquois nations should have a government-to-government relationship to the United States. The Tuscarora leader was initially fearful that the NIYC would become a pawn of the BIA, but his younger sister and Witt convinced him otherwise. The older sibling relented and, according to Witt, "was entirely gracious" when the young people finally met in his home.[30]

Witt and Karen Rickard had sent out invitations and posters to all tribal communities within a thousand-mile radius of Witt's home in South Hadley, Massachusetts. Local television and newspaper outlets in and around the Tuscarora reservation in New York State, including the *Niagara Falls Gazette* and Buffalo's WKBW Evening News, covered the gathering. Blatchford donated a Navajo blanket, which the two Iroquois NIYC leaders raffled off. Although the turnout was limited, Witt, Rickard, and Blatchford believed their efforts successful in linking the East with the West and hence fostering wider intertribal unity. According to Blatchford, the meeting stood as a "milestone" in overcoming the "old European strategy of divide and conquer," which had proved especially problematic for the Haudenosaunees. Observing the proceedings, William Rickard came to admire the young activists and gave his unequivocal support to the NIYC, declaring, "As long as your organization operates on honesty, it will have the blessing of the Great Spirit. . . . I offer my assistance to the Council whenever it needs it."[31]

As plans for the eastern regional meeting of the NIYC unfolded, Witt and Blatchford worked on the first edition of *Aborigine*. Without any antecedent, the two had to determine the content and direction of the newsletter, as well as resolve printing and distribution dilemmas. Blatchford envisioned a publication that was not overly lofty or political in its language but nonetheless insightful and intelligent. As it turned out, they had little in the way of opinion pieces or essays for the first issue and thus resolved to reprint the proceedings from the inaugural meeting in Gallup. Witt, who had named the publication, worried that readers would "yawn and then toss the whole booklet out," as the minutes seemed "boring, trite, ungrammatical, irrelevant, vague, ponderous, and obscure." To avoid such a predicament, she suggested that they summarize the proceedings rather than print them verbatim. Witt's involvement turned out to be an asset because of her literary skills and proximity to eastern media outlets. As Blatchford noted, "Our hick newspapers here do not carry much of good quality news on Indian affairs." Due to their limited finances, the two resolved to print up just one hundred copies, asking each charter member to foot a portion of the bill and pay for distribution costs.[32]

When it finally appeared in March 1962, *Aborigine* introduced both Native and non-Native people throughout Indian country and beyond to the NIYC. Karen Rickard sketched the council's seal, which emblazoned the cover of the newsletter and would become the organization's permanent symbol. Inside the cover, the newsletter listed the organization's officers, bylaws, and articles of incorporation and contained a summary of the first annual meeting

Shirley Hill Witt and Herb Blatchford developed and edited the NIYC's newsletter, *Aborigine*, which served as a recruiting tool for the organization. Karen
Rickard created the seal of the NIYC. (*Aborigine*, Shirley Hill Witt Papers [MSS
591 BC, box 3, folder 36], Center for Southwest Research, University Libraries,
University of New Mexico)

in Gallup. Despite Blatchford's concerns, the first issue also had
hints of an underlying nationalism. In his "Statement of the National Indian Youth Council," Mel Thom argued that the history of
the United States was one of suppression of American Indians. He
called for the preservation of the traditional values and beliefs of
Native people, stressing, "WE BELIEVE IN A FUTURE WITH HIGH PRIN-
CIPLES DERIVED FROM THE VALUES AND BELIEFS OF OUR ANCESTORS."
Native Americans could also play an "important role" in modern
society. "The Indian people are going to remain Indians for a long
time to come," he reminded his readers, but first they needed to

navigate their way through "a changing world of good and bad influences."[33]

Aborigine resonated with many of its readers, bringing in two hundred contributions and new memberships. Executive director Blatchford took stacks of "Abbies" to college Indian clubs throughout the Southwest, hoping to spread the news of the new organization and attract potential recruits. He informed Thom that he would attend the 1962 Regional Indian Youth Council at Brigham Young University, as "our future members will be coming to us from that direction." The Workshop on American Indian Affairs served a similar purpose. Students such as Browning Pipestem, Fran Poafpybitty (Comanche), Charles Cambridge, and Bruce Wilkie joined the NIYC after their workshop experience.[34]

The second annual NIYC meeting drew some of these new recruits. Again, the council organizers planned the gathering after the workshops to coincide with the Gallup ceremonial in early August. For much of the meeting, attendees focused on Indian identity and strategies for Native people to preserve their culture. Mirroring the philosophy of her older brother, Karen Rickard argued that Indians needed to reject the concept of forging a middle ground between Indian and white worlds and instead fully embrace the Native way. Blatchford agreed, contending that the Indian's way of viewing the world was more dynamic than the "either/or philosophy" of mainstream white society. One way they resolved to do this was by holding the annual NIYC meeting on Indian land. Joan Noble suggested her tribal community at Fort Duchesne on the Ute reservation in Utah as the next venue, to which the council's officers agreed. Besides such ruminations, much of the discussion revolved around housekeeping matters, such as finalizing the organization's bylaws and constitution before resubmitting them to the county commissioner's office for incorporation.[35]

When the second annual NIYC meeting ended on August 8, once again the young activists parted ways and scattered thousands of miles all over Indian country, with only the tenuous lines of the telephone and the U.S. postal service holding them together. Witt and Rickard followed Bernadine and Thomas Eschief back to their home on the Fort Hall Reservation in Idaho before heading back to the East Coast. As they made their way through the Upper Peninsula of Michigan, a pickup truck smashed into the side of Witt's Toyota Crown Custom. The two young women slowly regained consciousness to the sounds of startled voices asking whether they were Indians. "Yeess . . . Get help for us please," begged Rickard, as she bled profusely from the forehead. One man responded, "Don't do nothing. They're Indians. They'll go away." Finally a doctor stopped and called for an ambulance, which had to transport the two council founders across the Wisconsin state line, because hospitals in Michigan would not treat them. For ten days they languished in hospital until John Winchester drove six hundred miles from Ypsilanti, Michigan, to take the two women to the Detroit airport, where they caught a flight back to New York.[36]

In many ways, Rickard and Witt's car wreck stood as a metaphor for the nascent NIYC. Indian affairs were at a critical juncture, but the organization seemed unable to do anything about it. Little of substantive value had come out of the second annual meeting, as the founders searched for some way to move forward to make their organization purposeful. The struggle continued into the following year. Blatchford sent out applications for monetary aid to numerous philanthropic foundations, getting little response. The executive director and Vice President Witt managed to cobble together another edition of *Aborigine* that year, but its centerpiece essay—a rambling history of Native people from contact through World War II—seemed mundane and uninspired. To make matters worse, the distance separating the council's leaders complicated the coordination of NIYC activities, resulting in no national campaigns or activities during the council's first few years of existence.[37]

When the NIYC assembled for its third annual meeting at Fort Duquesne, there was an air of importance, despite the relative stagnation of the previous year. Clyde Warrior chastised all in attendance for their inactivity and lack of initiative. Moreover, actor Marlon Brando attended the gathering and even brought a crew to film the council's proceedings, adding a further element of drama to the meeting. Those in attendance discussed a myriad of issues, including termination as a violation of treaty rights. The officers spoke of unifying Indians and even carrying their plight to foreign nations, making the case that if America had violated Indian treaties, "other international treaties cannot be qualified as worthy documents." Others expressed concern over the media's continued use of negative images of Native people, especially the widely disseminated stereotype of the drunken Indian.[38]

With Brando's film crew hovering in the background in search of the perfect camera angle and quotable sound bites, council members went on to initiate a debate on whether they should unite with African American students and join the civil rights struggle. Many argued such action would "divide the tribes" and that "the unity of Indians would suffer" if they forged such an alliance. Native people had different goals from those of blacks. Indians had no desire to integrate into white society; rather, sovereignty was their foremost concern. As one person succinctly put it, "Indians want to retain what they have and the Negro wants something the whites have." This fundamental difference rooted in each group's distinct historical experience would remain a recurring problem for Native activists and would serve as a barrier that inhibited any major, lasting coalition between Native activists and their African American counterparts.[39]

Still, many of the founding NIYC members realized that they could find common cause with black people. As subalterns, both groups sought greater freedom and justice from a society and a political system that had oppressed them for centuries. Some pointed to the discrimination that Indians in the Deep South suffered, noting that, like African American communities, many southeastern tribes were more or less barred from voting by white authorities. Others, such as Rickard, attended the March on Washington in 1963 to show solidarity with other people of color. But in the end, they concluded that such injustices were minor when compared with their larger agenda of treaty rights, sovereignty, self-determination, and cultural preservation. Indians had always been outside white society's electoral process, as treaties brokered with the federal government gave most tribes a unique trust relationship with the United States. If Native people followed the black students' lead, they might jeopardize their special status.[40]

Exchanging ideas on treaty rights, media stereotypes, and the civil rights movement may have fostered lively dialogue for Brando's film crew, but at the end of the day, many still wondered how they could achieve something tangible. As one attendee asked, in the long run would "words and personality exercises be enough?" They spoke of informing the public at large of Native people's plight to sustain treaty rights and overturn forced termination, but how, they pondered, could they best do this? Some in attendance believed the NIYC needed to take action and "make a stand on an issue." The organization should "place its aims at something it can accomplish," one member suggested. The problem, however, was to pinpoint a prominent issue and determine what type of action to take.[41]

Some thought that a new national publication that focused on major issues confronting Native peoples could act as "a sounding board for ideas" and foster better dialogue on how best to proceed. Accordingly, the organization established *Americans Before Columbus*, which, like *Aborigine*, began as a mimeographed newsletter. Unlike its predecessor, however, *ABC*, as it came to be known, reported on major issues affecting Native Americans, while also giving young people a venue to express their opinions. Along with Thom's regular column, "For a Greater Indian America," opinion pieces on a multitude of issues promulgated the NIYC's core philosophy of treaty rights, sovereignty, self-determination, and cultural preservation. With its premier issue, *Americans Before Columbus* became the first Red Power publication.[42]

Tillie Walker (Mandan) of the United Scholarship Service (USS)—an organization devoted to helping Native students financially—acted as *ABC*'s initial coordinator. Described as "a really big-hearted person," Walker possessed the know-how and necessary experience to get the newspaper off the ground. "She knew how to facilitate things and how to get things done," Gerald Brown recalled, "[and] she saw that [we] needed assistance." Walker, along with Ansel Carpenter, Jr. (Sioux), and Fran Poafpybitty, both veterans of the Workshop on American Indian Affairs, published the newspaper out of the USS office in Denver. The first issue, released in October, contained articles that reflected the NIYC's growing discontent and restlessness. One anonymous piece took shots at the

National Congress of American Indians, critiquing the organization's recent convention and noting how "disheartening" it was to see its members "waste time, energy and talent on petty tattle tailing and personal vengeance." A two-part essay entitled "Law and Order" ripped into Public Law 280, which transferred federal trust responsibilities to individual states without the consent of the affected tribes. According to the article, the law proved especially troublesome in Washington State, where authorities failed miserably in administering services.[43]

The second issue of *ABC* hit the press two months later and continued its focus on Washington State. The second installment of "Law and Order" turned up the heat, blaming state authorities for trampling Indian sovereignty and self-determination while failing to live up to their trust responsibilities. Another article on Native fishing rights exposed the state's failure to abide by treaties brokered between the United States and the Muckleshoot, Puyallup, and Quinault Indians. The NIYC reported that Native people were "engaged in a great battle to preserve their aboriginally-derived" rights. This protracted "war" took a toll on the Indians of western Washington, as their resources and ability to continue the fight waned. "The opposition grows stronger and is joined by the machinery of state government," which used local courts to extinguish fishing rights and even questioned the legitimacy of the Puyallup tribe. State game wardens forcefully prohibited the tribes from freely fishing along the rivers in the region. Moreover, a biased media, buoyed by wealthy sports fishermen associations, reported only Washington State's position. The article concluded, "It seems essential that the Indians of Western Washington unite in a spirit of common concern and cooperation to develop a program of control and conservation of their fisheries."[44]

In yet another article, "Washington State Shifts War Strategy," the NIYC declared that the state's game department had "virtually declared war on Indian fisheries." Using an "armed militia," game wardens confiscated nets and seized the Indians' catches, depriving them of their food source and income. The article went on to draw parallels with the past and placed the blame for salmon depletion on white sportsmen:

Like the buffalo of the Great Plains, the whiteman saw great profit and
pleasure in exterminating as many buffalo as possible. So too with the
salmon. The Indians are not guilty of depleting the salmon run. The
Indian take of salmon has actually diminished during the past few
years. Through exorbitant catches facilitated by modern equipment,
and pollution of streams and immediate areas by heavy industry and
logging operations the whiteman created the problem. If any one group
is to blame for depleting the salmon run it is the non-Indian. . . .

The facts are plain. The Indians have treaty rights to fish and the
moral right of every person in this country, to make an honest living.
Indian fisheries provide the larger part of the Indians' livelihood. The
state on the other hand, not willing to tackle the real contributors to
salmon depletion, bully the Indians. For the mere pleasure of the sports
fisherman the State is attempting to sacrifice the livelihoods of Indian
citizens. Every man has a right to make a living.[45]

The NIYC had sounded the alarm, stressing that something had
to be done to combat Washington's "new strategy." As discussed
at the Fort Duchesne meeting the previous summer, the organization had found an issue on which to take a stand. Council members
failed, however, in pinning down exactly what sort of action they
needed to take.[46]

ABC's emphasis on Washington State and fishing rights was due
to the addition of two new dynamic leaders, Bruce Wilkie and Hank
Adams. Wilkie, a Makah from Neah Bay on Washington's Olympic
Peninsula, studied political science and economics at the University of Puget Sound in Tacoma. He cut his teeth in Indian policy
at the 1962 Workshop on American Indian Affairs, where he also
met Clyde Warrior. Adams, on the other hand, was an Assiniboine
from the Fort Peck Reservation in eastern Montana. He grew up
on the coastal Quinault reservation in Taholah, Washington, where
he learned the traditional subsistence patterns of his adopted tribe.
Adams's sharp mind and firm grasp of federal Indian policy im-
pressed all who knew him; Vine Deloria, Jr., described Adams as
"one of the most intelligent" people he had ever met. Like Wilkie,
Adams was a college student, studying education at the University
of Washington in Seattle.[47]

The influence of Adams and Wilkie would prove decisive in shaping the direction the NIYC took in 1964. As the crisis over fishing rights in the Pacific Northwest heated up, Thom and the organization's officers called a special mid-year meeting on December 28 and 29 at the Olin Hotel in Denver. Joined again by Marlon Brando, who offered his support and media connections to help bring the NIYC's cause to the public eye, council members discussed what the organization could do in the way of direct action to solve Indian problems. Gearing up for some sort of engagement, officers appointed Pachel Sherman as their legal counsel. Weeks later, Wilkie, Warrior, and Thom met again with Brando in New York City, where they told local and international media correspondents about their new "campaign of awareness." According to Thom and the others in attendance, they devised this new agenda to bring light to the plight of American Indians and treaty rights. Still, they failed to adopt a resolution that committed the council to any specific cause. Part of the reason for the hesitancy may have been their desire to receive a petition from a tribe specifically requesting their assistance.[48]

Such an appeal came the following February. Learning of the NIYC through Adams and Wilkie, the Puyallup, Nisqually, and Muckleshoot Indians requested the organization's support in the fight to preserve their traditional fishing rights as guaranteed by the federal treaties negotiated in 1854–1855. Council officers called an emergency meeting on February 8, again in Denver, where they decided to take action. On the suggestion of Wilkie and Adams, the organization planned to hold a series of "fish-ins" to demonstrate against Washington State's policies. When the March edition of *ABC* came out, Thom announced that the NIYC would make its stand. Days later, the fish-in campaign began.[49]

As Mel Thom packed his bag for Washington State, he and the other founders of the National Indian Youth Council could take pride in their achievement. Those committed young people who founded the council had constructed an organization from the ground up. With only the most meager of resources at their disposal, they relied on their own ingenuity and vision "for a greater

Indian America" to build their council. To be sure, they took the organizational structure of the Regional Indian Youth Council and the lessons from the Workshop on American Indian Affairs, but the NIYC arose as something new—it was the first independent Native student organization.

Thom and his coconspirators went on to found *Americans Before Columbus*, which broke ground as the first Red Power publication, hitting the press more than a decade before *Akwesasne Notes* and other subsequent newspapers. *ABC* served as the voice of the NIYC and acted as a sounding board for ideas, which eventually led the council's leadership to confront the crisis unfolding on the banks of the Nisqually and Puyallup rivers in Washington State. The NIYC's efforts would bring international attention to the Indians of the Pacific Northwest and their struggle to preserve treaty rights. The fish-ins would also lift the NIYC out of obscurity and transform it into a nationally recognized and respected organization.

CHAPTER 5

"THE TIME COMES WHEN WE MUST TAKE ACTION!"

The Fish-in Campaign and the Rise of Intertribal Direct Action

Before Mel Thom, Clyde Warrior, Shirley Hill Witt, John Winchester, and other activists crossed into Washington State to inaugurate the fish-ins of 1964, American Indians' experience in conducting intertribal civil disobedience was limited. In the late 1950s the Haudenosaunee engaged in direct action to protect tribal lands and deflect state and federal government attempts to circumvent treaty rights by building massive public works projects, such as Kinzua Dam, on Seneca land. Tuscaroras William Rickard and Wallace "Mad Bear" Anderson rose to local infamy with their relentless defense of Iroquois sovereignty, clashing with authorities and even spending time in jail for their actions. However, the localized nature of the Iroquois struggle failed to draw intertribal involvement. The National Congress of American Indians considered their fight but never committed to actively joining the cause. The NCAI, indeed, believed that any kind of protest or direct action was distasteful and contrary to the Indian way. Well into the 1960s, the organization displayed a banner that read, "Indians Don't Demonstrate."[1]

The new direction the National Indian Youth Council blazed in early 1964 made activism a part of the greater intertribal fight to preserve Native culture, uphold treaty rights, push for self-determination, and promote tribal sovereignty. Years before the Indians of All Tribes took over Alcatraz Island or militants in the American Indian Movement descended on Wounded Knee, Native students—both men and women—from throughout the United

States joined with the Indians of the Pacific Northwest to confront government authorities, risking arrest and bodily harm. The fish-ins paved the way for future intertribal activist endeavors. "It was a major source of encouragement and hope to have a Ponca from Oklahoma, a Paiute from Nevada, a Tuscarora from New York, a Flathead from Montana, a Navajo from New Mexico, a Mohawk from Michigan, and a Pottawatomie from Ford Motors among others offering to fight for their cause," Hank Adams reflected shortly after the protest. The NIYC's efforts escalated the fight for treaty rights and gave national exposure to the nascent Red Power movement. In mid-1964 the National Indian Youth Council stood as the foremost intertribal protest organization in operation.[2]

By the time the NIYC launched its fish-in campaign, student activism in the United States was in full swing. As early as 1958 the NAACP youth council of Wichita, Kansas, with the support of local black churches, had coordinated a series of sit-ins throughout Oklahoma. In Oklahoma City, Tulsa, Enid, and Stillwater, African American students challenged Jim Crow laws that had been on the books for decades. This first cluster of student sit-ins sparked subsequent action in other cities. In 1959 the Congress of Racial Equality (CORE) held civil disobedience workshops in Miami, Florida, where they prepared black students for a second wave of sit-ins. Students descended on segregated lunch counters throughout the city, resulting in multiple arrests and violent attacks from racist whites. Similar action occurred in Greenville, South Carolina; Atlanta, Georgia; and, most famously, Greensboro, North Carolina.[3]

The events in Greensboro in early 1960 led to a flurry of sit-ins in some sixty-nine cities throughout the upper South, but as sociologist Aldon Morris explains, all of these demonstrations "grew out of a context of organized movement centers." Contrary to popular perception, the black church, the NAACP, the SCLC, and CORE—not student-based organizations on college campuses—organized the sit-in movement. Similarly, it was Ella Baker, a veteran of the NAACP and the SCLC, who brought young leaders together to form the Student Nonviolent Coordinating Committee. Indeed, SNCC, the student organization that emerged as the vanguard of direct action in the early 1960s—the movement that inspired and influenced student activists across racial, ethnic, and gender lines—was the brainchild of the established leadership of the civil rights movement.[4]

Unlike the sit-in campaign, which elders in the NAACP, CORE, and the SCLC devised and organized, the fish-ins were planned and executed by Native students without the guidance of a larger organization such as the NCAI or any other group for that matter. Certainly the NIYC found inspiration from those African American students in the South, and without a doubt the council borrowed their direct action tactics—for Native students too were products of the Cold War political climate, viewing the world through a highly moralistic lens. But the leaders of the NIYC functioned independently, without extensive training in civil disobedience or the backing of a church or larger organizational structure. The NIYC received a request from the Native fishers who were sick of being arrested and harassed, and the council decided, quite boldly, to take action.

This is not to say that the fish-in movement simply materialized in a vacuum. The roots of the struggle for fishing rights in Washington extend back well into the nineteenth century when whites first began settling the Pacific Northwest. Isaac Ingalls Stevens, who became the first governor of the newly established Washington Territory in 1853, employed the Indian Treaty Act, purchasing land from the Native inhabitants and granting it to white settlers. Despite his attempts to extinguish Native land claims, the territorial governor recognized the importance and centrality of fishing to the Indians of the region. Not only were the salmon and steelhead trout their primary source of food, but the fish also kept their world in balance; there was a spiritual, even symbiotic, connection between the two.[5]

Of course Stevens was no culturally sensitive government agent seeking to carve out a pluralistic social utopia in the Pacific Northwest. More than anything, the governor wanted the land, not the fish. Besides, if the government prohibited the indigenous people from fishing, it would have to provide some sort of alternative subsistence. Hence Stevens set about dividing the Salish villages in the region into "tribes" so that he could more effectively employ the

Indian Treaty Act and broker binding agreements. The signatories of the Treaty of Point Elliot came from villages in the northern Puget Sound region, while those who signed onto the Treaty of Medicine Creek were concentrated further south. Several other treaties followed, including the Treaty of Point No Point for the people living in the Kitsap Peninsula, and the Treaty of Neah Bay for those from the northern Olympic Peninsula.[6]

Together the treaties resulted in the loss of millions of acres of land, but they guaranteed "the right of taking fish, at all usual and accustomed grounds and stations" and confirmed that Indian peoples held their right to fish "in common with all citizens of the Territory." Stevens even personally assured them of the validity of the documents, telling one group of signatories, "This paper secures your fish." Such promises lived on in the oral traditions of the Native people from the Oregon Country. Andy Fernando of the Upper Skagits, for example, recalled that more than one hundred years after the treaties were signed, his grandparents reminded him of Stevens's pledge, noting, "To the elders, a promise made was a promise kept."[7]

Beginning in 1887 the federal government further threatened the Native land base through the Dawes Severalty Act, which broke tribal lands into individual allotments and sold off all surplus lands. The Nisquallys had claimed 4,700 acres as set forth in the Treaty of Medicine Creek, but by the mid-twentieth century only 835 acres of the original reservation still existed. Similarly, the Puyallups lost 17,463 of the 18,000 acres of their original reservation. As tribally owned acreage in the Pacific Northwest dwindled and Indians began adopting white forms of subsistence, some observers questioned the continued existence of certain tribes. Moreover, many of the "usual and accustomed places" were no longer located within tribal boundaries. Changing demographics and territorial displacement begged the question of whether Native people could fish within the reservation boundaries as they had existed in the 1850s or even in the modern day.[8]

Matters became more complicated when increased logging and urban sprawl began to affect watersheds. Pollution, sportfishing, and the proliferation of massive fisheries led to a decline in salmon runs and forced state authorities to enact conservation measures.

The first such restrictions came in 1877, but authorities typically overlooked Indian subsistence fishing and recognized the validity of the treaties that Stevens had brokered roughly twenty years earlier. In the decades that followed, however, as public memory of the treaties faded and the popularity of sport fishing increased, the Washington State government began to crack down. New restrictions in the 1890s prohibited out-of-season fishing at stations Native people traditionally frequented. Into the twentieth century the state proceeded to erect more laws, which its Department of Game and Fish began enforcing with vigor.[9]

Native people, however, continued to fish as they had for generations. Their actions angered many white fishers who blamed the Muckleshoots, Puyallups, Nisquallys, and other Puget Sound Indians for the declining numbers of trout and salmon. They called for more sweeping restrictions that would bring the Indians of the Pacific Northwest in line with state fish and game laws. After World War II the Washington State Sportsmen's Council—the political lobby and mouthpiece of recreational fishers—took the lead in opposing Indian fishing. The Washington State Department of Game and Fish buoyed the organization, as many employees attended meetings and involved themselves in the council's affairs.[10]

Although the primary concern of the Sportsmen's Council remained conservation, members of the organization adhered to the civic nationalist spirit of the era, believing that the virtues of American civilization should extend to all peoples. The council therefore supported the termination of the federal government's trust responsibilities and concurred with many government officials that assimilation of Native people into American society should stand as the United States' goal. Floyd Whitmore, an active member of the council, voiced this sentiment at one of the organization's meetings in March 1955, when he stated: "The long-range solution is the integration of the Indian population rather than their segregation on reservations. Education of the Indians in conservation principles is necessary." This philosophy drove the council in its protracted legal and political battle with the Native people of the Northwest.[11]

The passage of Public Law 280 in 1953 only worsened things for Native people. Also known as the Enabling Act, the measure shifted

jurisdiction over Indian affairs from the federal Department of the
Interior to state governments. Eventually the law took effect in thir-
teen states, including Washington. For Native fishers, the Enabling
Act further jeopardized their efforts to preserve long-standing
treaty rights, as the State of Washington's Department of Game and
Fish had proven to be their greatest opponent. Although the law
nominally exempted hunting and fishing from state control, Native people rightly viewed PL 280 as a threat to their sovereignty. It
would be much more difficult to solicit federal involvement under
the measure's provisions.[12]

Their fears came to life when game wardens began arresting fishers shortly after passage of the Enabling Act. The first such arrest
came in 1954, when Robert Satiacum (Puyallup-Yakama) challenged
state game laws by intentionally gillnetting out of season and without a license. The case eventually made its way to Washington
State's Supreme Court, which split 4–4 on whether the Department
of Game and Fish had the authority to limit or regulate Indian fishing. Although the court had to drop charges against Satiacum, the
simple fact that it heard the case implied that such matters fell under
state jurisdiction—a troubling prospect for those who favored federal treaty rights. To make matters worse, the court declared it
"would permit the state to abrogate [Indian] treaty rights at will."[13]

The conflict between state authorities and Indian fishers escalated in the early 1960s, as game wardens began raiding Native fish
camps. In one instance, armed Skagit Indians responded by intimi-
dating game wardens with the possibility of violence. "They have
been crowding us," complained chief enforcement officer Walter
Neubrech. "They've threatened us and there has been some bodily
contact with some of our people." Undaunted, wardens stepped
up their raids. In September 1963 they arrested and took into cus-
tody fifteen Muckleshoots who had set up nets across the Green
River. Judge F. A. Walterskirchen ruled in the subsequent trial that
the accused were members of the Skope-Ahmish band and hence
not signatories of the Point Elliot Treaty. Although Walterskirchen's
ethnographic knowledge of Salish-speaking peoples may have been
questionable, his decision stuck and temporarily halted Muckleshoot fishing along the Green River.[14]

In 1963, Native people received another blow with the ruling in *State v. McCoy*. The case stemmed from the arrest of a Swinomish Indian who had been fishing along the Skagit River using a six-hundred-foot gillnet. The defendant had been commercially selling his catches, which no doubt affected the Washington State court's verdict. In its decision, the court gave sweeping regulatory powers to the state's Game and Fish Department. State control over off-reservation fishing was both "reasonable and necessary" for conservation purposes, the judge declared; it did not matter that the defendant was a member of a tribe that had signed a treaty guaranteeing the right to fish at usual and accustomed places.[15]

The *McCoy* decision reverberated throughout tribal communities in western Washington. Some Native fishers drove to the state capital in Olympia to meet with the governor and air their grievances, while others simply ignored the decision and continued to fish as they always had. On January 1, 1964, a group of Nisquallys made their way to Frank's Landing on the Nisqually River, only to find that game wardens—possessing an injunction from the Pierce County superior court—had closed the entire river to fishing. Arrests followed as the fishers attempted to cast their nets. Days later, the court issued a restraining order. "We are certain the Indians will not continue fishing after receiving copies of the restraining order," game warden Neubrech told reporters. Raising an American flag at Frank's Landing, Janet McCloud, a Tulalip who joined the crusade announced, "Our people have fought and died for the United States and we have an agreement with it to fish these grounds. We plan to do so . . . and this flag will give us courage." The Indians cast their nets; arrests followed.[16]

By February the situation had spiraled out of control. Tribal leaders met with NIYC representatives Bruce Wilkie and Hank Adams—both of whom had strong ties to the region—to discuss the crisis. Wilkie, who served as both executive secretary of the NIYC and treasurer-manager of the Makah Tribal Council, suggested that Indians turn out in force to voice their grievances to Democratic governor Albert Rosellini. Some members of the Affiliated Tribes of Northwest Indians and the Intertribal Council of Western Washington Indians expressed concern over the use of protest tactics to protect treaty rights. They feared such methods might associate Indian fishers with southern blacks, a circumstance that many believed would tarnish their cause. Wilkie remained ambiguous about NIYC's strategy. He told reporters for the *Seattle Post-Intelligencer* that Indians would not engage in protest marches or sit-ins but would find their own way to convey their message. However, that same day, he announced to the *Seattle Times* that Native activists might employ the same tactics used by civil rights activists to present their case.[17]

Although they made contrary statements publicly, behind the scenes council staffers had already decided on launching a campaign of direct action. Years later, NIYC president Mel Thom recalled that whites had proscribed certain modes of behavior for Indians to follow and that his organization aimed to break this trend. He noted that it was a radical idea to employ demonstrations, but the adage "Indians don't demonstrate" seemed outmoded and needed to be "done away with." The NIYC sought to do something "dynamic and different"—its members wanted to prove they "had guts to take direct action."[18]

Shortly after meeting with tribal leaders, Thom announced, "The time comes when we must take ACTION!" He informed the council's membership that the organization would finally make its stand on the protection of treaty rights in the Pacific Northwest. Herb Blatchford sent telegrams to Shirley Hill Witt and John Winchester in Michigan, who promptly purchased plane tickets from Ann Arbor to Washington State. Thom, Clyde Warrior, Karen Rickard, and Gerald Brown also made travel arrangements, while Wilkie and Hank Adams began coordinating upcoming events and a plan of attack. They gained the support of nearly all the tribes in Washington. Besides such regional backing, Seminoles from Florida, Winnebagos from Nebraska, Blackfeet from Montana, Shoshones from Wyoming, and Sioux from the Dakotas all committed to the cause and made their way to the Northwest. Blatchford later noted that the fish-ins were "the first full-scale intertribal action since the Indians defeated General Custer on the Little Big Horn," while Thom added, "We were ending the government's divide-and-rule system among Indians."[19]

Along with gaining wide intertribal support, the NIYC secured the services of Marlon Brando, who announced he would join the NIYC in its campaign. Wilkie and Adams believed his presence would attract greater media attention to their crusade and aid the larger goal of sustaining treaty rights. Brando's involvement did not revolve solely around media exploitation. According to Reverend John J. Yaryan, an Episcopal priest from San Francisco's Grace Cathedral, the actor was "very, very sincere" and completely dedicated to the cause. John Winchester further observed, "Brando's strictly on his own. We don't channel what he says. Sometimes he just gets so roaring mad over some of the things that have happened to Indians we have to hold him down." Other activists, however, viewed Brando's past involvement with the civil rights movement as detrimental. One staffer told journalist Hunter S. Thompson, "We're happy to have Marlon on our side . . . but he's one of our big problems too, because he keeps making statements comparing Indians and Negroes; the two movements are entirely different."[20]

Indeed, many NIYC organizers feared that association with the African American civil rights struggle would hurt their campaign. Part of the problem was the widespread racism against blacks. "The Negroes don't have the law on their side yet and they have a lot of popular prejudice against them, while the Indians' problem is the Federal bureaucracy; we almost have the law on our side in the form of treaties, and all we ask the white man to do is live up to those treaties," one activist explained. NIYC president Thom took an even harsher tone, accusing NAACP attorney Jack Tanner of "meddling" in Washington Indian affairs. "This is Indian business," Thom pointedly told reporters, "and he should not bring his group into it. This is an Indian treaty, not a civil right issue."[21]

After soliciting involvement and coordinating events, the NIYC settled on the first three days of March to hold the fish-ins and a subsequent protest rally at the state capitol in Olympia. Wilkie notified local and national media outlets of their plans. Like civil rights strategists, NIYC leaders recognized that news coverage of the fish-ins was vital to spreading the message of Indian treaty rights and Washington State's suppression of those rights. "We knew the game wardens would make arrests," recalled Thom. The key was catching the wardens on film harassing and arresting Indians who were peacefully fishing as they had for generations.[22]

The night before the big fish-in, Wilkie's Makah tribe held a special potlatch ceremony for the activists, giving them necklaces, baskets, and paddles in tribute to their efforts. The following day, on March 1, NIYC organizers, local Indian fishers, reporters, and game wardens crowded along the banks of the Puyallup River. "You could feel the hostility that was being built up against the game wardens," recalled Thom. The tension temporarily ceased when some Indians took out cameras and began taking photographs of the visibly angry authorities. Soon a near carnival-like atmosphere pervaded, as demonstrators continued to snap pictures and Indian children ran and played along the riverbanks.[23]

The fun ended, however, when Brando and the Episcopal priest Yaryan cast gillnets into the Puyallup. To ensure their arrest, Bill Satiacum had filled the bilge of their boat with salmon he had caught the night before. Authorities quickly descended on them, charged the two with violating the state's restraining order, and carted them off to jail. An entourage of activists, journalists, and speculators followed them to the police station, intensifying the media spectacle. Lining the hallways outside the jail, the crowd grew increasingly loud in their protestations until finally the authorities released Brando and Yaryan. Pierce County prosecutor John McCutcheon even dropped the charges against Brando, explaining, "I don't see any purpose in prolonging it or allowing him to sit in jail and make a martyr out of himself. This was done for show only and we are not going to make a mockery out of the law or our own office." McCutcheon, however, was too late. News of the fish-ins and Brando's arrest splashed across the front pages of Washington newspapers and flowed through national newswires.[24]

The night following their initial fish-in, NIYC activists and Brando gathered in the lobby of the Olympia Hotel to strategize how to proceed. The following day they would hold a massive protest at the state capitol, but many council staffers worried about future action. Shirley Hill Witt put it this way:

The arrest of Brando and Yaryan was heady stuff, but then what? Certainly it was imperative to capture the moment and capitalize on the

Shirley Hill Witt *(second from right)*, Gerald Brown *(far right)*, and other NIYC leaders journeyed to Washington State in 1964 to help organize and participate in the fish-ins. (National Indian Youth Council Records [MSS 703 BC, box 1, folder 15], Center for Southwest Research, University Libraries, University of New Mexico)

event. The news media went into a paroxysm during which interviews with "talking heads" flooded the television screens. The local NAACP representatives had problems with the Indian action, insisting that the Black political movement "would take care of Indian problems" with the implication that the Indians should quiet down and let them handle Indian grievances. Even more unlikely, comedienne Phyllis Diller told them simply "to go home" since it was un-American to behave like that. . . . The newspapers and talk show hosts called the members of NIYC a variety of colorful names, among them was "Red Turks," "Red Muslims," and, picking up on the American ambiguity toward England's famous musical export, "Red Beatles." Also muttered, combining impacted racism, was "Red Niggers." All of this, along with the expectations of the fishing people, made it imperative that concrete steps should be taken and not just for the short term but for the future, too. Otherwise, the effort would amount to no more than *Sturm und Drang* with no lasting benefit.[25]

They talked late into the night, each offering his or her opinion. Even gonzo journalist Hunter S. Thompson interjected. Witt remembered that Thompson "discarded any pretense to impartiality as a recorder for his *National Observer* newspaper, springing forth with one scheme after another, all of which were exceedingly weird and politely rejected by the NIYC planners." Brando proved more pragmatic and suggested that activists meet with Governor Rosellini and directly confront him with Washington State's blatant violation of Native peoples' treaty rights. The evening ended on an upbeat note, with Brando and Witt tango dancing into the wee hours of the morning.[26]

The media frenzy over the fish-ins and Northwest Indians' treaty rights followed the NIYC to Olympia for its planned mass protest. Estimates of the size of the crowd gathered at the state capitol varied, ranging anywhere from to 1,500 to 5,000, but whatever the figure, it remained the largest intertribal protest ever assembled. As the energy mounted, Makahs from Neah Bay performed traditional dances on the steps of the capitol, while others danced in front of the governor's mansion. Several organizers gave speeches, demanding change in Indian affairs and Washington's acknowledgment of Northwest tribes' treaty rights. Hank Adams, as part of the NIYC's "Proclamation of Protest," issued a series of demands to the state government. Adams called for the appointment of a state Indian advisory committee consisting of Native members; a joint state and federal scientific study of Indian, recreational, and commercial fishing in Washington's rivers; and an immediate halt to arrests of Indians fishing at "usual and accustomed" places.[27]

Clyde Warrior's fiery speech followed Adams's more reasoned platform. The Ponca asserted that the fish-in marked "the beginning of a new era in the history of American Indians." He maintained that, for the first time, Indians from diverse tribal backgrounds had congregated and protested peacefully, seeking to rid America of "a cancerous sore" that made a mockery of the United States and defiled the nation's integrity. "From time immemorial," Warrior exclaimed, Native people of the Northwest had fished the rivers of western Washington, and they would continue to do so for generations to come. Taking a religious tone, he blamed state authorities not only for breaking treaties but also for severing "the sacred relationship between the Indian and God." Thus, Indians faced "an indignity to the human spirit" and "the worst kind of discrimination."[28]

Warrior, Adams, Thom, Blatchford, Winchester, Wilkie, and Brando then met with Governor Rosellini in the capitol rotunda to talk about Indian fishing and federal treaty rights, while Witt spoke with the press corps gathered outside. Refusing to pull any punches, NIYC leaders and tribal leaders issued a joint statement, which read:

> The past and present history of treaties between the federal government and their captive Indian nations exemplify a treaty as a "convenient way of license to steal" for the government. If this be so, then perhaps our next appeal must be to the governments and people of the world. For it would seem that Hanoi, or Moscow, or London, or France should be deeply concerned with the United States treaties and the violation of them. For if Justice is denied to us today because we are weak and defenseless by you who have the power to mete justice, then the day will come when you or our children will also appeal for justice to the deaf ears of your conquerors. "The seeds you sow are the crops you reap."[29]

The governor received the memorial and met with the activists for nearly four and a half hours. He agreed to some of the demonstrators' demands, including Adams's suggestion that the state create an advisory board consisting of Native members. The governor also paid lip service to protecting treaty rights and upholding Native sovereignty. Overall, however, the meeting with Rossellini proved to be, to use Brando's word, "unsatisfactory."[30]

The governor related his and the state of Washington's stance in a speech he delivered to the crowd. Complimenting those in attendance, Rosellini began by stressing the "progress and accomplishments" of Native people in recent history. He reminded them of all the state services available to Indians, including public schools, welfare assistance, and health care. "As always state agencies stand ready to cooperate with you," he told his listeners. Rosellini then quickly took a more resistant position, proclaiming the state's fisheries to be essential to Washington's economy, while their "proper care and management" was "of importance to everyone who resides in the State, both Indian and non-Indian." Outlining the threats that pollution, river damming, and irrigation posed to the salmon runs, the governor noted that the state could not "condone a new [threat] in the form of an unregulated or uncontrolled fishery by Indians at such times and at such places as they and they alone shall choose."[31]

Rosellini attempted to defuse the anger of many demonstrators by noting that the state sought only to regulate fishing when studies revealed conservation necessary to maintain a healthy fish population. "Without such regulation," he contended, "the Pacific Salmon would be as rare as the Dodo Bird." The governor concluded his speech, reminding his audience that his administration hoped to aid Native people by improving their standard of living, expanding educational opportunities, and securing citizenship rights. "I urge you to maintain your cultural heritage," he exclaimed, "[a] heritage that is not necessarily lost by working in a changing society."[32]

Rosellini's speech disheartened many of his listeners, but it strengthened the resolve of NIYC activists and the Native fishers who relied on the salmon for their livelihood. Brando forcefully voiced his discontent, contending that the Indians were "prepared to go all the way to the wall with this thing." Others, however, celebrated the governor's firm stance against unregulated Indian fishing. Days after delivering his speech, Rosellini wrote his friend Lowell Johnson, of the Sportsmen's Council, declaring, "As you probably are aware . . . I took a position on the fisheries question that is virtually the same as the position advocated by the State Sportsmen's Council." Enclosing a copy of his address, he requested that Johnson bring his remarks "to the attention of the other members of the Council."[33]

Johnson responded to the governor, commending him on handling the demonstration "with great discretion." The sportsmen went on to denounce the NIYC and its tactics. "The Washington

State Sportsmen's Council regrets that certain unscrupulous individuals have chosen to equate the current Indian commercial fishing situation to the Negro civil rights issue," the council proclaimed. Accordingly, the council asserted that those who protested represented only a small minority of Indian people—most of whom were satisfied with the treaties of Medicine Creek and Point Elliot. In the opinion of the sportsmen, the demonstrators had taken phrases of the treaties out of context, refusing to acknowledge their full wording: "The right of taking fish at all usual and accustomed grounds and stations is further secured to said Indians *in common with all citizens of the Territory*" (emphasis mine). Hence, the NIYC and those who participated in the fish-ins had demanded "special privileges not guaranteed by the treaty." Therefore, proclaimed the council, "*they are in* reality the treaty violators" (council's emphasis).[34]

Rosellini's stance and its firm backing by the Sportsmen's Council proved the NIYC and the Native fishers of the Pacific Northwest had a long and arduous battle ahead of them. The March fish-ins failed to bring immediate change, but as Adams wrote, they "achieved a new spirit and renewed courage" among Native people throughout Indian country. Indeed, the show of intertribal strength was impressive, as some forty-seven tribes took part in the fish-ins and the protest at the state capitol. So electrified were NIYC staffers over the intertribal unity and show of force in Olympia that Wilkie sent out a memo proclaiming, "THIS HAS BEEN THE GREATEST INDIAN VICTORY OF MODERN DAY!"[35]

The battle in the Northwest, however, remained far from over. Thom, Adams, Wilkie, and others resolved at the NIYC annual meeting, held at Neah Bay on the Makah reservation, to establish a field office in Olympia to direct the fight. The organization also helped found a regional outfit that spearheaded future fish-ins—the Survival of American Indians Association (SAIA). With NIYC and SAIA support, the fish-ins continued after the rally in Olympia, and on March 11, game wardens arrested Don McCloud (Puyallup) and five others for violating state conservation laws and the court's restraining order. Federal district judge George Boldt declined their petitions for writs of habeas corpus and incarcerated them for thirty days. Adams, Janet McCloud, and others picketed their hearing, brandishing signs that read, "We Ketchum to Live—You Ketchum to Kill" and "We'd Rather Fish than be on Welfare."[36]

The continued conflict in Washington prompted U.S. senator Warren Magnuson to introduce legislation "to bring order to a fishery that is being damaged by the unregulated fishing of a very small number of our citizens." Concurring with the Sportsmen's Council, Magnuson believed the "in common with" provision in the treaties of Medicine Creek and Point Elliot meant that Native fishers had to abide by state conservation laws. "I believe that these treaties should fit present day conditions in the overall consideration for maintaining our fishery resources," the senator declared. "I believe it is absolutely necessary that the Indian fisheries be managed as a part of the total management picture." Senate Joint Resolutions 170 and 171, therefore, built upon the Enabling Act, giving states the power to pass sweeping conservation measures without violating federal treaties.[37]

Sportsmen's Council president Lowell Johnson wrote Magnuson to express the council's satisfaction that the senator was "now taking the appropriate action." Lobbying for SJ 170 and 171, the council also wrote the Senate subcommittee considering the measures, stating that legislation was necessary because Native people had proved unable to regulate their own fishers effectively: "The present unregulated Indian fishing contains within itself the seed of its own destruction. *No regulation* can only result in extinction. Such cannot be the intent of the various Indian treaties." Believing that Magnuson's bills were the best hope of sportfishers in Washington and elsewhere, the organization called on additional support from its membership base.[38] In a letter addressed to "Fellow Sportsmen," council officer Bob Hart posited:

> Your rivers are being destroyed. The most dangerous force at this time is the Indian fishery that exists in our rivers with total disregard for all accepted conservation principles. . . . The people of Washington and the other 49 states think of the Indian as the "Poor ignorant Redman who has been deprived of all of his rights." The fact of the matter is that, since 1924, he has had all of the rights you have, plus many more, and in addition, doesn't have to play most of the games by the rules. . . . Help eliminate ignorance by informing the public of the truth.[39]

At the same time that the Sportsmen's Council endorsed SJ 170 and 171, the NIYC attacked them full force. Wilkie rightly contended that the measures gave the state of Washington power to circumvent Indian fishing and, hence, chip away at Native treaty rights. The NIYC executive secretary warned, "Should the sportsmen of Washington State get their way, it would mean that Congress would be sacrificing the livelihoods of the Indians for the mere pleasure of a few boastful sportsmen." The National Congress of American Indians also testified in hearings on the measures. The organization called on the Senate to launch a comprehensive study of the fishing industry in the Pacific Northwest rather than passing Magnuson's bills, believing such an investigation would show that the catch Indian fishers brought in was meager in comparison with what commercial outfits harvested.[40]

Besides the NCAI, the myriad tribes of western Washington issued a collective statement arguing against state control over Indian fishing. Representatives of the Makah tribe asserted that Magnuson's bills "once again bring into question the integrity of the US government with respect to its treaties," while Eagle Seelatsee, the chairman of the Yakama Tribal Council, claimed that most tribes already had their own conservation measures in place. Tribes even received a measured degree of support from the Department of the Interior. Assistant Secretary John Carver concurred with Seelatsee, asserting that Indians had as much interest in conservation as Washington's fish and game commission. Carver further noted, "The unwillingness of the states to recognize any special Indian need is probably the reason for the Indians' unwillingness to be subjected to state regulation."[41]

Proponents of the measures also turned out in full force. Though the Sportsmen's Council opted to forgo the hearings, the organization's president sent game warden Neubrech specific instructions to "enumerate what we consider the key points." Neubrech fulfilled the council's wishes when he told committee members the state of Washington sought only to regulate off-reservation fishing in order to conserve fish resources. Assuming a conciliatory tone, the game warden claimed that Indians could do as they pleased on their own reservations. Others took a harder stance. Washington attorney general Joseph Coniff declared that unregulated Indian fishing had proved to be "incompatible with any intelligent management program designed to conserve this great natural resource," while the chairman of the fish and game department for Idaho contended that Indians, not commercial fisheries, were responsible for the depleted state of salmon and trout resources in the Northwest. Similarly, the director of the Oregon Fish Commission argued that the treaty makers of the nineteenth century did not intend for Indians to "take all the fish."[42]

Just how much fish Native fishers actually brought in proved detrimental to Magnuson's cause. Figures from the state of Washington's Department of Fisheries indicated that the Indian catch was but a small fraction of what white fisheries claimed. The total salmon catch for Indian fisheries in 1964 stood at 110 metric tons, whereas that for the United States as a whole was 160,300 metric tons. A narrower comparison between Indian fishers, sportfishers, and commercial fisheries is even more revealing. In Washington State alone between 1958 and 1967, Native people took 6.5 percent of the total catch, sportfishers 12.2 percent, and commercial operations 81.3 percent. Such figures provided ammunition for the NIYC and other opponents of SJ 170 and 171.[43]

The NIYC and Indian fishers in the Northwest achieved a major victory when Magnuson's bills failed to move out of committee and onto the floor of Congress. The measures' demise, however, did nothing to stop authorities from arresting Nisqually, Muckleshoot, Puyallup, and other Native fishers. To combat the continued threat to treaty rights, Adams proposed that the NIYC expand its operations in the Northwest by spearheading educational projects, lobbying efforts, and a new "sustained campaign of awareness." In a report from October 1964, Adams further detailed his vision. He contended it would be necessary to continue supporting fish-ins, but also they must work within judicial channels. If the NIYC could offer legal assistance "wherever necessitated" and build a case "eking out all relevant information from the past that would work toward strengthening the Indian claims today," perhaps the Northwest tribes could achieve a sweeping judicial victory. At the time he issued his report, few observers could have guessed that Hank Adams, a young, unknown student activist from Poverty Flats on

Hank Adams was the mastermind behind the fish-ins. He worked tirelessly for Native fishing rights until the famed Boldt decision of 1974. (Hank Adams, photograph, National Indian Youth Council Pictorial Collection [PICT 000-703-0035], Center for Southwest Research, University Libraries, University of New Mexico)

the Fort Peck Reservation, had just devised the strategy that would ultimately secure the treaty rights for Native fishers in the Pacific Northwest.[44]

Besides a legal front, Adams believed the NIYC should devote efforts to fostering economic development and full utilization of fishery resources. He noted that "scores of non-Indians" had become millionaires by tapping into Washington's fishery resource. If the Native people of the state could develop such a full-scale fishery, he believed, "it could prove to be a financial bonanza." The visionary Adams was not just blowing hot air. He built upon his suggestion, offering a detailed market analysis of the fishing and cannery industry, as well as a general assessment on how and why an organized Indian fishery would succeed. He concluded, "The development of the fishery resource could well have the effect of permanently entrenching Indian fishing rights into the economic structure of the state." Acknowledging his plan had "more theory than substance," Adams nevertheless maintained that the NIYC could fulfill such objectives through dedication and hard work.[45]

NIYC officers may have approved of Adams's plan, but the dispersed nature of the organization made fulfilling such a project nearly impossible. With the executive director in Gallup, New Mexico, the president in Schurz, Nevada, the vice presidents in Ann Arbor, Michigan, and Fort Duquesne, Utah, and the *Americans Before Columbus* editorial office in Denver, the neophyte organization had enough difficulty simply calling its annual meeting. By late 1964, Adams and the SAIA therefore assumed control over operations in Washington State. To be sure, the officers of the NIYC continued to keep close watch on events unfolding in the Pacific Northwest, but with their heightened profile, they broadened their activities in hopes of having as great an impact on Indian policy as possible.

Although the NIYC's officers faded from the Northwest fishing battle, the young council activists who inaugurated the fish-in movement could take pride in their achievement. Through their savvy engagement of the media, use of direct action tactics, and ability to bring together Native people from myriad tribes, these Red Power warriors put the battle over fishing rights on the political map and set a course that would ultimately secure the treaty rights of Native fishers. Their efforts stood as the first instance of united intertribal direct action, and they encouraged subsequent Indian activists to use civil disobedience and mass protests as a means to make changes in Indian policy.

Moreover, the fish-ins gave the NIYC the necessary exposure to act as one of the foremost intertribal outfits in operation. Increasingly, the organization viewed education and the fight against poverty as Native peoples' greatest concern. If American Indians had more resources at their disposal and armed themselves with higher education, they could better confront the dominant society that threatened their existence as a people. The newfound fame resulting from the fish-ins opened doors, allowing the women and men of the NIYC to initiate a myriad of new programs and projects in the mid-1960s.

CHAPTER 6

"We Cannot Be Afraid of Power; We Must Use It"

The Growth of Red Power Militancy

In 1964, shortly before the National Indian Youth Council's annual meeting, Mel Thom issued a memorandum to the organization's board of directors: "We are ready to define the best approaches to strike at that great monstrosity that threatens to engulf Indian people and destroy Indian life. . . . We cannot be afraid of power; we must use it." Basking in the success of the fish-ins, Thom argued that the NIYC operated at "the grass-roots level" and, hence, best represented Native peoples' concerns and interests while "other Indian organizations are mostly echoing what their White Brothers tell them." Thom also rejected the civic nationalist agenda of the era and criticized the dominant society's attempt to "rehabilitate" the American Indians and make them "first-class American citizens," which, in reality, meant stripping them of their culture. Such a policy only caused Native people to "destroy themselves" because they saw no other recourse or meaning in life. "You have to be angry if you can see all this," he concluded.[1]

The fish-in campaign recast the NIYC from what was essentially an obscure student social club into a nationally recognized and respected intertribal organization. The council even achieved a degree of international fame, as admirers from as far away as England and New Zealand gave their encouragement and support. Membership nearly tripled, ballooning from fewer than 40 members in 1963 to more than 120 the following year. *Americans Before Columbus*, the NIYC's chief publication, evolved from a mimeographed newsletter into a lithographed newspaper. Mel Thom, Clyde Warrior, Joan Noble, and other staffers received numerous invitations to speak at conferences and universities around the country, while both Thom and Bruce Wilkie were elected to their respective tribal councils.[2]

The NIYC's newfound fame, however, did not translate into any sort of acquiescence. To the contrary, the NIYC only became increasingly militant in its stance on treaty rights, tribal sovereignty, and cultural preservation. While the failure of Governor Albert Rosellini and the federal government to protect Northwest Indians' fishing rights angered and disillusioned the organization's officers, Washington State's actions remained a reflection of a greater, more deeply rooted problem in the United States. The activists of the NIYC believed that America must change its long-standing disregard of Native communities and that it must make the change immediately. There was no middle ground. For the young women and men of the NIYC, they were confronted with a dark force that sought to carry on a prolonged war of destruction against Native peoples. Like other student activists of their time, they steadfastly believed in the possibility of a moral universe and that it was their duty to make it a reality.

The NIYC's growing militancy manifested itself in their rhetoric and writings. Thom's essay, "Indian War 1964," which appeared in *American Aborigine*, argued that Native people needed to view the struggle to preserve treaty rights and Indian culture as a protracted conflict with the American social and political structure. "We are convinced, more than ever before, that this is real war," Thom wrote. America sought to destroy Native culture and life, and it was up to the NIYC to "rally our Indian forces" and unite in confronting this threat. He posited that NIYC members needed to "hit strategically" at their opposition, and since Indians were few in number, they "must make every effort count." They should know their enemy and gain a "full understanding of the present American system" in order to force change effectively.[3]

Shirley Hill Witt bolstered this position in her essay "Right Flank and Left Flank," which appeared alongside Thom's article in *American Aborigine*. The first vice president called for a new spirit of sweeping pan-Indian unity between Native people who lived on reservations and those who dwelled in cities, asserting that "blood lines are inalienable." Witt argued that the fight was much more than simply a battle to hold onto parcels of land; it was a crusade for cultural preservation against a power structure that threatened the very survival of Native people everywhere. "We all stand or fall together in our struggle for survival as Indians," she maintained. "We are all fighting for our birthright. . . . Let us then fight united."[4]

Unity, however, was just the first step in solving the major problems plaguing Native people. During the mid-1960s, the NIYC struggled—with varying degrees of success and failure—to devise new campaigns to bring about the kind of change that Witt and Thom advocated. Often confused over its direction, the organization worked within established political channels, while simultaneously railing against them. NIYC staffers devised new approaches to Indian education and leadership training but bitterly attacked Great Society programs for reform as colonialist and racist. In short, the fish-ins may have brought the NIYC success, but the still-nascent council wrestled with its competing roles as a respectable student Indian organization and an antiestablishment protest movement.

In its crusade to combat poverty on reservations and reform Indian education, the NIYC took its cue from the sociopolitical changes unfolding in Washington, D.C. On January 8, 1964, in his first State of the Union address, President Lyndon Johnson called for an "unconditional war on poverty." The president's "Great Society" campaign gave birth to the Office of Economic Opportunity (OEO), a new government agency that oversaw community action programs designed to provide the poor with resources to help devise their own solutions to problems gripping their communities. A large number of the OEO's activities targeted education. Johnson's education acts earmarked federal funds to aid poor school districts on a per-pupil basis.[5]

Allocating funds to poor districts that needed them most, however, proved much more complicated than Johnson and his allies expected. In the Deep South, African American leaders who hoped to use the funds to improve the dismal state of education in black districts had to contend with the white political establishment. For example, congressional leaders targeted the Child Development Group of Mississippi, which was only marginally affiliated with the Student Nonviolent Coordinating Committee, as a communist, black nationalist front organization that would funnel funds to advocate revolution. Mississippi senators John Stennis and James Eastland more or less controlled how OEO funds were allocated, leaving African Americans with little community control.[6]

In Indian country, things turned out differently. Head Start and Upward Bound programs remained free from Indian Bureau domination, giving Native communities a much greater degree of self-determination. Throughout the 1960s, Indians took steps to address the grinding poverty that plagued reservations, as well as the inadequate educational programs of the postwar era. One of the best examples of this new wave of self-determination in education was the creation of the Rough Rock Demonstration School on the Navajo reservation in 1966. The school used OEO funds to devise a curriculum that incorporated Diné tradition, culture, and language. The Navajo Tribal Council oversaw and sponsored the school's development, which served as a precursor to the creation of the first tribal college—Navajo Community College—in 1968.[7]

Initially, NIYC staffers were concerned more with mimicking the success of the fish-ins than with education programs. Shirley Hill Witt, John Winchester, and Karen Rickard hoped to hold a massive demonstration in New York State to protest the construction of Kinzua Dam and the flooding of Allegany Seneca lands. The NIYC leadership urged members of the organization to "TELL ... OR THREATEN" congressional representatives and even the president to stop the dam project. If the government failed to meet their demands, one memo stated, they should take the case to the international community and spread the word that American treaties were "not worth any more than any other piece of paper." Ultimately, the Senecas cut off Witt, Winchester, and Rickard's plans and opted against holding a public protest, for fear of jeopardizing a possible settlement with the federal government. Although the NIYC held a successful rally in Reno, Nevada, that drew eight hundred people from tribes in California, Utah, Arizona, and Nevada, the council's staffers failed to find a new venue where they could employ the sort of direct action used in the fish-ins.[8]

Instead, the heroes of the fish-ins focused increasingly on spreading their message of self-determination, cultural preservation, sovereignty, and treaty rights at regional councils, conferences, and workshops throughout the United States. Receiving multiple invitations, members of the NIYC traveled all over Indian country. Mel Thom attended conferences and meetings so frequently that his "luggage" consisted of a toothbrush, a tube of toothpaste, shorts, and an extra pair of socks. And he typically wore a seersucker suit because, according to one friend, it didn't show any wrinkles. "He could sleep in that thing. He would just shake it out, put it on, and jump around. He travelled light," Dan Edwards remembered. Clyde Warrior too journeyed far and wide. Shortly after the fish-ins, he attended and spoke at the Northwest Regional Indian Youth Council meeting at the University of Montana in Missoula and the Southwest Youth Council at Fort Lewis College in Durango, Colorado, where admirers in the Shalako Club asked him to impart "words of wisdom . . . on any subject of your choosing." Blatchford joined the Ponca in Durango, and the two distributed one hundred copies of *Aborigine* in hopes of recruiting future members.[9]

Charlie Cambridge was one of those new recruits who would go on to serve as a leader in the NIYC. Born near the sacred Huerfano Mountain in the heart of Dinétah on the Navajo Reservation, Cambridge attended the youth council in Durango, where he met Blatchford and Warrior. He immediately took a keen interest in the NIYC and its activist politics, leading him to enroll in the Workshop on American Indian Affairs. After the six-week crash course in federal Indian policy, social theory, and Native history, Cambridge took a position on the NIYC board of directors while pursuing his education at the University of Colorado in Boulder. Cambridge was just one of many young Native students captivated by the charisma of the council leaders and the urgency of the message the organization was spreading throughout Indian country.[10]

The women and men of the NIYC reached out to Native students like Cambridge by attending Indian youth councils in the West, but geography did not restrict council activists. Warrior and Joan Noble courted students from the Great Lakes region when they accepted invitations to attend the "Accent on Youth" conference at Wisconsin State University in Eau Claire. The Ponca delivered the keynote speech, "Time for Indian Action," which encouraged Native students to join the emerging international student movement. As people in Eastern Europe, Asia, and Latin America made strides to overcome the colonialist structures of the past, American Indians were "sitting on the side lines." Rather than resign themselves to such complacency, Native youth needed to take action to forge their own destinies. "Youth is a time of freedom," Warrior declared, and it was vital that they "not be left out of this exciting time in history."[11]

The International Youth Conference held in Bismarck, North Dakota, afforded NIYC leaders yet another venue to express their emerging intertribal nationalism. Noble and Hank Adams took primary responsibility for coordinating the event, which was jointly sponsored by the NIYC and the Foundation of North American Indian Culture. The two organizers chose "How an Indian Youth Looks at His Culture" as the theme but hoped to tie American Indians' situation to that of indigenous people throughout the colonized world. Bruce Wilkie delivered a speech entitled "Can the Indian Culture Survive?" while Dumont spoke on Native and cross-cultural education.[12]

While such conferences provided the NIYC with multiple venues to press its message, it was the American Indian Capital Conference on Poverty held in Washington, D.C., that gave the council its biggest audience. Designed to provide Congress with input as it considered the Economic Opportunity Bill, the conference drew hundreds of Indians and other interested parties. Commissioner of Indian Affairs Phileo Nash and his eventual successor Robert Bennett both attended, as did representatives of the National Congress of American Indians, who, along with the Indian Rights Association, were instrumental in organizing the event. NCAI president Walter Wetzel (Blackfeet) served as the honorary chair of the conference, while NIYC members Robert Dumont and Tillie Walker took seats as committee members.

The conference took place between May 9 and 12, 1964, at the Washington National Cathedral in the District of Columbia. Thom,

Witt, Warrior, and Karen Rickard, among others, also attended in addition to Dumont and Walker, taking up residence in the Alban Towers just across the street from the cathedral. Native folksinger and guitarist Buffy Sainte-Marie also traveled to D.C. for the event and shared a room with Rickard. Before long, the Towers hummed with the sounds of drumming and Buffy's Spanish guitar. The NIYC activists, as usual, brought a heightened energy to what otherwise may have been a stodgy policy-making discussion. And again council activists flirted with trouble. At one stage, a man who identified himself as a member of the Communist Party from Czechoslovakia approached council staffers and expressed his desire to form a coalition between the Communist International and the NIYC. As Witt recalled, "Warrior, naturally, was enthusiastic about the concept, but other officers—in the majority—pointed out that Indians had enough problems already and needed no further encumbering issues to deal with, given the country's abhorrence to anything that smacked of [being] 'communistic.'"[13]

Once under way, the Capital Conference on Poverty served as a forum where attendees discussed and debated Indian education, unemployment, health care, and housing. They broke into several workgroups to further flesh out these problems. Nearly all concurred that something had to be done to amend current policy and remedy the grinding poverty affecting Native people. Echoing their actions at the American Indian Chicago Conference, the students who attended the gathering drafted their own statement, which they duly delivered to Wetzel and the other conference organizers.[14]

Robert Dumont coordinated the youth report. An Assiniboine who grew up at Wolf Point on the Fort Peck Reservation in Montana, Dumont, like other NIYC staffers, had excelled academically. He attended the Workshop on American Indian Affairs in 1961 before receiving a John Hay Whitney fellowship a year later. At the time of the Capital Conference, Dumont was working toward his master's degree in human development in the Graduate School of Education at Harvard. His educational pedigree served the students well when they penned a statement they hoped would influence Congress in its vote on the Economic Opportunity Bill. In the final draft, the students concurred with the bulk of the attendees that poverty stood as one of the foremost problems facing Native people, but insisted that in combating the situation, the government should not push Indians into the mainstream of white society. Any poverty programs the government devised must work within a "cultural framework" that respected traditional tribal values.[15]

The youth report, by most measures, lacked any pretense of militancy or underlying anger, prompting Clyde Warrior to add a little muscle to it in an impromptu speech. Shirley Hill Witt, knowing Warrior would take the stage, recalled being "scared but determined" as she handed Annie Wauneka (Diné) the NIYC's request to speak. Wauneka interrupted the current speaker and asked those in attendance to give the youth representative their full attention. Warrior then let them have it. "Our leaders become impotent and less experienced in handling the modern world," he exclaimed. Those chairing the Capital Conference, however well-meaning, were not true representatives of the poor; otherwise they would recognize that poverty was only a symptom of a much larger problem. The lack of self-determination—tribes' inability to control their own destinies—stood as Native peoples' greatest obstacle. When the government deprived Indians of such responsibility, they could only live in "ignorance and frustration." Warrior concluded by saying, "No amount of formal education or money can take the place of these basic life experiences."[16]

Warrior's pointed speech "horrified all the tame Indians in the room," recalled Witt, as did the subsequent alcohol consumption of some NIYC staffers. After the meeting, Rickard reprimanded those who had been drinking at the conference. "We cannot afford to be frowned upon because of liquor," she scolded. Such behavior might have a "lasting effect" because "a drunken NIYC member will be spotted very quickly." For many tribal elders and other Native representatives accustomed to a moderate approach, the Capital Conference on Poverty signaled their first encounter with the increasingly militant and often rowdy architects of Red Power.[17]

Although the NIYC had myriad speaking engagements and rose as one of the foremost intertribal organizations in operation, staffers still were unsure about the council's future direction. When the organization met at Neah Bay in August 1964 for its annual meeting, members attempted to come to some sort of understanding on how best to proceed as an up-and-coming intertribal outfit. The fish-ins had given the organization much needed exposure and a greater chance at securing financial resources, but many wondered about the council's future. Where was the NIYC coming from and in which direction would it proceed?[18]

Toward the end of the meeting, educational reform emerged as the paramount issue. With the new political direction emanating from Washington, D.C., opportunities to introduce changes in Indian education opened up. Attendees stressed how the government had often used education as a tool to assimilate Native people, "retarding Indian children" and leaving them confused about who they were. A dearth of parental involvement in educational curricula and "a lack of Indian long-hair intellectuals" stood as the primary obstacles in achieving greater self-determination in the classroom. Assuming the new educational programs panned out, the NIYC could perhaps devise its own agenda to amend past deficiencies.[19]

The council took its first step by becoming an active member in the United Scholarship Service. Based out of Denver and sponsored by several nonprofit associations, including the Carnegie Corporation, the Association on American Indian Affairs, and the Executive Council of the Episcopal Church, the USS sought to expand educational opportunities for Native and Hispanic students. Several NIYC staffers worked for the service. Dumont proved to be instrumental in securing the NIYC leadership's involvement, informing Thom that "in terms of power, prestige, and status, [it] would be an important move." Members resolved to pool their meager resources to fund a single scholarship. Warrior recommended that they name it after the recently deceased William Rickard—the fiery Tuscarora leader who railed for complete tribal sovereignty and respect for treaty rights. Eventually, however, he suggested "Geronimo Scholarship."[20]

In committing to the USS, the NIYC began the process of transforming itself from a group of political activists that some found abrasive into a respectable educational organization. The council successfully secured funds from the Charles F. Kettering Foundation after the donor lectured Thom on the necessity to erase

NIYC's image as a "[rabble-]rousing and irresponsible group."
After the lecture, Thom—whom some people began calling "Mao
Tse Thom"—wrote to a friend, lamenting, "I failed to convince him
that NIYC has to go along the lines of a revolutionary and dynamic
movement. . . . I tried to point out to him that it was some of the
basic structures of the present system that are responsible for Indian conditions as they are today." Kettering, however, would have
none of it, making the foundation's $20,000 donation contingent on
the condition that the NIYC reject militant rhetoric and demonstrations as a means to achieve social change.[21]

Holding their fire proved too difficult for some members of the
NIYC. In an essay entitled "Which One Are You?" Warrior captured
the anger and frustration that pervaded much of the NIYC. He
spoke of a "pathetic scene . . . a very sick, sad sorry scene" among
Native youth, who seemed to suffer from an identity crisis. Warrior proceeded to label five types of Indian students, perhaps with
certain NIYC staffers in mind. He identified "Type A" as the "slob
or hood who gets his identity from the dominant society, drops out
of school and turns to alcohol and crime." The second type was the
"Joker," a "bungling clown" whom others failed to take seriously.
"Type C" he described as the "Redskin 'white noser' or the sell
out." This disdainful character, Warrior wrote, was a "little brown
American" and a "fink" who served as the white society's peon.
"Type D," or the "ultra-pseudo Indian," sought to identify herself
as Indian but had no experience with traditional culture or knowledge of the past. Such Native people were "proud yet phony." Finally, Warrior appeared to model the "Type E" Indian after himself,
whom he defined as an angry nationalist who upheld Native culture and disliked "uncle tomahawks."[22]

Although Warrior contended that none of his identified types
were ideal, he argued that Indian students had to adopt a nationalist philosophy and turn away the "religious workers and edu-
cationalists incapable of understanding" and the "pseudo-social
scientists who are consciously creating social and cultural genocide
among American Indian youth." Warrior went on to target government bureaucrats who continually promoted ill-fated programs
that sought to acculturate and assimilate:

I am sick and tired of seeing my elders stripped of dignity and low rated in the eyes of their young. And I am disturbed to the point of screaming when I see American Indian youth accepting the horror of "American conformity" as being the only way for Indian progress. . . . The National Indian Youth Council must introduce to this sick room of stench and anonymity some fresh air of new Indianness—a fresh air of new honesty and integrity, a fresh air of new Indian idealism, a fresh air of a new "greater Indian America."

How about it? Let's raise some hell.[23]

In the subsequent months, some NIYC staffers set aside attempts to recast the organization as an educational agency and fulfilled Warrior's request to "raise some hell." Council members brashly called for the impeachment of former U.S. senator Arthur Watkins of Utah, one of the foremost proponents of termination and full assimilation who served on the Indian Claims Commission. Noting that Watkins made "prejudiced and biased" statements and that he remained "an offense" to American Indians, the NIYC declared his "senility and poor judgment" as grounds for removal from his position. At a subsequent NCAI meeting in Washington, D.C., Thom noted that congressional leaders "fled in terror" when he showed them his organization's impeachment resolution.[24]

Then, in May, Thom wrote to the Pentagon about the military's practice of awarding medals to men who had fought in the Indian wars of the nineteenth century. He wondered how and why the army celebrated "campaigns for which this country cannot truly be proud of." Those who fought to dislodge Native people who were only defending their homelands and lives had committed "atrocities" rather than heroics. "Some of the cruelest acts perpetuated upon man were committed in the Indian campaigns," Thom argued. Sending copies of his remonstrance to the House Committee on Veterans Affairs and even the Wadsworth Veterans Administration Hospital, he concluded that although "it is good to be nice to old men," the army's actions seemed "detrimental" from a Native perspective.[25]

Thom also contacted the well-established Association on American Indian Affairs to reprimand its officers for claiming to represent

Native people. He pointed out that no Indians sat on the AAIA's board, and he demanded that the organization send the NIYC carbon copies of all letters sent out on Native people's behalf. The dispute stemmed from a Calvert Distilling Company advertisement that depicted American Indians in a less than positive light. Claiming to represent Indian interests, the AAIA had attacked the company for promoting the ad and, in the process, negative stereotypes. Thom, in turn, chose to lambaste the association rather than Calvert. He went so far as to write the company to explain that the AAIA did not truly represent Native Americans and only used Indians for its own gain.[26]

In June, Warrior further shook up the establishment when he told students at the University of South Dakota that people in power wanted to convert Indian students into "well-behaved, orderly, submissive 'peons.'" Many young Indians fell into the trap, as they attempted to "curry favor with the powerful in hopes of getting a few crumbs of rank." Taking a page from Robert K. Thomas, his old instructor at the Workshop on American Indian Affairs, Warrior compared the American Indian to the Irish and the Jew who fomented change by "demanding respect." If Native people wanted to halt the process of becoming whites' "'pet' Indians," they would have to take control of their own destinies, "start anew and . . . think about their problems in a new way."[27]

Through their letters, petitions, articles, and speeches, Thom and Warrior succeeded in raising hell and probably angering their primary donor, Charles Kettering, and others within the political establishment. However, at the same time, many NIYC members hoped to foster a more respectable image and work toward educational reform. At the 1964 midyear meeting in Denver, staffers continued to argue about the council's future direction. Board member Ed Johnson contended that the NIYC lacked stability, while Secretary Gerald Brown believed members should agree upon a more realistic platform. Hank Adams opined that the council had to move from mere concern to complete commitment, Blatchford complained about faltering finances, and Thom announced that council members needed greater discipline. With such a degree of conflict and dissatisfaction, it is a wonder the organization survived.[28]

The debate continued into the 1965 annual meeting on the Flathead reservation in Montana, where the discord of the preceding year ultimately resulted in the election of new officers. First Vice President Shirley Hill Witt, who continued her studies in anthropology at the University of Michigan and later at the University of New Mexico, relinquished her post, effectively ending her active involvement in the NIYC for the time being. Similarly, Joan Noble, the second vice president, also distanced herself from the increasingly militant and fractious council and chose to devote her attention to the Great Society's Volunteers in Service to America program before heading to Tonga on mission for the Mormon Church. "Mister Ed" Johnson (Paiute-Yakima) and Angela Russell (Crow), a veteran of the Colorado workshops, took over as first and second vice presidents, respectively. Both Warrior and Wilkie resigned their positions on the board of directors. Warrior married his college sweetheart and former workshop student, Della Hopper, and moved to Tahlequah, Oklahoma, where he studied the cultural effects of education among the Cherokees. Wilkie, on the other hand, pursued high office on the Makah Tribal Council and greater involvement in the NCAI. Wilkie, Warrior, Noble, and Witt each had her or his own individual reason for departing, but taken collectively, the shake-up in 1965 can be attributed largely to the NIYC's inability to re-create the success of the fish-ins and its struggle to find a new direction.[29]

The ouster of Blatchford as executive director starkly illuminates these growing fractures. Many council members blamed the Navajo leader for the financial and organizational problems that plagued the NIYC. Brown, during his stint as secretary, complained to other staffers that the central office in Gallup needed to begin producing records of all deposits if the council hoped to retain its tax-exempt status. Thom also criticized Blatchford for not being able to keep the council's finances in order. He told Dumont that queries into the matter were futile, as "we get no response out of Gallup." For his part, Blatchford believed the problem resided with the confusion and disagreement over the future of the NIYC. At the 1964 meeting at Neah Bay, he contended that the council had simply "glossed over" the budget, giving no input on how monies should be appropriated. Much of this discord was due to internal dissent. "If they meet they argue for four days straight until you think they will never agree on anything," he later recalled. Blatchford further resented those who criticized *American Aborigine* as "a childish high school annual" that was out of touch with the rising tide of Red Power, especially since he and Witt had edited and maintained the newsletter from its inception.[30]

After 1965, Blatchford severed his ties with the council. The NIYC founder instead devoted his attention to serving as president of the Northwest New Mexico Economic Opportunity Council. He also took over as director of the Gallup Indian Community Center, which helped relocated Navajos and Hopis adjust to their new surroundings in the city. The loss of Blatchford would prove to be great for the NIYC. As Witt later acknowledged, "It was he who kept rationality functioning amongst us." Thom continued his leadership role within the council by succeeding Blatchford as executive director. He moved the central office to his home in Schurz, Nevada, on the Walker River Paiute Reservation. After marrying Fran Poafpybitty, one of the coordinators of *ABC*, Thom also assumed control over that publication from Nevada.[31]

Following the shake-up at the 1965 meeting, some members of the NIYC continued to rail against the establishment, while others sought to work within it. Thom himself embodied the organization's competing visions. Though he would continue his rhetorical assaults on mainstream society, the new executive director recognized that the success of the American Indian Capital Conference on Poverty and the subsequent passage of the Economic Opportunity Bill opened new doors for the organization. In his regular *ABC* column, "For a Greater Indian America," Thom acknowledged a "conflict of basic philosophy" between Native people and the United States. He posited that government policies "bury the hopes and destroy the dreams" of Indian communities. Nevertheless, Thom seemed to have some faith in the Great Society and its new direction in American Indian policy, despite all his past criticisms. Through the Office of Economic Opportunity's programs, Native people could offer their unique perspectives and contribute to the development of poverty and education programs. He maintained that Indian control over such programs and the continuation of the tribes' special trust relationship with the federal government could very well work to the advantage of America's First Nations.[32]

The OEO's new programs and the agency's goal of involving Native people in the creation of those programs also encouraged NIYC's education czar, Robert Dumont. More than anyone else in the organization, Dumont believed that the council could flourish as "an active agency" in the new sociopolitical climate by directing Indian education and establishing new revolutionary programs. Like other Indians concerned with the future of their children's education, Dumont believed that part of the reason for the high dropout rates among American Indians rested with the complete separation of students from their homes and their tribal communities. If the NIYC could devise new ways to bridge the gap between school and community, perhaps statistics on Indian education would not be so abysmal.[33]

Dumont, along with other NIYC members such as Thom, Rickard, Winchester, Russell, Johnson, Adams, Tillie Walker, Charlie Cambridge, and Browning Pipestem took seats on the Indian advisory committee of the OEO's Upward Bound program. The committee arranged to meet in Washington, D.C., to hammer out new Indian educational programs. Hoping to draw the charismatic Clyde Warrior into the fold, Upward Bound directors petitioned the wayward Ponca to attend the committee's sessions, even sending him an airline ticket. Eventually he acquiesced, and in April 1966 he joined his cohorts in the nation's capital for two days of discussion.[34]

When the session opened, Warrior immediately went on the offensive, suspecting the officials at Upward Bound of trying to "wash students in white paint." He argued that, under present conditions, Native youth should be allowed to drop out if they wished. The educational structures in place remained completely alien—whites had little knowledge of Native culture and taught children courses in English, a foreign language to many students. Such a curriculum resulted in "warped and twisted" children, Warrior asserted, adding, "It is a miracle if [one] makes it through high school." The goal of Upward Bound should be to "make the shit we all waded through a little shallower for those who follow." To do this, Indians needed to have a better self-image, and programs must "fit into the context of the world of the kids—so they won't be scared." Echoing Dumont, he opined that new programs should integrate parents and members from students' tribal communities.[35]

Other NIYC staffers agreed. If Upward Bound programs were to succeed, noted Adams, teaching methods needed to change completely. He discussed his observations of educational endeavors on the Nisqually Reservation in western Washington, which had "improved enormously" due to parental involvement. Dropouts waned as the curricula changed to favor traditional Native culture. Bringing Indian culture into the classroom, however, did not mean that Upward Bound programs should completely reject white culture. Tillie Walker expressed skepticism of past educational projects labeled as culturally sensitive. "There should be instruction in Indian culture only if the person giving it is really good," she contended. Browning Pipestem likewise rejected the complete expulsion of European cultural forms from the classroom, declaring, "White culture should be taught so the Indians can learn to take advantage of it."[36]

The coordinators of Upward Bound held a follow-up meeting in Denver a month later. There the participants moved from mere philosophizing about Indian education to a more detailed assessment of what should be done to reform it. They concluded that recruiters should seek out the "silent, invisible" student, as well as the "hell-raiser." Staff training should utilize Indian consultants who, in turn, would instill a degree of cultural sensitivity in those who entered Native communities to teach. Moreover, visits to the homes of students enrolled in Upward Bound projects would do much to improve parental participation.[37]

Involvement in Upward Bound gave the NIYC further experience in developing educational programs that instilled a sense of pride and cultural retention in Native youth. The organization drew on these lessons when it joined the NCAI, USS, and American Friends Service Committee between July 21 and 22 at the Boone Leadership Conference. Organized by Richard Boone, the executive director of the Citizens Crusade against Poverty, the conference aimed to develop leadership training programs. Boone believed that future leaders could remedy the lack of economic independence on many reservations if they had the "management ability" to fully control and exploit resources available to them. Gerald Brown sat on the conference's executive committee and aided in drafting a proposal that called for government internships that would give young students training at the management level. Budgeted at over $70,500, the program would recruit one thousand Native youths over ten years. After interns had gained four years of experience, a placement service would help them find jobs in areas "directly relevant to the future of the American Indians." More often than not, this would mean work within tribal councils, the OEO, or the Indian Bureau.[38]

Not all NIYC members agreed with such reforms, rejecting the idea of working within established channels. Warrior remained apprehensive of leadership development, the OEO, and other government ventures designed to aid Indians. When the council met on the Lac Courte Oreilles Chippewa reservation in Wisconsin, Warrior challenged Brown for the council's presidency—the same opponent he faced in the 1961 election for the presidency of the RIYC. The Ponca sought a new direction for the NIYC. Believing that "radical and drastic changes in Indian affairs" were needed, he explained that "nothing meaningful for tribal people has ever been accomplished in the world unless it has been with a drastic change." He wanted to strengthen the organization's militant image and pursue avenues of direct action rather than the more moderate course Brown staked out. Employing the slogan "Up, up with persons" in his campaign, Warrior attacked both the Indian Bureau and the OEO as government agencies full of "white colonialists, racists, fascists, uncle tomahawks, and bureaucrats . . . who could care less about the average Indian."[39]

When staffers finally tallied the ballots, the ever-popular Warrior again defeated Brown in a landslide. The NCAI reported in its publication *The Sentinel* that the result signaled "the hottest political upset since the days of the Roman Empire." To observers, the election symbolized a contest between generations, with Warrior representing the younger, more militant students. Brown supporters were disheartened with the outcome and its implications. One backer lauded Brown's record, noting that it seemed "tragic to

hand over the organization to a bunch of kids just out of college."
Brown himself thought that Warrior would take the organization in
a radical new direction and, hence, was "confident that next year
they shall return to the proven leadership."[40]

Despite such predictions, Warrior retained firm control over the
NIYC for the remainder of his life. He consolidated his power at
the next midyear meeting by approving an age requirement for
the council's board of directors, which stipulated that 75 percent of
those who sat on the board had to be under age twenty-one. Moreover, the new president made good on his promise to move the
council in a more militant direction. Thom, who had always been
especially tight with Warrior, took heed when he promised "to put
out a tough issue of *ABC*" to strengthen the NIYC's image. In the
December issue of the publication, the executive director echoed
Warrior's sentiments on the OEO and the Indian Bureau. Shedding
the optimism he held the previous year, Thom asserted that bureaucrats who cared only about themselves staffed the agencies. He
ridiculed Natives who worked for the federal government, point-
ing out that few spoke their traditional language, knew tribal songs,
or even felt comfortable in Indian communities. There remained an
overall lack of self-determination on reservations, Thom declared,
and poverty was still widespread.[41]

When he testified before the U.S. Senate Subcommittee on Executive Reorganization in December 1966, Thom continued his assault,
refusing to pull any punches. The government's "simple-minded"
solutions were failing, he maintained. Cities had become "dumping
grounds," as the discredited policies of relocation and termination
created urban ghettoes. The Paiute pointed out that over the past
one hundred years the United States had spent over $4.2 billion on
poverty programs for Indians. Between 1948 and 1965 alone, it had
spent $2.5 billion. Still, the government's efforts had failed to rem-
edy the "Asiatic-type poverty" that plagued Native communities.[42]

Warrior also gave government officials an earful when testify-
ing before the President's National Advisory Commission on Rural
Poverty in February 1967. In his famous speech "We Are Not Free,"
he admonished the Indian Bureau for making decisions for Native
people without their consent or input:

We are not free. We do not make choices. Our choices are made for us; we are the poor. For those of us who live on reservations these choices and decisions are made by federal administrators, bureaucrats, and their "yes men," euphemistically called tribal governments. Those of us who live in non-reservation areas have our lives controlled by local white power elites. We have many rulers. They are called social workers, "cops," school teachers, churches, etc., and now OEO employees. They call us into meetings to tell us what is good for us and how they've programmed us, or they come into our homes to instruct us and their manners are not always what one would call polite by Indian standards or perhaps by any standards. We are rarely accorded respect as fellow human beings. . . . We are the "poverty problem."[43]

The young Ponca leader went on to demand self-determination and power over the decisions that affected the Native American community. Otherwise, warned Warrior, "there will be a generation of Indians growing to adulthood whose reaction to their situation will make previous social ills seem like a Sunday School picnic."[44]

Shortly after Warrior's speech, Thom and Hank Adams took to the streets of the nation's capital to lead a demonstration against the OEO and federal Indian policy. They protested the lack of jobs for Indians in cities and on the reservations. Adams later issued a statement to the Senate Interior and Insular Affairs Subcommittee on Indian Affairs, which was considering a bill to extend the Indian Claims Commission until 1972. He proclaimed that the ICC was "no great boon" and that Indians would be much better off if they could create a plan themselves to combat the poverty that plagued tribal communities.[45]

The NIYC's anger extended beyond the federal government and even white society. Some members began attacking the NCAI, an organization that had supported the youth council and shared the same vision for the future of Native America. In the past, staffers had always poked fun at the more established outfit, referring to the NCAI as the "National Congress of Aged Indians." Vine Deloria, Jr., who served as its executive director during the mid-1960s, later recalled that many of the quarrels between the two organizations were for "public consumption," explaining that they sought to gain "some leverage on the BIA." However, by 1967 the quarrel had evolved into an outright conflict. Frustrated by the plodding pace of reform, Thom blamed the NCAI and its "self-appointed spokesmen" for bolstering the status quo and selling out to the White power structure." In a speech before the Wisconsin Indian Leadership Conference in Eau Claire, he ripped the NCAI's "finky leadership" for passing resolutions that condemned NIYC's protests. "Did the so-called leaders have the 'guts' to come out and counter picket?" Thom asked. "No, they didn't. They would rather sit down and pass resolutions." Deloria responded by leveling accusations at NIYC leaders. He criticized their left-leaning politics and labeled board member Charlie Cambridge "the V.C. [Viet Cong] of the Indian world." Cambridge immediately shot back, calling Deloria "the V.D. of the Indian world."[46]

Such militancy, however, never translated into radicalism. The Red Power warriors continued to support the same principles of sovereignty, self-determination, cultural preservation, and protection of treaty rights that the NCAI had favored. The difference, therefore, rested in the methods and rhetoric each organization chose to employ. Staffed by angry young students who witnessed the rising militancy in the Student Nonviolent Coordinating Committee, the Black Panther Party, and the antiwar movement, the NIYC shared the same generational anxieties that were part and parcel of the Cold War sociopolitical landscape. Their world was one of right and wrong, black and white, good and evil. Warrior, a staunch supporter of Barry Goldwater during the 1964 presidential contest, must have surely identified with the Arizona Republican's words, "Extremism in the defense of liberty is no vice." This growth of militancy may have given form to the Red Power movement, but it also led to serious fractures within the NIYC.[47]

After the fish-ins of 1964, the National Indian Youth Council employed whatever means necessary to make a "greater Indian America." The organization attempted to change the system from within by working alongside government agencies to devise OEO programs that would reform Indian education and federal poverty efforts. But it also attacked the establishment and called for a complete upheaval of the system. Perhaps the immediate cause for the council's identity crisis stemmed from its inability to replicate the success of the fish-ins or to take advantage of OEO funds and launch a successful educational venture. Whatever the trigger may have been, the NIYC was most certainly a product of the greater sociopolitical environment that gripped the nation.

In June 1966, NIYC leaders had their ears to the ground when Stokely Carmichael shocked mainstream Americans by shouting out the words "Black Power!" at a rally in Greenwood, Mississippi. A month later, at a Fourth of July parade in Oklahoma City, Clyde Warrior painted "Red Power!" on one side of his car and "Custer Died for Your Sins" on the other. He and Mel Thom wreaked havoc that day when they proceeded to force their way into the parade and disrupt the event. Such action starkly symbolized that the NIYC was growing more militant and extreme. The undisciplined nature of that militancy, however, would ultimately lead the organization and its newly elected president down a path of self-destruction.[48]

CHAPTER 7

"Slug Them in the Mouth or Shoot Them"

Reform, Revolt, and Reorganization in the NIYC

In July of 1966, journalist Stan Steiner contacted Clyde Warrior in hopes of interviewing the militant president of the National Indian Youth Council. Steiner was working on a book that would shed light on the emerging Red Power movement and the ideology of its leaders. Warrior accepted Steiner's request, and in the waning weeks of the summer the journalist made his way to Tahlequah, Oklahoma, where the Ponca was helping conduct a study of Cherokee schools and Indian education. Sporting a Hawaiian shirt, Bermuda shorts, and a straw hat, Warrior ranted about the racist social structure in Oklahoma. "The only way you change that structure is to smash it. You throw it over sideways and stomp on it," he lashed. He warned about a new generation of angry Indian youth who had few opportunities and saw armed revolution as the only solution. "Violence will come about," Warrior contended. "And as far as I am concerned, the sooner the better."[1]

During the late 1960s, the militancy of NIYC staffers continued to grow. Warrior, Mel Thom, and others in the youth council upheld the principles of their elders but did so through angry, even violent rhetoric. At the same time, however, the NIYC evolved as an organization seeking new approaches to Indian education as the best means to bring about change. At its annual meeting in August 1967, council officers amended the articles of incorporation to fit this direction. The revised charter declared that the NIYC sought to reform Indian education by "conducting and supporting research and demonstration projects," sponsoring student workshops, and funding scholarships. The organization secured several massive grants to work toward these ends. Thus the NIYC attempted to identify itself as both a respectable educational agency and a militant Red Power front. But by the summer of 1968 the organization's leaders were no longer able to continue the juggling act, and the resulting upheaval tore the council apart.[2]

The NIYC's direction in the mid- to late 1960s echoed the growing militancy of student activists across the United States. In September 1966, Stokely Carmichael of the Student Nonviolent Coordinating Committee penned his famous essay "What We Want," which explained that black people needed sovereignty over their own communities and greater political power. Soon African American youth in both the North and the South echoed Carmichael's sentiments, questioning the integrationist agenda of the mainstream civil rights movement. Meanwhile, in Oakland, California, Huey Newton and Bobby Seale formed the Black Panther Party for Self-Defense to resist what they saw as a white colonialist power structure. "Off the pigs!" they declared, as they called for blacks to arm themselves to defend against racist white police officers. Both SNCC and the Black Panthers also advocated change through education by establishing community schools that employed an Afro-centric curriculum.[3]

Advocates of Black Power were not the sole activists detaching themselves from the American mainstream. The escalating violence and destruction in Vietnam led antiwar protesters to question traditional American values. Increasingly, the demonstrators viewed the United States as a racist and imperialist state that needed radical change. Some radicals in the Students for a Democratic Society openly supported Ho Chi Minh and the North Vietnamese in their independence struggle against American military forces. Though such militants remained a small minority, their political voice proved greater than their numbers, as media outlets broadcast their demonstrations and marches to every corner of the country— including Indian country.[4]

The young women and men in the NIYC could easily identify with the anti-imperialism of the peace advocates and the separatism of the Black Power movement. Indeed, sovereignty and self-determination stood as ideological pillars among Native student activists. Although the NIYC never took up arms as the Black Panthers did, nor advocated the complete revolution called for by some antiwar protesters, it did concentrate on educational reform, believing that if future generations of Native people held the intellectual tools to understand American society and government policy, they could change it. With an educational goal similar to that of SNCC or even the Black Panthers, the NIYC hoped to create culturally sensitive classrooms where a Native-centered curriculum would replace the Euro-centric agenda that had been imposed on American Indian pupils for generations.

Many NIYC staffers had developed their outlook on Indian education during the Workshop on American Indian Affairs. There they heard Robert Thomas and others stress cultural relativity and the need for a more inclusive curriculum. Thomas collaborated closely with tribal communities, observing Indian education efforts and devising means by which they might be improved. In the summer of 1962, Thomas and his student aide Clyde Warrior had investigated cross-cultural education among the Cherokees near Tahlequah, Oklahoma. Funded by the Carnegie Foundation, the project had been initiated by Sol Tax as one of his action anthropology endeavors, hoping ultimately to revitalize traditional Cherokee culture.[5]

Murray Wax launched a subsequent study that built upon Thomas's work with the Cherokees of eastern Oklahoma. As part of the Indian Education Research Project at the University of Kansas, Wax employed Warrior and Robert Dumont to help in the research. Their efforts culminated in an article, "Cherokee School Society and the Intercultural Classroom," published in the social science journal *Human Organization*. Wax and Dumont—who coauthored the essay—concluded that Indian education was "a process imposed upon a target population in order to shape and stamp them into becoming dutiful citizens, responsible employees, or good Christians." Even Native youth who attended public schools faced their instructors' overt attempts at acculturation. This "unidirectional" learning process failed to incorporate Indian cultural contributions and ignored indigenous languages and traditions.[6]

Warrior took a more militant stance than Dumont and Wax. He believed the problem with Indian education among the Cherokees was rooted in the southern racist culture of eastern Oklahoma, which held Native people in a "system of peonage." In this region, Indians worked like slaves and had little self-determination. Although they were "just like any other poor people," their subservient status prohibited them from relating to urban America. Warrior contemplated how best to bring about change, concluding that violence offered the best option. "Slug them in the mouth or shoot them," he declared, as that was the only thing "Southern rednecks" understood.[7]

Although Warrior may have chosen violence as the best solution, others within the NIYC took a more pragmatic view, believing they could reform education to incorporate Native culture. Dumont and Mel Thom looked to the Navajos' Rough Rock Demonstration School as a blueprint for how they might proceed in developing new approaches to Indian education. The school's founders were tribal leaders who transformed the Diné oral tradition into a written curriculum. The faculty at Rough Rock also stressed the Navajo language in their curriculum, believing that, as one instructor put it, "whenever anyone learns any language, you learn a complete new way of thinking, a new way of looking at the world." To be sure, Rough Rock had its critics. Donald Erikson, an education professor at the University of Chicago whom the Indian Bureau had hired to report on Rough Rock, believed that the new community school went too far, ignoring academics and focusing too much on the economic development of the local community.[8]

The NIYC, however, brushed aside the criticisms of Erikson and others. Rough Rock had devised the type of bicultural education that staffers in the organization had been talking about for years. Shortly after Rough Rock's founding, Dumont wrote Thom to discuss the possibility of an NIYC-sponsored education venture. He maintained that any such endeavor should involve better teacher training, major staff administration changes, and greater community control. The Indian Bureau's hierarchical system had proven ineffective. Most important, of course, remained the infusion of intercultural perspective into the curriculum.[9]

Articulating an approach to Indian education was easy; actually starting an NIYC-sponsored program proved more difficult. Then, in May 1966, education specialist Jack Forbes of Far West Laboratory for Educational Research and Development contacted Thom about launching a new Indian-controlled institution. Forbes, who claimed Powhatan ancestry, had long been involved in Indian education, having proposed a "Native American University" to the Department of the Interior in 1961. In a letter to Vice President Lyndon Johnson, Forbes had argued, "The integration of Indian students into existing public universities is but a temporary measure and cannot be seen as a real solution to the major problems of the Indian people." Forbes envisioned a multilingual institution where Natives from all over the Americas could convene and discover their shared experiences as indigenous peoples. Some Native leaders, however, staunchly opposed Forbes's plan. Cherokee leader W. W. Keeler believed that separate education would only hinder Native children's ability to integrate into mainstream society. Government leaders also rejected Forbes's Native American University, arguing that it would not meet the needs of Indian students.[10]

Despite the temporary setback, Forbes continued to work toward greater self-determination in Indian education. In 1966 he served as a guest lecturer at the Workshop on American Indian Affairs, while also founding the Center for Tribal Research to advocate for "an inter-disciplinary comparative approach to the problems of tribal and folk (sub-national) groups." That same year, he took a position as the research program director of Far West Laboratory, an organization founded to work with the Office of Equal Opportunity in developing new culturally sensitive curricula and teaching methods. Under Forbes's influence, Far West Labs sought to incorporate Native perspectives when devising new educational programs. In one of its reports, Far West declared that neither the BIA nor public schools had met the needs of Indian children, as both lacked adequate funding for textbooks and classroom equipment and were often located in poor, remote areas that required long commutes from home to school. Furthermore, high dropout rates and teacher turnover, along with poor communication with the students' parents, had created a dire situation that Far West hoped to remedy.[11]

Forbes tapped the NIYC, an organization he described as "a non-profit educational agency," to bring in a fresh Native perspective to Far West's projects. Together, the NIYC and Far West proposed an in-depth, fifteen-month survey of ten Indian schools located across the United States. The NIYC and Far West would closely observe the schools, searching for ways to make Indian education more effective. Relying on the study, they would establish several experimental demonstration schools, which, like Rough Rock, would involve the local tribal community and include Native language, history, art, music, and literature in the curriculum. Head Start grants from the OEO would help cover the schools' operating costs, but the NIYC would contribute funds to help get the ventures off the ground.[12]

In the spring of 1967, NIYC executive director Thom contacted Charles Kettering about donating funds. Kettering, who had contributed to NIYC in the past, was enthusiastic about the project, calling it "one of the most exciting efforts ever to be undertaken in the Indian field." His faith in the project, which he expected to make "a tremendous and significant impact," persuaded him to offer $5,000 toward the initiation of the demonstration schools. The OEO, in turn, would contribute $1,000 for each model school to purchase equipment and pay a $1,700 salary per teacher. The contributions of Kettering and the OEO helped launch the project, but they still were not enough to see the project through to the end. Fortunately, Thom and Dumont proved to be savvy grant writers, successfully petitioning the Carnegie Foundation for $95,000 and the Ford Foundation for $27,500. Never before had the NIYC seen so much money come its way. With the largesse of this financial backing, the council could now take steps to remodel Indian education and position itself as one of the foremost intertribal organizations in operation.[13]

At its sixth annual meeting in the summer of 1967, the NIYC temporarily put its anti-establishment rhetoric to rest when staffers invited Commissioner of Indian Affairs Robert Bennett (Oneida) to deliver the keynote address. Bennett lauded the council for its efforts in Indian education and for discovering new ways of coping with the problems facing Indian country. Following Bennett,

Dumont outlined NIYC's educational mission for the commissioner and others in attendance. The education czar told his audience it was time to begin incorporating Native values into the
classroom. As it stood, Native students experienced a "rapid and
intense cultural change" when they entered the classroom at any
given BIA or public school. They were forced to adjust to an entirely
alien society that had no knowledge of Indian culture or traditions.
Drawing from his field experience among the Cherokees in Oklahoma, Dumont noted that even small details, such as the seating
arrangement in a classroom, affected a child's learning ability and
could lead to detachment and alienation.[14]

Silent withdrawal, however, signaled an Indian form of resistance—"an intricate and complex method of defense" against the
one-way learning process found in most classrooms. Although
Indian students learned in the classroom, Dumont maintained that
what they learned was not exactly what the instructor was teaching. Rather, they learned about the sorts of classroom social dynamics employed in white educational institutions. Such "underground
learning" indicated that a "war of cultures" had unfolded in
schools run by whites. High dropout rates signaled another means
by which Native students fought this war. When students dropped
out, Dumont contended, it indicated that the teachers and administrators had failed—not the students. The NIYC education specialist concluded by suggesting some remedies, such as introducing a
greater degree of respect and worth into the classroom; involving
tribal members, parents, and the students themselves when devising curricula; and making learning a two-way process.[15]

Dumont's speech outlined the NIYC's philosophy on Indian
education, but it also provided a model for what the organization
was attempting to do in its demonstration school endeavor with
Far West Labs. The address and the meeting at White Eagle seemed
to prove the NIYC had successfully remodeled itself into, in the
words of Jack Forbes, "an educational agency." Thom confirmed
this transformation in a letter to members of the NIYC, observing
that the council had "changed structure": "Instead of being only
a fraternal association of Indians, we are now a fully tax-exempt
charitable and educational agency." He went on to note that the

council could no longer consider itself a purely activist outfit: "While we are in position to be militant," he noted, "we are also in a better position to use private and public resources for our causes." Educational research and reform had seemingly become the organization's top priorities, not protesting or "raising hell," as Warrior had once proclaimed.[16]

Relying on the funds from Kettering and the Carnegie and Ford foundations, Thom and Dumont made plans in the fall of 1967 to move NIYC's main operations to the Hotel Claremont in Berkeley, California, where Far West Labs was headquartered. Thom's wife, Fran Poafpybitty, took a job as Forbes's secretary, while Dumont and the NIYC executive director hired Sam English (Ojibwe) as an office secretary and bookkeeper to handle the organization's growing finances. Trained as an electrician, English had served as office manager of a small machine shop when he developed a great concern for relocated Indians and their rising suicide rates. English worked for the council twenty hours a week, while also attending classes at the University of San Francisco. He had his work cut out for him, as the council's records were in a state of complete "disarray."[17]

As Thom and Dumont devoted their full efforts to the demonstration schools, Warrior and NIYC board member H. Browning Pipestem took steps to develop what they called the Institute for American Indian Studies. Pipestem had attended the Workshop on American Indian Affairs with Warrior and served with Dumont, Thom, and Rickard on the Indian advisory committee for the OEO's Upward Bound program, before enrolling in law school. Like Warrior, Pipestem was charismatic and took great pride in his full-blood background, claiming to friends that he was "8/4's Indian." Pipestem also possessed a dynamic intellect. "He was smart," recalled Gerald Brown. "Of the whole bunch he was the biggest intellectual." Della Warrior agreed, adding, "Browning was a true scholar. . . . [He was] very analytical." Pipestem's physique made him all the more imposing. Charlie Cambridge characterized him as "a big big big person" and a "big monster football player," while Brown insisted that the giant Pipestem was "three times the size of me."[18]

In conceiving the Institute for American Indian Studies, Pipestem and Warrior modeled the project after the Workshop on American Indian Affairs, which had so profoundly influenced them. Like the workshops, the institute would bring Native college students from across the United States together for six weeks of intensive study of social theory and its application to issues facing Indian people. They hoped the institute would correct the false histories of Native Americans taught in BIA and public schools, while helping students realize their own marginality. "The educational system is a white man factory. . . . Individualistic thinking is a trap," Pipestem had declared at the Upward Bound meeting of April 1966.[19]

Although D'Arcy McNickle and American Indian Development, Inc., still held the summer workshops in Boulder, Warrior and Pipestem believed that AID's curriculum was no longer in tune with the younger, angrier generation. Moreover, despite AID's sponsorship, whites devised the curriculum and essentially ran the workshops. The NIYC's new Institute for American Indian Studies would bring in a Native teaching staff and hence a stronger Indian perspective. "It is a unique undertaking since it is probably the only all-Indian institution ever conducted in higher education," Pipestem told Forbes. As with their annual meetings, Warrior and Pipestem further resolved to hold the summer institute in an Indian setting, selecting Haskell Indian School for the first year's gathering.[20]

For funding, Warrior and Pipestem tapped the OEO and the BIA. Requesting $67,000 for the project, the council outlined the institute's three-phase program. During the first phase, the NIYC would hold four regional college conferences in the spring of 1968 to arouse interest in the institute and to recruit students. Phase two consisted of the actual six-week workshop, which up to thirty students would attend. Finally, phase three launched the Coordinating Office and Resource Center that would act as a training depot for college students seeking to become involved in the political and social affairs of their home communities. The OEO allotted the NIYC a $29,000 grant for the project, while Commissioner Bennett promised Warrior that the BIA would provide room and board at Haskell and that Upward Bound would likely furnish additional funds for travel and transportation. Though the council had to trim back its ambitious agenda, the institute was off the ground.[21]

Topics of discussion included culture and identity, folk and urban society, poverty in America, and issues confronting contemporary Native America. The NIYC also used many of the same books assigned at the workshops, including John Collier's classic *Indians of the Americas*, Ruth Benedict's *Patterns of Culture*, and Edward Spicer's *Cycles of Conquest*. For the first institute, the NIYC devised an "American Indian Reader," which organizers called "the blue bible" because of the color of its cover. The reader reprinted essays by Warrior, Sol Tax, Robert Thomas, Albert Wahrhaftig, and Rolland Wright. Despite Pipestem's proclamation that "Indian people conceived [the institute], raised money for it, organized it and are now operating it," the NIYC brought in non-Indians such as Wright, Nancy Lurie, Robert Rietz, and even the Waxes to serve as instructors, guest lecturers, and advisers.[22]

The similarities between the Institute for American Indian Studies and the Workshop on American Indian Affairs fomented tension between the NIYC and AID. Those who participated in the former organization felt that whites dominated the workshops and thus infringed upon the self-determination of Native people. Alternatively, leaders in AID criticized the NIYC staffers who directed the institute for their radical and overly militant approach. In light of the council's institute, McNickle, Tax, Rietz, Galen Weaver, and others instrumental in the creation and operation of the workshops held a meeting during the summer of 1968 to discuss the future of their project. Tax believed that the workshops still had a purpose, as they afforded Native students the opportunity to engage in "mutually helpful dialogue." The Chicago Conference coordinator chuckled at the workshops' initial focus on the marginalization of Native students, but he believed they retained a certain "political action" component relevant to the times.[23]

The organizers of the institute and the workshops may have clashed further over the recruitment of participants, though the younger, more vibrant institute probably appealed to a greater number of college students in an increasingly politicized nation. Rolland Wright, who taught in both venues, believed NIYC purposely recruited Native youth who fit its more militant ideal, with the hope of bringing in future council members. Organization building remained central, Wright maintained, noting, "The curriculum was clearly only an incidental part of the institute, not central as it had been in the workshops." The institute's more militant image attracted urban-based Indians, unlike the workshops, which drew students primarily from reservations.[24]

In planning for the first institute, the NIYC relied on word of mouth for recruitment. The publication of Stan Steiner's book *The New Indians* in the spring of 1968 gave the council added exposure. The book featured Thom, Warrior, Shirley Hill Witt, and Herb Blatchford, among others, as the angry voice of a new generation of militant young activists. "Academic Aborigine[s]," Steiner dubbed them, stressing their activist agenda and anti-establishment stance. The journalist traced the origins of this "Powwow of the Young Intellectuals" back to the Regional Indian Youth Council and showed how the leaders of this "youthful rebellion" sought to preserve traditional values while fighting against, in Thom's words, the "poisons of the dominant society." Steiner's celebratory narrative showcased the fish-ins and how the NIYC had brought hope to the Native people of the Pacific Northwest. Despite its sometimes sensational approach, *The New Indians* nevertheless captured the mood of the rising Indian youth movement and broadcast its message to Native students throughout the United States.[25]

After the publication of *The New Indians*, the NIYC gained further exposure for its institute when several newspapers featured articles on the organization and its founders. Herb Blatchford, the subject of one such article, attempted to diffuse some of Steiner's sensationalism when he told the *Gallup Independent* that Steiner's account dwelled too much on Indian militancy and not enough on the council's "lobbying and quiet, but effective diplomacy." Shirley Hill Witt, alternatively, seemed to bolster the fiery picture of *The New Indians* when she blasted the government for its continued efforts at assimilating Native people. She lauded traditional Indian ways, while denigrating the fast-paced rat race of Anglo culture. "Slavery of the Anglo to his watch," she explained to reporters from the *Albuquerque Tribune*, was the problem: "A little ticking piece of metal. It rules. It's a monarch." The tone of these articles, along with Steiner's book, undoubtedly appealed to young Indians, who were very much a part of the highly politicized youth culture of the late 1960s. If the Institute for American Indian Studies benefited from such exposure, Clyde Warrior's increasing despondency and losing fight against severe alcoholism threatened both the success of the institutes and the stability of the NIYC itself.[26]

It was no secret that Clyde Warrior enjoyed drinking. At the Boulder workshops, he had earned a reputation for his uncanny ability to consume large quantities of alcohol into the early hours of the morning, while managing to excel in the classroom, despite splitting hangovers compounded by just a few hours of sleep. Perhaps a fire burned deeply within the Ponca, compelling him to up-lift himself and his people. Or maybe it was just a youthful vivacity. By 1966, however, shortly after his election as NIYC president, Warrior's ability to balance his boozing with his professional life began to waver. Employed for twelve months during the 1966–67 academic year as Murray Wax's assistant in a study of Oklahoma Cherokees, Warrior simply neglected his duties. Shortly after he moved to Tahlequah, capital of the Cherokee Nation and the center of Wax's educational study, Warrior turned his home into a party haven for those young Cherokees attracted to his warm and mag-netic personality. Sometimes he would hold special thematic par-ties that lasted for days, such as his "Annual Celebration of the Crucifixion."[27]

All of the partying, however, began to catch up with him. An ir-ritated Wax complained that the NIYC president "submitted a very small quantity of work." To be sure, Wax noted, the work he did complete was of "a high quality" and revealed that Warrior un-derstood "the dynamics of Indian education and of Indian affairs as well as anyone." However, Wax still reprimanded his student aide for failing to live up to his role as social researcher. "Since you lack a formal background in social science and do not seem to have been improving it by intensive study, I do not see what meaningful participation you could then have in the project," Wax scolded.[28]

Warrior's disorganization further angered Wax, especially his failure to itemize the phone calls he made on behalf of the study. Wax suspected the Ponca of using monies earmarked for research for his personal "pleasure." "I told you long ago that I did not wish to get financially involved on a personal level with you," the sociologist fumed. "I refuse to get involved any deeper with your finances." Wax insisted that Warrior compensate him for misappropriation of study funds and threatened to have his phone disconnected.[29]

Wax nearly reached his breaking point when Warrior took part in a much publicized NIYC demonstration in July 1967. Fearful that the administration and the Office of Education at the University of Kansas (KU) would cut the funding for his study, Wax blasted Warrior for his "latest escapade." "NIYC means Clyde Warrior, and that means KU project, and accordingly I expect inquiries and criticism both from KU and the Office of Education," he fretted. "If they should make such an attack, I don't see how we can defend ourselves, but at least for my own satisfaction I should like to know—immediately!—what happened and how you were involved." Warrior attempted to explain himself and apologized if his "inebriated self got out of line."[30]

The NIYC president must have recognized that his tenure as Wax's assistant was not going smoothly, as he increasingly turned his attention to building his academic credentials. In the spring of 1967 he applied to several programs, including a postbaccalaureate fellowship at Haverford College and the graduate program in American studies at KU. Despite their troubled relationship, the sociology professor wrote Warrior a stellar letter of recommendation. He described his aide as a person of "insight, ability, and tenacity." D'Arcy McNickle also wrote a glowing letter for Warrior, calling him "one of the outstanding young Indians in the country." The University of Kansas admitted the Ponca, and he also received a three-thousand-dollar John Hay Whitney Foundation Opportunity Fellowship to fund his study.[31]

Warrior relocated to Lawrence in the summer of 1967, and he enrolled in classes during the fall semester. However, he soon dropped out of the program and moved back to his hometown—Ponca City, Oklahoma—the following spring. Shortly after the publication of *The New Indians*, Charles Powers of the *Kansas City Star* drove out to the oil refinery town to interview Warrior. The smell of petroleum permeated the air as the reporter spoke with the unemployed and bitter leader in his three-bedroom bungalow. "I don't know a single white man who's helped the Indian," Warrior asserted. "Oh, they're all sincere and dedicated. And stupid. I don't know any who have done the Indians any good." As he downed glass after glass of "cola," the despondent NIYC founder lambasted the Bureau of Indian Affairs, declaring everyone over thirty should be fired. He ridiculed the "racists and incompetents" in the BIA for antiquated policies rooted in the pre-Collier era that had led to a "neurotic, almost insane attitude toward joining 'the mainstream.'" However, Warrior made no claim that he had the answers on how to rectify the problem: "Do I know what to do? No, I guess not. If I had an answer it would be on the tip of my tongue. But it's not."[32]

The NIYC president's spirit and energy were sapped. Lacking the fire he had once exuded, Warrior, in the words of Vine Deloria, Jr., "had gone off the deep end in his drinking." Browning Pipestem had to assume control over the Institute for American Indian Studies as Warrior's involvement waned. Warrior's wife, Della, began conducting all of the family's business on top of caring for their two daughters. Warrior attempted to save himself by entering alcohol rehabilitation in Los Angeles, but the brief interlude failed to end his excessive drinking. The Ponca leader suffered a further blow when his mother died that spring. In the summer of 1968, when his liver began to fail, he and his family moved to nearby Enid, Oklahoma, where Della's parents lived. There, at the age of twenty-eight, Clyde Warrior died.[33]

News of Clyde's death spread around Indian country like wildfire, leading to a profound sense of sadness and even hopelessness. After hearing of the tragedy, Shirley Hill Witt, who had not been active in the council for three years, thought, "Clyde's struggle had come to an end, taking ours with it." At his funeral, friends and family members gathered around to remember Warrior and his efforts to create a brighter future for Native people. Mel Thom, accompanied by Sam English, flew in from Berkeley to pay his last respects to his close friend and colleague.[34] In a rousing address, Thom lauded the fearless Ponca for his bravery and dedication to the uplift of all Native people:

Our leader is gone. But the spirit of such a leader is never gone. We can still hear him teasing, laughing, cussing, singing, and talking as few men would. We will always hear him. His words made Indian people feel good. He had an unusual ability to bring honesty out of people.

It is sad that men have best understood Clyde after his passing on. Although, sometimes, unacceptable to modern tradition his words and deeds were those of honesty and love for his people. In his short life he brought us a long way ahead in our struggle for human equality.

Clyde gave us a new hope. He gave us courage at a time when we were scared. He led us to know what freedom might be for our people. For many of us he turned the tide when Indian life seemed to be on a one-way road to oblivion. He frightened people with his fight against oppression of Indian people. With crystal clear words he could talk of our American system[,] which few American people understood.

Clyde was a great American; Clyde was a great Indian patriot; Clyde loved his country. He wanted this country to do right not only for his Indian people but also for men of all races. He was a free man held in bondage.

Clyde leaves us with our great struggle just beginning. This may be American Indian's last rally against oppression. We need Clyde, but he is gone. He opened the doors of self-realization for us. For opening those doors he was struck down by white man's alcohol, as surely as the assassin's bullet has struck down so many great men. It is indeed a tragedy that so many great Indian men have to go this way.

Clyde is gone but never forgotten.[35]

After the funeral, Thom called on the council's membership to donate money for a headstone, as Warrior's grandparents could not afford one. The NIYC later rechristened their summer institute as the Clyde Warrior Institute on American Indian Studies and declared August 31 "Clyde Warrior Day," ensuring the date was a paid holiday for the organization's staff.[36]

Warrior's death marked the beginning of the end for NIYC's founding board of directors and officers. In Berkeley, Thom and Dumont's model demonstration school project began to fall apart because the leaders failed to find the time or necessary staff to follow through with their initial blueprint. NIYC officers blamed Far

West Labs, asserting that the study did not successfully incorporate Native systems of learning. The educational process in the model schools "remained alien and [had] not been integrated into the cultural norms of the community." They contended, "The school retains the position of the colonizer and the community that of the colony."[37]

Discouraged, Thom and Dumont neglected the heavily funded project and turned their attention to other matters. In May 1968, Thom, Dumont, and Sam English joined Hank Adams and Tillie Walker of the United Scholarship Service in the Poor People's Campaign. Conceived by Martin Luther King, Jr., the Poor People's Campaign brought together economically underprivileged Americans from diverse backgrounds. King hoped a massive show of force would prod lawmakers to step up the War on Poverty by passing an "Economic Bill of Rights" that would end job discrimination and guarantee all people reasonable employment. Though the great civil rights leader had been assassinated in April, the campaign's Committee of One Hundred continued with King's plans. Dumont, Thom, Walker, Adams, and Leo LaClair (Muckleshoot) were among the fifteen Indians on the committee. Together they formed the Coalition of American Indian Citizens and made plans to march on Washington to press forward with King's vision and bring an end to the widespread poverty that plagued Native people.[38]

The coalition drafted a statement, which they presented to Secretary of the Interior Stewart Udall. Indian people, according to the coalition, remained the poorest people in the nation; they were victims of a "racist, immoral, paternalistic, and colonialistic system." The government's paternalism was like a virus, they clamored, and the secretary of the Interior was the host. The Interior Department had failed Native people, and its efforts to include them in the BIA were mere "tokenism." "We make it un-equivocally and crystal clear that Indian people have the right to separate and equal communities within the American system," the statement read. In hopes of forcing Interior and Indian Bureau officials into "meaningful negotiation," the coalition proceeded to picket and temporarily occupy the BIA building. Thom, Dumont, and Walker were arrested and summarily sentenced to thirty days in jail.[39]

Mel Thom *(at left, behind microphone)* and Hank Adams *(at center, wearing glasses)* join Ralph Abernathy *(on Adams's right)* and Reijes Tijerina *(on Adams's left)* at the Poor People's Campaign in Washington, D.C., 1968. Detractors from both inside and outside the NIYC criticized Thom for his involvement. (Karl Kernberger Collection [PICT 2000-008-00843], Center for Southwest Research, University Libraries, University of New Mexico)

Meanwhile, Sam English headed back to Berkeley to tend to business at the council's office at the Hotel Claremont. On the return flight, the NIYC office secretary, along with fifteen to twenty other Native activists who had attended the Poor People's Campaign, held an impromptu powwow in the airplane's main aisle. Stewardesses and other passengers soon joined the fun as the plane made its way toward the Denver airport. Swept up in the moment, English decided impulsively to join activists from the Three Affiliated Tribes in a protest they were planning in Bismarck, North Dakota, rather than return to the Bay Area. Using NIYC funds, English purchased plane tickets for himself and several of his friends.[40]

Neither the arrest of NIYC staffers nor English's detour boded well with the organization's chief funding sources. The Ford Foundation charged that the council's involvement in the Poor People's Campaign violated the terms of its grant, believing that the Berkley office had used funds for protesting rather than educational development. The foundation had earmarked its donation of $27,500 for the model demonstration schools and educational development, not for protests. Indeed, the terms of grant specifically stated, "No major deviations will be made . . . without approval by the Foundation." However, according to English, Thom and Dumont had never used the Ford Foundation grant money for anything other than the model demonstration schools. "I should know," English recalled. "I wrote the checks." Regardless of how the NIYC used the grant, the organization's old rabble-rousing image was again haunting the council. Even Far West Labs distanced itself from the NIYC in order to protect its chief sources of funding. One of its donors wrote to Forbes expressing his displeasure with the council's protest activities, noting, "It is understood that you will direct your project without the involvement of Mr. Thom, Mr. Dumont, members of their families, or the Coalition of American Indians." The NIYC was unraveling fast, and neither Thom nor Dumont could stop it.[41]

On top of the problems with their chief sources of funding, the main office in Berkeley had virtually lost all contact with the NIYC staffers in White Eagle, Oklahoma, who ran the Clyde Warrior Institute for American Indian Studies. Browning Pipestem, who had his own separate NIYC stationery printed, wrote to Forbes in July 1968 to tell the Far West Labs director about the summer institute. Though Forbes kept an office in the same building as NIYC executive director Thom and Dumont, Pipestem asked him if he would serve as one the institute's guest lecturers, reflecting a breakdown in communication between Berkeley and White Eagle. Pipestem had also called a secretive board meeting in Norman for the staffers in Oklahoma, discarding tradition by closing the gathering to the public.[42]

Matters came to a head at the council's annual August meeting in Gallup, New Mexico. Pipestem, who had taken full control over the Institute for American Indian Studies after Warrior's death, led a group of newly recruited students from the institute to Gallup. Donning black sunglasses and flanked by a posse of young Native students, the giant Pipestem confronted the NIYC board of directors, who he believed had allowed the organization to fall into financial disarray. Many of the organization's founders also attended, including Herb Blatchford and Shirley Hill Witt, but Pipestem and his entourage kept them standing in the back of the room, never even offering them seats or an opportunity to speak. When the council held its annual election, Pipestem and his followers ousted nearly all of the old board members, staff, and officers. Even Mel Thom, the founder and long-standing figurehead of the council was removed as executive director. The new officers withdrew from the Poor People's Campaign and completely severed all ties with the Coalition of American Indian Citizens.[43]

Witt recalled that neither Thom nor any of the board members sought to retain control of the NIYC, asserting that they "looked forward to turning over the organization to a new generation and, perhaps, a new brand of operation." Hence, it came as a shock when Pipestem and company greeted the founders with "an unmistakable air of hostility." Sam English, one of the few staff members to retain a position within the organization, believed that Pipestem's actions were nothing short of a coup that irreparably altered the NIYC. Still, Thom accepted the takeover. English believed that the NIYC founder and onetime president and executive director had always "considered the progress of the youth" first and foremost and therefore thought a change in leadership would "lead to a new era." Thom and the other Red Power warriors who had founded and led the NIYC in its formative years may have stumbled and lost control by that fateful summer of 1968, but they accepted it. They constructed their movement and articulated an ideology that they hoped the younger generation would co-opt and build upon. The change of guard, which so fittingly took place in Gallup—the very place the NIYC was born—proved that they had succeeded.[44]

For a political entity to remain vital and dynamic, more often than not, there must be change. This axiom especially held true for the

National Indian Youth Council in 1968. Council leaders had secured massive grants and had devised promising educational programs, but at the same time, their growing militancy clashed with their reformative goals. In the end, they chose confrontation and protest (or drowning their anger at the bottom of a bottle) over education and reform. Following the ouster of Thom and the other board members, the NIYC regrouped, but remained loyal to the founding ideals of sovereignty, self-determination, treaty rights, and cultural preservation. Under the leadership of its soon-to-be-appointed new executive director, Gerald Wilkinson, the organization set about expanding its activities, broadening its focus, and securing its legacy.

CHAPTER 8

"THE NATIONAL INDIAN YOUTH COUNCIL IS A PROCESS, NOT AN EVENT"

Continuity and Transformation in the 1970s and Beyond

In August 1968, following the National Indian Youth Council's annual meeting in Gallup, H. Browning Pipestem and the newly elected board of directors ordered executive secretary Sam English back to Berkeley to clean out the NIYC office at the Hotel Claremont. English was to move the organization's operations to Albuquerque, a city that the new NIYC leaders viewed as more centrally situated in Indian country. Driving across the Great Basin at breakneck speeds in a rented U-Haul truck, English transported the organization's files and belongings into an office in Albuquerque's Nob Hill district near the University of New Mexico.[1]

With just eight thousand dollars remaining in the council's coffers, Pipestem next directed English to New York City to seek out new sources of funding for the struggling council. A "scared shitless" English navigated his way through the Big Apple and met with several potential donors. When he returned to New Mexico, he and other staffers launched a recruitment drive that drew in nearly four hundred members by the end of September. These sure-footed steps ensured that the NIYC would survive the tumultuous events of 1968. But even more significant to the future of the second-oldest intertribal organization was the recruitment of Gerald Wilkinson as executive director in May 1969.[2]

Wilkinson, more than anyone else, was responsible for rebuilding the NIYC and securing its legacy. During his nearly twenty years as executive director, he broadened the council's membership base,

CONTINUITY AND TRANSFORMATION IN THE 1970S AND BEYOND

secured new sources of funding, and expanded the NIYC's activities, overseeing new programs and initiatives that transformed the council into a multifaceted organization that continues to advocate for Native people to this very day. Under Wilkinson's tenure, the NIYC carried on its efforts to reform Indian education, but the council also joined up with the American Indian Movement to protest federal Indian policy. The NIYC hired attorneys to fight for Native rights in the courts, at the same time lobbying legislators at both the state and federal levels. All the while, Wilkinson and the council leadership remained dedicated to issues affecting reservations or rural tribal communities and held true to the founding members' commitment to sovereignty, self-determination, treaty rights, and cultural preservation. However, with their headquarters in Albuquerque, they also became increasingly focused on urban Indians. The organization's development of a job training and placement agency proved to be one of the most crucial transformations in the 1970s. It was this ability to adapt that enabled the organization to look back at the 1960s and proclaim, "Of all the activist groups started during that tumultuous time in U.S. history, NIYC is the sole survivor."[3]

When viewed in a wider historical context, the survival of the National Indian Youth Council through the late 1960s is nothing short of astonishing. Just as the NIYC sought to cauterize its wounds and start anew, other student movements spiraled out of control and eventually imploded. Factionalism grew rampant within the Students for a Democratic Society, as the organization split between a progressive labor faction and self-proclaimed revolutionaries. By 1969 this latter faction called itself "Weatherman" and joined with the militant Black Panthers in advocating a "united front against fascism." That same year, SDS held its final national convention in Chicago. As the organization folded, the Weatherman faction declared a "state of war" and embarked upon a violent campaign against what it saw as an irreparably corrupt American power structure.[4]

The Student Nonviolent Coordinating Committee suffered a similar fate. As with SDS, factionalism tore the organization apart in the late 1960s. After the election of Stokely Carmichael as chairman in 1966, SNCC moved in an increasingly radical direction, eventually resulting in the removal of all whites from the organization. Many of the new militant leaders began advocating violent revolution and cultural nationalism. Before long, radicals targeted and ousted veteran staff members who clung to the ideal of nonviolent, collective political action. Even Carmichael himself was ejected in 1969. That same year, SNCC held its final staff meeting in New York City, where the fiery H. Rap Brown seized control of the organization and renamed it the Student National Coordinating Committee. Brown's SNCC continued on in name for a few more years, but for all intents and purposes the SNCC of old no longer existed as a functional organization.[5]

As SDS and SNCC faltered, other student organizations began hitting their stride. In March 1969, Mexican American students met in Denver for the first National Chicano Youth Liberation Conference. Embracing their culture and heritage, they self-identified as "Chicanos" and advocated political action and racial pride, which they outlined in "El Plan Espiritual de Aztlán." The manifesto condemned the "brutal 'gringo'" for the invasion of the Mexican homeland and for his exploitation of the Chicano people. "We declare the independence of our mestizo nation," the authors announced. "We are a bronze people. . . . [W]e are Aztlán." The following year, Chicano students again met in Denver for the second Youth Liberation Conference. Under the leadership of Rodolfo "Corky" Gonzales, the 2,500 attendees established La Raza Unida Party to give their movement greater structure and political leverage.[6]

Around the same time, Asian American students at San Francisco State College, like their Chicano counterparts in La Raza Unida Party, began advocating racial pride and consciousness. Influenced heavily by the Black Panther Party in nearby Oakland, students from the Inter-collegiate Chinese for Social Action and the Asian American Political Alliance joined forces with other students on campus to launch a series of strikes under the auspices of the Third World Liberation Front. "Shut it down!" they declared as they walked out of classrooms in protest of the institutional racism that plagued the college and American society in general. The strikes spread to the University of California at Berkeley and eventually led to the development of the first Asian American studies programs.[7]

Native students in the Bay Area also rode the wave of activism. At the University of California at Berkley, Professor Jack Forbes and two students, LaNada Means (Shoshone-Bannock) and Lee Brightman (Cheyenne-Sioux), founded a Native student movement called United Native Americans (UNA). Forbes, who had worked closely with Mel Thom and Robert Dumont in developing new approaches to Indian education, served as the mastermind of the organization. In their publication *Warpath*, they advocated "the brotherhood of all Indian peoples without regard to the whiteman's boundary lines" and condemned the Indian Bureau as a "colonial office" controlled by "white bureaucrats and their Indian collaborators." To illustrate their point, they called for the creation of a "Bureau of White Affairs," which would give non-Indians a taste of the paternalism and oppressive oversight that Native people had to cope with on a daily basis. "It is obvious that whites are being badly discriminated against," the UNA reported sarcastically. "They are also becoming too soft and need to go through a toughening experience with the help of the ever-ready federal government."[8]

As the UNA pushed its agenda in *Warpath*, on the other side of the San Francisco Bay the American Indian Nation, another intertribal organization founded to help Indians adjust to an urban environment, began plans for transforming the dilapidated federal prison on Alcatraz Island into an American Indian National Center. The center would serve as a "living cultural memorial" to all Indians in the United States, while the actual construction project would act as a sort of domestic Peace Corps venture that would give the would-be Native worker "the opportunity to pull his own bootstraps' rather than federal apron strings." The federal government could live up to its democratic ideals and redeem itself from "100 years of shame" by authorizing such a center.[9]

Forbes, who as early as 1966 had suggested that Native people could use surplus federal land for an all-Indian university, took notice of the American Indian Nation's efforts and, along with Native students from the University of California at Los Angeles and San Francisco State College, joined the cause. Their efforts were further invigorated when the San Francisco Indian Center mysteriously burned to the ground in October 1969, leaving the Native people in the city without a central community center. Realizing that the federal government would never hand over title to Alcatraz, Indian leaders in the Bay Area decided to take matters into their own hands and simply seize "the Rock." On November 20, 1969, Native students calling themselves Indians of All Tribes landed on Alcatraz and commenced an occupation that lasted until June 1971.[10]

The Indians of All Tribes issued a proclamation, laying claim to the former prison for all Native peoples "by right of discovery." "We wish to be fair and honorable in our dealings with the Caucasian inhabitants of this land," they asserted. "We will purchase said Alcatraz Island for twenty-four dollars in glass beads and red cloth, a precedent set by the white man's purchase of a similar island about 300 years ago." The occupiers went on to declare they intended to develop a center for Native American studies where young people could learn about Native culture and art; an American Indian spiritual center to rejuvenate ancient religious practices; an Indian center of ecology to train Native youth to restore Indian lands and water resources; an Indian training school that would include a center for arts and crafts, as well as a restaurant that would serve Native foods for the public; and finally, an American Indian museum to "show the noble and tragic events of Indian history."[11]

The Indians of All Tribes ultimately failed in their bid to make Alcatraz "Indian land forever," but they succeeded in pushing the Red Power movement into the American conscience by garnering massive media exposure. It was this attention that led the public and academics alike to conclude that Alcatraz had served as the springboard for the Red Power movement. The takeover, to be sure, was an incredibly dramatic historical moment. News footage of the event was broadcast throughout the United States and beyond, raising awareness of issues facing urban Native people. The Alcatraz occupation also inspired a fresh new wave of intertribal activism. Richard Oakes (Mohawk), John Trudell (Sioux), LaNada Means, and the other occupiers became heroes to so many young Native people who wanted to make a difference. And Alcatraz made the takeover the main form of protest for so many Native activists. The takeovers at Fort Totten, the BIA in Washington, D.C., and Wounded Knee would all draw their inspiration from the takeover of Alcatraz. But the Alcatraz occupation, for all its drama, inspiration, and influence was still a continuation of an ongoing struggle guided by young people that had begun nearly a decade earlier. Both the militancy and the intertribal direct action that academics and nonacademics have ascribed to the Alcatraz occupation began with the NIYC.[12]

Ironically, the newly reorganized NIYC would ultimately benefit from the spotlight the Alcatraz occupation shined on issues facing Native people. The council's membership base ballooned as new chapters at colleges, universities, high schools, Indian schools, and reservations cropped up across the United States. The NIYC claimed as many as five thousand members in 1970 and fifteen thousand in 1972. Distribution of *Americans Before Columbus* widened; some eight thousand copies of the newspaper made their way to all corners of Indian country in 1969 alone. Such growth, however, had as much to do with the new executive director, Gerald Wilkinson, as it did the Alcatraz takeover.[13]

Born of Cherokee descent in North Carolina, Wilkinson arose as a star running back for his high school football team before suffering an injury that resulted in the loss of his right eye. He went on to study at Duke University, the Sorbonne in France, and Columbia University, where he earned a master of arts degree. Fluent in French and well versed in Marxist thought, he served as youth coordinator for the OEO program Oklahomans for Indian Opportunity in Norman, Oklahoma, during the 1960s. Initially, some did not trust Wilkinson, because he revealed little of his past and "didn't look Indian." Vine Deloria, Jr., recalled, "Gerry was so mysterious that half the time I wondered if he was a government agent keeping track of us. . . . Sometimes I made stuff up so it would look like I knew things—when I didn't have any idea—just to see how much information I could get from him." Deloria, however, came to trust Wilkinson, noting that he "worked harder than anyone I knew and took virtually nothing in salary."[14]

James Nez (Diné) bolsters Deloria's assessment. In the mid-1970s, Wilkinson recruited Nez to serve on the NIYC board of directors after the young Navajo student's successful tenure as president of the University of New Mexico's Kiva Club. Wilkinson and Nez immediately bonded and formed a lifelong friendship. "No one could

Gerald Wilkinson stabilized the NIYC and expanded its operations when he took over as executive director in 1969. Wilkinson served in his post until his death in 1989. (Gerald Wilkinson, photograph, National Indian Youth Council Pictorial Collection [PICT 000-703-0032], Center for Southwest Research, University Libraries, University of New Mexico)

come close to what he was doing for Indians," Nez testified. "He was a tireless worker" and a "kind and generous man." Although Wilkinson couldn't even afford an apartment in Albuquerque (he slept on the NIYC office floor), he managed to keep the struggling council afloat. Many questioned the new executive director's ability, while others seemed angered that a "white man" controlled the council. Nez recalled, "Some doubted he was Indian at all. I said, 'I don't care.' He's very dedicated to the Indian cause, more so than many so-called Indian activists of the day."[15]

Wilkinson was not the first choice to serve as the NIYC's new executive director. The reorganized board of directors initially hired Thomas G. Lentz to stabilize the council and reinitiate activities. Lentz, however, bolted once he realized the council had no coffers or payroll. Facing disaster, Pipestem took matters into his own hands and personally recruited Wilkinson. Charlie Cambridge remembered that for a considerable period of time Wilkinson worked as executive director extralegally, as Pipestem had installed him without an official vote from the board. It would take months before the board met and voted on the matter.[16]

Once on board, Wilkinson conceptualized the new NIYC as a national organization with semiautonomous affiliates. He believed that the best way to expand the membership base and build upon the momentum of the Red Power movement would be to allow local chapters "independent action." In short, local affiliates should handle local situations. "We need to establish more regional offices which are locally controlled," the new leadership proposed. "These offices should develop a constituency and meet their needs.... These offices should develop local contacts and have their own funds." Hence, new NIYC chapters would grapple with their own issues without interference from the central office in Albuquerque. About the only requirement was that new members subscribe to the overarching mission of self-determination, tribal sovereignty, cultural preservation, and protection of treaty rights.[17]

Starting a new NIYC chapter under Wilkinson's leadership could not have been easier. All one needed to do was submit an application card with the names of the charter members and wait for the main office to mail back a certificate of affiliation. This informal, easy process led to the creation of new chapters all over Indian country and beyond. Chapters formed in large western and midwestern cities like Salt Lake City, Tulsa, Milwaukee, St. Paul, and Phoenix, as well as smaller college towns such as Stillwater, Oklahoma; Logan, Utah; Durango, Colorado; Davis, California; Flagstaff, Arizona; and Las Cruces, New Mexico. As Indian activism grew in the early 1970s, chapters were founded even in remote locales like Elko, Nevada; Hobart, Oklahoma; and Cibecue, Arizona. Indeed, new affiliates cropped up at such a rate the main office had difficulty keeping track of them all.[18]

Besides growing the organization, the main office continued to focus on Indian education. Although the NIYC cut Thom and Dumont's model demonstration school project from the organization's operations, the council continued to sponsor and even broaden the

During the early 1970s, Native students launched new NIYC chapters at high schools and colleges across Indian country. (NIYC Rally, photograph, National Indian Youth Council Pictorial Collection [PICT 000-703-0082], Center for Southwest Research, University Libraries, University of New Mexico)

Clyde Warrior Institute for American Indian Studies. In the summer of 1969, the NIYC organized institutes at the University of California at Los Angeles, Stout State University in Wisconsin, and the University of Colorado in Boulder. The 120 students who participated enrolled in two courses—"American Indians and Contemporary American Society" and "Issues in Change and Development in American Indian Communities"—enabling them to receive up to six credits toward their college degrees. The council funded the institutes through an Upward Bound grant of $159,000, most of which the organization paid out to the sponsoring universities.[19]

A separate endeavor initiated in the summer of 1970, the Educational Intern Training Program, sought to give students hands-on experience in problem solving and policy implementation. Participants spent five weeks in Washington, D.C., where they met in a series of seminars to discuss federal Indian policy. NIYC veterans Vine Deloria, Jr., Browning Pipestem, Robert Dumont, and Bruce Wilkie, who had been recently elected as executive director of the National Congress of American Indians, served as guest speakers. After their stay in the nation's capital, the enrolled students headed out to western New Mexico, where they spent a week at Zuni Pueblo, observing traditional practices and gaining a greater understanding of some of the problems southwestern Native communities confronted.[20]

The informal, even loose structure of the NIYC in the 1970s allowed for individual chapters to initiate their own educational endeavors. In Hammon, Oklahoma, the local NIYC affiliate designed a "survival school" in response to mistreatment of Native children in the local public school. Viola Hatch was largely responsible for the project. An Arapaho born in Geary, Oklahoma, Hatch worked with Wilkinson in Oklahomans for Indian Opportunity while also organizing local youth councils for Cheyenne and Arapaho students. In 1972 she was elected to the NIYC board of directors after forming a local council affiliate in Hammon. Hatch and other activists brought in Native instructors who implemented a culturally relevant curriculum for the survival school. The project received a $30,000 grant from the Bureau of Indian Affairs, enabling some sixty-five students of all ages to enroll.[21]

The survival school did not sit well with whites in Hammon, leading to a standoff that lasted nearly three weeks. During that time, local authorities harassed the school's instructors and administrators, questioning the legitimacy of the project and charging the NIYC affiliate with political subversion. At times it seemed as if the matter would descend into an outright war. "At night the cowboys would come out with a rifle in one hand and a beer in the other," remembers Hatch. "The police refused to do anything about it. . . . There were cars and pickups lined up and down the street. They were demanding that we come out and fight them." On another occasion, vandals assaulted the school itself, breaking nearly all of the windows. Despite such intimidation, Hatch, Wilkinson, Nez, and other council activists stood their ground and refused to back down. They kept the school open for over three years until finally

In 1973, Viola Hatch helped organize an NIYC survival school in Hammon, Oklahoma. She continues to serve on the council's board of directors today. (Viola Hatch, photograph, National Indian Youth Council Pictorial Collection [PICT 000-703-0075], Center for Southwest Research, University Libraries, University of New Mexico)

local officials agreed to meet NIYC's demands for fair treatment of Native children by putting an end to discrimination.[22]

The NIYC chapter in Hammon was not the only affiliate to experience a backlash from local authorities. In Brigham City, Utah, site of the notorious BIA boarding school known as Intermountain, NIYC student affiliates reported being harassed on a daily basis by the city's police department and residents. The situation stemmed from Diné students' having complained of Intermountain's draconian regulations, which limited free speech, forced Mormon conversion, and authorized excessive disciplinary action. Students told NIYC staffers that school officials had handcuffed them, shaved their heads, and injected them with the tranquilizer Thorazine for breaking Intermountain's strict rules. In response, Wilkinson devised a student "Bill of Rights" and charged the BIA with failing to implement a culturally relevant curriculum and violating the Diné's treaty rights by establishing a school seven hundred miles away from the reservation. NIYC staffers in Brigham City and Albuquerque organized protests to bring attention to the situation at Intermountain, shocking local residents whose Mormon community had been relatively quiet up to that point.[23]

Indeed, political protest, like education, remained a cornerstone of the reorganized NIYC. The council launched its first protest under Wilkinson's direction against the Indian Bureau's Albuquerque data center. Keypunch operators at the center charged the BIA with discrimination in its hiring and promotion practices. The NIYC went on to help organize the American Indian Movement for Equal Rights in Indian-Native Development (AMERIND), a watchdog group that represented BIA employees and helped them file complaints and lawsuits. Founded in Gallup eight years after the inaugural NIYC meeting, AMERIND forcefully argued for an all-Indian BIA that was independent of the Department of the Interior. NIYC leaders headed the new outfit, and the council paid for all of its printing, mailing, and traveling expenses.[24]

Just as NIYC staffers founded AMERIND in the desert Southwest, another group of council activists immersed themselves in a very different battle out on the northern Plains. In Fort Totten, on the Spirit Lake Sioux reservation in North Dakota, a near war broke out between competing factions seeking control of the tribal council. Florence Joshua, who had served as the tribal chairperson challenged usurper Lewis Goodhouse, whom she accused of stuffing ballot boxes in the recent tribal election. According to Joshua, the local BIA agent, Richard Bauer, had conspired with Goodhouse in the recent coup because the bureau found him more "easy to control." Wilkinson and the NIYC sided fully with Joshua and, at her behest, held a massive protest powwow to criticize Goodhouse and call for a new election. Held weeks before the Indians of All Tribes descended on Alcatraz Island, the protest drew some six hundred people, including activists from another organization based out of Minneapolis—the American Indian Movement (AIM).[25]

In late 1969, just as the protest powwow at Fort Totten unfolded, NIYC remained the most stable and recognized Native activist organization in operation. For over half a decade, its newspaper, *Americans Before Columbus*, had kept Native people across Indian country up to speed not just on pressing issues but also on the NIYC's activities, personalities, and growing militancy. The paper, along with Stan Steiner's book *The New Indians*, found an especially receptive audience in the founders of AIM. NIYC secretary Sam English recalled AIM founder Clyde Bellecourt (Ojibwe) running around at the 1969 NCAI meeting in Albuquerque, hoping to meet Mel Thom. "He had a copy of *The New Indians*," noted English. "You could see the excitement on his face." Although Thom was no longer affiliated with the NIYC, Bellecourt made contact with English and other council staffers in hopes of forging an alliance between the two organizations.[26]

AIM had a very different background from that of the NIYC. Founded by former Ojibwe convicts Bellecourt, Dennis Banks, and Edward Benton Banai, the urban-based organization fought racism and discrimination in Minnesota's Twin Cities. They originally called themselves Concerned Indian Americans and organized an "Indian patrol" to monitor the police in Native communities and prevent episodes of brutality. Armed with two-way radios, cameras, and tape recorders, they confronted police, broke up fights, and escorted home those too intoxicated to drive. Although Bellecourt, Banks, and other patrol members suffered regular police beatings for their efforts, their success proved astonishing. The Minneapolis police went twenty-two weeks without making a single arrest in the Native community. By 1968, Bellecourt, Banks, and Banai decided to change their organization's name to the American Indian Movement, which provided a better acronym than "Concerned Indian Americans."[27]

The NIYC entered into an alliance with AIM shortly after the Fort Totten protest. The two organizations resolved to cooperate in their efforts and support one another's programs. On November 10, 1969, the NIYC, AIM, the NCAI, and other intertribal organizations joined together to form the American Indian Task Force, which would present a statement to Vice President Spiro Agnew calling for greater Native involvement in shaping federal Indian policy. The formation of the American Indian Task Force

Clyde Bellecourt of AIM *(left)* and NIYC staffer Stanley Snake strategize to-gether. AIM and the NIYC collaborated regularly during the early 1970s. (Clyde Bellecourt and Stanley Snake, photograph, National Indian Youth Council Pictorial Collection [PICT 000-703-0090], Center for Southwest Research, University Libraries, University of New Mexico)

dramatically showed that although intertribal organizations such as the NIYC, AIM, and the NCAI differed sharply in the tactics they employed, each subscribed to the same principles of treaty rights, tribal sovereignty, self-determination, and cultural preservation, allowing for a general statement that included the signatures of Gerald Wilkinson, Dennis Banks, and D'Arcy McNickle. Such co-operation stood in sharp contrast to the African American struggle, which experienced acute divisions in the late 1960s between Black Power proponents calling for separation and moderate leaders ad-vocating integration.[28]

The alliance between such disparate factions of the Indian move-ment failed to hold together through the 1970s. The breakdown,

however, resulted from disagreement over tactics rather than ideology. NCAI officials distanced themselves from militant activism
when, in March 1970, the NIYC and AIM picketed the BIA's Plant
Management Engineering Center in Littleton, Colorado. The two
organizations charged that the Bureau discriminated against Native people in promotions and job training. Employing face-to-face
confrontational tactics that would become AIM's trademark, representatives of the two organizations cornered assistant BIA chief
Stewart Edmonds in his office and proceeded to give the frightened
government worker a verbal lashing. Roughly one hundred NIYC
and AIM members held a protest powwow and occupied the office
for three days until Bureau commissioner Louis Bruce (Mohawk-
Sioux)—who had also served as executive director of the NCAI—
finally arrived and signed their protest petition. As the ink dried,
Littleton police rolled in and arrested nine of the occupiers. The
arrests only led to further protests and picketing in Minneapolis,
Albuquerque, Sacramento, Cleveland, and Chicago.[29]

The conflict with the BIA spilled over into 1971, when John Crow,
who served as Louis Bruce's deputy commissioner, effectively assumed control over bureau affairs. Recognizing Bruce as an ally
and lauding him for signing their protest petition a year earlier,
the NIYC and AIM issued a declaration of support calling for the
reinstatement of the commissioner's full powers. Staffers for the
two organizations made their way to Washington, D.C., where they
marched into the BIA building and attempted to force their way
up the stairs into Crow's office. Security officials blocked the protesters and threw AIM member Ted Means (Sioux) off a stairwell.
A fistfight ensued, leading to the arrest of eighteen men and eight
women activists. Once the dust settled, Bruce met with the protesters, ordered hot meals for them, and engaged in a "mutually supportive" discussion that resulted in a temporary truce.[30]

Such goodwill came to a brisk end in the fall of 1972, when activists from the NIYC, AIM, and other organizations marched cross-
country from California to Washington, D.C., on what they termed
the Trail of Broken Treaties. When the caravan reached the national
capital in late October, just days before the 1972 presidential election,
they issued a twenty-point proposal that called for the restoration of

treaty rights and the treaty-making process. The demonstrators also insisted a new "Office of Federal Indian Relations and Community Relations" replace the outdated and ineffective BIA. Finally, they demanded the protection of Native religions and the preservation of Indian culture. Fish-in organizer Hank Adams penned the proposal in hopes of drawing some sort of agreement with the Nixon administration before the upcoming election.[31]

Matters descended into chaos when the activists marched down to the BIA building and attempted to negotiate with bureau officials. With the memory of the 1971 confrontation still undoubtedly fresh in their minds, security officials demanded the protesters leave the premises at once. The rebuttal, coupled with the inability of the caravan leaders to find adequate lodging, led to the forced occupation of the building. Holed up for a week, the occupiers erected a teepee on the front lawn and unfurled a banner that read "Native American Embassy." When word spread that the bureau would not meet their demands and that the police planned on expunging the caravan from the building, the protesters took out their anger and frustration on the building itself—violently destroying furniture, artwork, office machinery, and file cabinets full of records.[32]

The sacking of the BIA building more or less ended the active alliance between the NIYC and AIM, as Hank Adams and the council's leadership condemned the action as wanton destruction. NIYC board member James Nez remembered that his organization's official support of AIM quickly dried up, noting, "By that time we had many grants and we couldn't support uprisings." Some AIM leaders, however, seemed oblivious or simply couldn't accept the broken alliance. "The AIM folks would come down to our office and shake us down. We'd arrange a speaking engagement for them and then they'd try to pass the bucket and extort funds out of our organization," Nez maintained.[33]

AIM went on to garner even greater media attention in 1973 when members of the organization occupied the hamlet of Wounded Knee in South Dakota to demand the removal of Dick Wilson, the notoriously corrupt chairman of the Oglala Sioux Tribe. Banks, Bellecourt, Russell Means, and other AIM leaders called for federal intervention to force Wilson out. Even though disgruntled residents of the

reservation had summoned AIM because Wilson had misappropri-
ated tribal funds and used a portion of the monies to hire "goon
squads" to enforce his will and silence his critics (charges that
proved accurate), NIYC leaders refused to actively join the cause
and instead only offered a few words of support.[34]

Despite the split with AIM, the NIYC continued to employ direct action to redress the grievances of Native people. Beginning in
1974, the council joined with the Coalition for Navajo Liberation to
take on large multinational corporations that sought to build several coal gasification plants in the Navajo Nation, which activists
feared would pose a health hazard to the local Diné people. The
council found itself at odds with the governments of the United
States and the Navajo Nation, both of which favored the proposed
venture. The NIYC lobbied relentlessly against the plants, while
seventy-five activists forced their way into the Navajo Tribal Council's governance chambers, where they proceeded to hold a sit-in
for nearly seven hours to protest the gasification plants. In 1977 the
U.S. Congress ultimately rejected the multibillion-dollar endeavor,
thus ending the campaign.[35]

The NIYC's efforts to stop coal gasification in Navajoland
proved to be one of the organization's last major demonstration
efforts. During the 1970s, America's social and political landscape
changed considerably, leading to the decline of the protest era.
For Native people, a slew of legislation that affirmed the tenets of
self-determination and tribal sovereignty brought a much brighter
future. The Blue Lake Restoration Act of 1970, the Alaska Native
Claims Settlement Act of 1971, the Indian Education Act of 1972,
the Indian Financing Act of 1974, the Indian Self-Determination
and Education Assistance Act of 1975, the Indian Health Care Improvement Act of 1976, and the Indian Child Welfare Act of 1978
stood as testament to the efforts of Native activists and their allies in Congress. Equally significant was the rejuvenation of Native culture. Sociologist Joane Nagel's research has shown that the
number of people who identified as American Indian tripled between 1960 and 1990.[36]

This changing political landscape called for a new approach
when confronting issues facing Native people. Beginning in the

In the mid-1970s, Gerald Wilkinson *(right)* and the NIYC challenged Navajo tribal chairman Peter McDonald *(left)* and the Navajo Tribal Council over the construction of several coal gasification plants in the Navajo Nation. (Peter McDonald and Gerald Wilkinson, photograph, National Indian Youth Council Pictorial Collection [PICT 000-703-0030], Center for Southwest Research, University Libraries, University of New Mexico)

mid-1970s, the NIYC branched out into the legal realm. Wilkinson devoted much of his energy to securing new sources of funding, which eventually enabled the organization to hire two full-time attorneys and take their fight from the streets to state and federal courts. This would prove a crucial step toward maintaining the organization's viability into the 1980s. One of the council's greatest concerns was what it saw as the federal government's protracted assault on traditional indigenous religions. The passage of the American Indian Religious Freedom Act of 1978 failed to preserve sacred sites, leaving many Native cosmologies under threat of extinction. Indeed, in the ten years after its passage, the federal courts ruled consistently against Indian plaintiffs seeking governmental protection of sacred lands.[37]

In the case *Sequoyah v. TVA*, NIYC attorneys filed amicus briefs on behalf of Ammoneta Sequoyah, a seventy-eight-year-old Cherokee medicine man and descendant of the founder of the Cherokee syllabary. Sequoyah maintained that the Tennessee Valley Authority's plan to construct a dam on the Little Tennessee River would flood the Cherokee people's place of origin. The NIYC argued that the federal agency would irreparably harm their plaintiff's religion and violate his first amendment rights. Federal district judge Robert L. Taylor, however, viewed the matter differently, ruling that the TVA's plans would in no way violate free exercise of Sequoyah's religious beliefs.[38]

Despite the setback, the NIYC forged ahead in its legal efforts to defend sacred lands and Native religions. Another case, *Wilson v. Block* brought suit against the Department of Agriculture for its plans to expand the ski basin in the San Francisco Peaks in northern Arizona. The NIYC claimed that such expansion would hinder the ability of both the Hopis and the Diné to practice their religion freely. For both tribes the mountains were sacred and remained at the very core of their cosmology. However, the district judge who handed down the verdict asserted that the expansion of the ski area would not infringe upon the free exercise of the plaintiffs' religions. Moreover, any governmental protection of the peaks on behalf of the Navajos and the Hopis would stand as state support of a religion and hence would violate the establishment clause of the Constitution's First Amendment.[39]

Often working closely with the Native American Rights Fund, the NIYC continued to fight for sacred lands and religious rights well into the 1980s, and although such cases accounted for a large portion of the organization's legal activities, the council did file many other suits during the period. In cases such as *Weahkee v. Powell*, the NIYC sought to highlight continued discrimination against Native people working within the federal government. Other cases, such as the class action suit against the Sunbell Corporation, which in the 1970s was the nation's largest manufacturer of assembly-line Indian jewelry, advocated for the rights of Native artists and artisans.[40] Although the council lost many of the cases, the NIYC as an organization viewed legal action as central to its overall strategy:

These actions are important not only for what they have or will win for our people. They are also important because they are events around which people can be organized for any number of things. Even if we lose a suit, the thing which has happened to the local Indian community, such as giving it backbone or prod[ding] the creation of an organization, or increasing awareness of issues may be more important than what was sought in the suit. . . . None of our legal actions are frivolous.[41]

Branching out into the legal realm not only helped the Indian community but also strengthened the NIYC as a viable organization, giving the council a higher profile in its bid to become a "first class legal office." The visionary Wilkinson did not stop there. Around the same time, the NIYC began its foray into job training and placement for Native people in New Mexico. The passage of the Comprehensive Employment and Training Act of 1973 (CETA) created a new workforce program under the direction of the Department of Labor that allowed local organizations to use funds for job training and placement. In 1974, Wilkinson applied for money and, to his astonishment, received a grant of $359,358—the largest single grant in the council's history. At once the executive director expanded the organization's staff, hiring new secretaries, an accountant, field counselors, and a CETA project director. He informed the NIYC board and membership that this new endeavor would further strengthen the council as a "forceful organization." He went on to explain that not only would the program deal with mounting unemployment among Native people who had relocated to the cities, but also its underlying philosophy was "to empower the Indian community."[42]

The new program proved successful beyond anyone's imagination. Within two years, the NIYC opened job training and placement field offices in Gallup, Farmington, and Santa Fe. By 1977 the organization had served more than 4,000 Native people who had relocated to urban areas in New Mexico, placing 1,500 of them in permanent jobs. Besides job training and placement, the council used CETA funds to initiate an ex-offender program, which was designed to help incarcerated Native people transition to life outside of prison. The NIYC therefore organized work release programs, pre-parole planning, and counseling services. The council even sponsored an Indian culture club at the New Mexico state penitentiary. "The CETA grant stabilized the organization. It gave the organization structure," James Nez recalled. Indeed, by the 1980s, NIYC's workforce services had become the organization's foremost program. In 1982 alone the NIYC/CETA budget stood at a whopping $1,036,625.[43]

The development and expansion of the job training and placement program dovetailed with the council's focus on urban Indians. In the past the NIYC had had no central office, with officers conducting council affairs in disparate parts of Indian country. Wilkinson's approach of giving autonomy to individual chapters while maintaining a central office in Albuquerque ultimately transformed the organization into an urban one. To be sure, the NIYC continued to fight for Indians on reservations and continued to uphold the founding principles of treaty rights, tribal sovereignty, cultural preservation, and self-determination for Native people. But helping Native people adjust to urban life became Wilkinson's and the council leadership's foremost concern.

The NIYC would continue to fight for Native people throughout the 1980s. Although the conservative ascendancy in national politics stunted political protest and left-leaning politics, a handful of dedicated activists carried on the movements initiated in the 1960s. Gerald Wilkinson remained one of those dedicated activists. The executive director continued to work for next to nothing, and he devoted the rest of his life to advocating for Native people. The political climate of the 1980s may have been unreceptive to political activism, but for Wilkinson that didn't matter. For the Cherokee, the welfare of all American Indians was what mattered.

On April 27, 1989, tragedy again struck the NIYC. While meeting with Comanche activist LaDonna Harris in the Americans for Indian Opportunity office in Washington, D.C., Gerald Wilkinson suffered a heart attack and collapsed. Legend has it that as the long-standing NIYC leader slipped away, he had a smile on his face. Wilkinson died doing what he did best—working for Native people.[44]

Wilkinson's passing was a great loss for the NIYC, as the long-time executive director had stabilized the council, grown its membership, and broadened its operations. Under Wilkinson's direction, the NIYC changed with the times, transforming into a dynamic, multifaceted organization unlike any other Native rights group in operation. The council expanded into the legal realm and filed massive lawsuits on behalf of Native litigants; it developed a job training and placement facility to help Native people who had relocated to Albuquerque and other urban centers in New Mexico; it lobbied both federal and state lawmakers for legislation beneficial to all American Indians; and it even continued to hold protests and demonstrations. Perhaps the NIYC itself best summed up its legacy when it noted in a report: "In history and principle, the National Indian Youth Council is a process, not an event."[45]

Epilogue

In winter, after a good snowstorm, the Sandia Mountains just east of Albuquerque radiate a brilliance, signaling a new morning to the million people below. Such was the case on the morning of January 24, 2009, when the National Indian Youth Council's board of directors met at the Homewood Suites in central Albuquerque. Much had changed and yet much had remained the same since the NIYC's founding years. The leaders were older and grayer than they once were, but their tenacity and sheer determination in the fight for Indian people remained as strong as ever.

During the meeting, executive director Norman Ration (Diné-Laguna), president James Nez (Diné), vice president Cecelia Belone (Diné), secretary Jenny Rodgers (Diné), and board members Viola Hatch (Arapaho), Shirley Hill Witt (Mohawk), Norbert Hill (Oneida), and Kay McGowan (Choctaw-Cherokee) expressed optimism that President Barack Obama would initiate much needed changes in federal Indian policy. Obama's initial plan called for the government to honor tribal sovereignty and its trust responsibilities, recognizing that a government-to-government relationship exists between Indian nations and the United States. The new president offered better health services and education, including full support for the revival of Indian languages and increased funding for tribal colleges. Upon taking office, he sought to protect sacred places and Native religious freedom, while also backing indigenous hunting and fishing rights. In short, Obama's plan reflected the very principles the NIYC had fought so hard for over the last five decades.[1]

Still, the optimism of the officers and board of the NIYC remained tempered with a degree of caution. During the meeting, Ration introduced a concept paper that called for a new self-determination act that would "provide services to *all* American Indians." The organization's main concern related to off-reservation Indian communities, especially those in cities such as Albuquerque. The paper proposed a new act that would stimulate job creation, provide more effective and efficient services, and replace the Bureau of Indian Affairs with a better service-providing agency for Native people living off-reservation. In no uncertain terms the paper stated, "President Obama's initiative needs more creative thinking. . . . We're not talking about money and programs but about reviving an economy. . . . We need a new Self-Determination Act and one that is adequately funded."[2]

In August 2009, Ration, Witt, Belone, and other NIYC representatives took their case to the United Nations conference on the rights of indigenous peoples at the Palais des Nations in Geneva, Switzerland. The only American intertribal organization in attendance, the council presented a concept paper on the international Declaration on the Rights of Indigenous Peoples. The NIYC pointed out that according to article 3 of the declaration, Native people have the right to "freely determine their political status and freely pursue their economic social and cultural development." However, U.S. policies—both past and present—have explicitly violated this right, the NIYC asserted. Believing that the United States must implement and respect the tenets of the declaration, council representatives demanded immediate justice "to enjoy our full humanity; to enrich our individual sovereignty; to enjoy our Mother Earth; and to live our lives to our full potentials as indigenous individuals."[3]

As one of the oldest intertribal organizations still in existence, the NIYC conducts most operations from its main office at 318 Elm Street in central Albuquerque. In the 1990s, when Norman Ration assumed the executive directorship of the organization, the NIYC remained a multifaceted organization that defied categorization.

Today the council leaders maintain the organization's legal interests, filing lawsuits and amicus briefs, while also engaging in the occasional protest. They lobby local, state, federal, and international lawmakers for legislation beneficial to indigenous peoples but continue to help find jobs and decent housing for Indians who have relocated to Albuquerque, Farmington, and Gallup. The organization has come a long way from its modest origins. During its first year of existence, the NIYC had struggled to stay afloat; it proved unable to secure a steady source of income or establish an expansive membership base. Fifty years later, the council remains a stable, viable, and dynamic organization that has never deviated from the cornerstone principles that had guided the council's founders. Tribal sovereignty, treaty rights, self-determination, and cultural preservation have remained the ideological foundation of the NIYC.

Many of the council's first leaders continued to work for Native people in varying capacities. Joan Noble was active in Volunteers in Service to America and spent two years in Tonga as a Mormon missionary before becoming a full-time elementary schoolteacher in Vernal, Utah, just outside the Uintah and Ouray Ute reservation in the northeastern part of the state. Bruce Wilkie served as executive director of the Makah Tribal Council and in 1970 was elected director of the National Congress of American Indians. Charlie Cambridge moved to Boulder, earned his Ph.D. in anthropology at the University of Colorado, and went on to work for the Office of Federal Acknowledgement. Robert Dumont continued to push for educational reform in Berkeley, serving as director of the Coalition of American Indian Citizens' Educational Research and Demonstration Project. He was also instrumental in the development of the Native American Educational Service College in Chicago before his death in 1997. Viola Hatch remained in her native Oklahoma and worked in varying capacities for the Arapaho and Cheyenne people. She also continues to serve on the NIYC's board of directors. Sam English eventually resigned his post as NIYC secretary and became a successful artist in Albuquerque. And Browning Pipestem took a high-profile job with Arnold and Porter law firm in Washington, D.C., before moving back to his native Oklahoma,

The main office of the NIYC at 318 Elm Street SE, Albuquerque, New Mexico. (Photograph by author)

where he became a born-again Christian and minister. In 1999 he died after a long battle with diabetes.[4]

Karen Rickard graduated from the State University of New York at Buffalo and went on to study at the Pratt Institute in New York City. She taught art in Niagara Falls, New York, before heading out to Los Angeles, where she was recruited to work with incoming Native American students at the University of California, Los Angeles (UCLA). Eventually she moved back east, to L'Anse, Michigan, and taught high school for twenty-five years before retiring in 2004. Karen Rickard Jacobson takes pride in her students' accomplishments and notes that several of them have won state honors in Michigan for their art. As is true for other NIYC founders, the friendships she forged in 1961 have lasted up to the present day.[5]

Shortly after the death of her husband, Clyde, Della Warrior and her two daughters moved from Oklahoma to Massachusetts. There she enrolled in the Graduate School of Education at Harvard University and in 1971 earned her master of arts degree. Warrior then landed a job with Albuquerque Public Schools but returned home to her native Oklahoma in the 1980s, where she served first as a council member and later as chairperson for the Otoe-Missouria Tribe. The Institute of American Indian Arts eventually lured Warrior back to New Mexico, naming her president of the prestigious school. Today Warrior works as chief operations officer for the Yocha Dehe Wintun Nation of southern California.[6]

Just as Della Warrior headed to Harvard, Gerald Brown enrolled in law school at UCLA and, after graduating in 1971, served as a legal adviser for his Flathead tribe. Two years later, Brown took a job at Navajo Community College in Tsaile, Arizona, where he worked as coordinator of special programs for over four years. The University of Washington eventually hired him as director of its Indian student division. From 1986 to 1999 Brown went on to work in desegregation centers in Washington, Oregon, and Colorado. Although he retired in 2004 and returned to his home on the Flathead Reservation in Montana, Brown proudly notes that his children work as attorneys, fighting for Native rights—just as their father did a generation ago.[7]

Hank Adams continued to lead the fish-in campaign in Washington State into the 1970s. On January 19, 1971, the Assiniboine activist was shot in the stomach while sleeping in his car near the Puyallup River. Tacoma police refused to investigate the case, claiming that barium and antimony found on his hands proved that he shot himself. Adams offered to take a polygraph test to challenge any discrepancies and clear his name, but Tacoma police chief Lyle E. Smith refused the proposition and closed the case. Adams eventually recovered from his wound and continued to gillnet alongside Native fishers. Adams's persistent efforts for Native fishing rights paid off when the U.S. Department of Justice finally filed suit against Washington State in federal court. In 1974, Adams and the Northwest Indians achieved the breakthrough for which they had fought so hard, when the U.S. district court ruled on the Department of Justice's suit. In *United States v. Washington*, Judge George Boldt declared that treaty Indians had the right to catch 50 percent of Washington's harvestable fish. Five years later, the U.S. Supreme Court upheld Boldt's decision and closed the case to further review. Today Adams remains involved in Native issues and lives in Olympia, Washington.[8]

Shirley Hill Witt earned her Ph.D. in biological anthropology at the University of New Mexico and taught at the University of North Carolina at Chapel Hill and Colorado College throughout the 1970s. Later she served as director for the Rocky Mountain regional office of the United States Commission on Civil Rights and as a foreign service officer for the Department of State's Information Agency. Witt has since returned to central New Mexico and lobbies regularly for indigenous peoples at the United Nations. She also serves as a board member on the council that she helped found.[9]

Herb Blatchford worked as director of the Gallup community center until 1972, when Frankie Garcia, mayor of the city and part owner of a bar that catered to Indians, fired the Navajo leader, allegedly for his active efforts to curb alcoholism among Native relocatees. Three years later, Blatchford rejoined the NIYC in Albuquerque and became heavily involved in the council's efforts to block coal gasification on the Navajo Reservation. Blatchford's attempts to remold the council he had once directed into an environmentally focused organization met resistance from executive director Gerald Wilkinson. Blatchford therefore split from the NIYC and attempted unsuccessfully to form a separate environmentalist outfit. On December 1, 1996, Herbert Blatchford died when a fire consumed his home outside of Gallup.[10]

After Mel Thom gathered his papers and belongings from the NIYC office at the Hotel Claremont in Berkeley following the council's reorganization in 1968, he moved back to his birthplace on the Walker River Paiute Reservation in western Nevada. There he served as tribal chair until 1974, when he established his own construction company. Although Thom continued to attend the annual meetings of the National Congress of American Indians, even serving as a floor leader during elections, the former president and executive director of the NIYC distanced himself from involvement in Indian education or political activism. Thom's deteriorating health undoubtedly sapped much of his energy. Suffering from arthritis aggravated by injuries sustained in a car accident years

earlier, he took his life on December 17, 1984. Vine Deloria, Jr., recalled seeing the leader a month before he died, noting, "He was
huddled over and hair was grey and face was badly distorted. . . . I
thought it was all over then but I guess he had to take action as he
was in such bad shape."[11]

At the time of his death, Mel Thom, along with Herb Blatchford,
Shirley Hill Witt, Hank Adams, Karen Rickard, Robert Dumont,
Bruce Wilkie, Joan Noble, Clyde Warrior, and others who figured so
prominently in the early NIYC, had been largely forgotten by activists and scholars alike. Until recently, those recalling early American Indian activism cited the takeover of Alcatraz in 1969 as the
beginning of the Red Power movement. They recounted the great
campaigns of AIM with their energies fixated on the organization's
male leaders and urban roots. But Red Power began much earlier.
It all started with the efforts of those young Native people who
boldly stepped forward to establish the first independent Native
student organization, the National Indian Youth Council.

The students followed a long legacy of intertribalism and pan-
Indian organization that stretched back to the early twentieth century. Although their agenda differed radically from that of early
reformers who founded the Society of American Indians, those
who initiated the NIYC worked equally as hard and believed in
their mission just as strongly as their forebears. Each organization
did what it thought necessary for the benefit of all Native people.
Ideologically, the NIYC had much more in common with the National Congress of American Indians, which has embraced a platform of tribal sovereignty and treaty rights since its founding in
1944. But unlike the NCAI, which saw litigation and lobbying as
the only respectable channels to make change, the NIYC was willing to use confrontation and protest anywhere and everywhere—
from the rivers of Washington State to the streets of Washington,
D.C. Ironically, some of those NCAI leaders who disdained direct
action were the very ones responsible for politicizing future leaders
like Karen Rickard, Clyde and Della Warrior, and Mel Thom at the
Workshop on American Indian Affairs.

The NIYC leaders also followed their forebears' example in
that the students who launched the Red Power movement were

both men *and* women. Unlike other student organizations of the late 1960s and 1970s, the NIYC lacked the stifling sexism that distorted power sharing and decision making. Following on the heels of the Regional Indian Youth Council and the workshops, where at least half of the participants were women, the founding of the NIYC could not have happened without the efforts of Witt, Rickard, Noble, Bernadine Eschief, and Mary Natani. These women, and their successors, created and held positions of leadership; they devised and amended their council's platform; they organized and participated in fish-ins and other demonstrations; and they edited and contributed to the first Red Power publication, *Americans Before Columbus.*

Moreover, like the founders of the NCAI, the women and men who started this movement came predominantly from reservations and rural tribal communities. Scholars have told us repeatedly that Red Power began in the cities when Native people who had relocated to places like San Francisco and Minneapolis found camaraderie at intertribal clubs and centers. Certainly this holds true for the Indians of All Tribes and the American Indian Movement, but the founders of the first Red Power organization, the NIYC, overwhelmingly had rural or reservation roots. When the backgrounds of Noble, Rickard, Eschief, Natani, Warrior, Thom, Blatchford, and most of the other charter members of NIYC are examined, the myth that Native activism began in the cities becomes glaringly apparent.

Despite these similarities with their forebears, the Red Power warriors of the 1960s were of a different generation. Like those young people who founded the Students for a Democratic Society and the Student Nonviolent Coordinating Committee, they were products of America's Cold War political landscape. And like those other students of the sixties generation, they believed the society around them was sick. It remained their job, even their duty, to fight that sickness. During its formative years, the NIYC cautiously approached the problems affecting Native America. But beginning in 1964 with the fish-in movement, they took bolder steps. Through heated rhetoric, direct action, and educational reform, they confronted head-on the simmering issues that plagued all Indian communities. Over the succeeding years, they marched in step with other student activists of the day, as their voices grew louder and angrier. But unlike the Student Nonviolent Coordinating Committee and the Students for a Democratic Society, which became casualties of political discord and undisciplined militancy, the NIYC transformed, adapted, and survived. Thanks largely to the efforts of Gerald Wilkinson to secure the organization's legacy, the council continues today as a viable organization that works for the betterment of all Native people.

That legacy began with the students who met in Gallup that fateful summer of 1961. Adhering to a philosophy of tribal sovereignty, treaty rights, self-determination, and cultural preservation, which they inherited from their elders, they believed unwaveringly in their mission to create a "greater Indian America." Those committed young people took a step into the unknown when they founded the National Indian Youth Council. Courageous and determined, they branded a new approach to the festering problems that Native peoples faced. And in launching the Red Power movement, they would forever change the face of intertribal politics.

NOTES

INTRODUCTION

1. During my career as a historian, I have heard many positions on how best to define and/or differentiate intertribalism and pan-Indianism. I can recall delivering a paper some years ago where the commentator insisted that I remove the term "pan-Indianism" and replace it with "intertribalism," claiming that the former was disrespectful and antiquated. In another instance, when I was a graduate student at the University of New Mexico, a colleague had devised a set of incredibly complex parameters on how to distinguish between intertribalism and pan-Indianism. What I remember most about that discussion was walking away totally confused and bewildered. To avoid such confusion, I take a simple position: "intertribalism" and "pan-Indianism" are synonyms. I therefore will use them interchangeably throughout this book.

2. Shirley Hill Witt to author, e-mail correspondence, 16 February 2009; Karen Rickard Jacobson to author, e-mail correspondence, 21 February 2009. Viola Hatch, who joined the NIYC in 1969, corroborates Witt and Rickard's position, insisting, "There was never any sexism. That was never true." Della Warrior agreed: "No, we weren't concerned about that. Women had powerful voices in the NIYC." Viola Hatch, interview by author; Della Warrior, interview by author.

3. Maurice Isserman and Michael Kazin, "The Failure and Success of the New Radicalism," in Fraser and Gerstle, *Rise and Fall of the New Deal Order*, 218; Shirley Hill Witt to author, e-mail correspondence, 4 December 2008. For more on how the Cold War fostered a sense of high moralism among Native political activists, see Rosier, "'They Are Ancestral Homelands,'" 1303.

4. Isserman, *If I Had a Hammer*, xviii; T. H. Anderson, *Movement and the Sixties*, 65; Greenberg, *"A Circle of Trust"*; Gerald Brown, interview by author; Sam English, interview by author.

5. See Josephy, *Red Power*, 145–53, 197–201; T. R. Johnson, Nagel, and Champagne, *American Indian Activism*, 9; Josephy, Nagel, and Johnson, *Red Power*, 101–18, 185–91, 260–65.

6. The origins of the slogan "Red Power" date to 1966. NIYC leader Clyde Warrior stated that he and other NIYC founders mimicked SNCC. Although "Red Power" had communist connotations, Warrior and his cohorts did not care. As Warrior remarked, "We thought it was kind of cute." "National Indian Youth Council, Inc., 1961–1975," n.d., box 1, folder 16, National Indian Youth Council Records (hereafter NIYCR); Charles T. Powers, "Uses of Red Power," March 1968, *Kansas City Star*, newspaper clipping in box 2, folder 28, NIYCR.

7. As noted above, the sheer volume of literature dealing exclusively with the takeover of Alcatraz is nothing short of astonishing. Some authors, such as Adam Fortunate Eagle and Troy R. Johnson, have written multiple works dealing with the subject. While each author has his or her own particular slant on the story, they all agree that the occupation remains the single most important event in postwar Indian activism that essentially gave birth to the Red Power movement. I would, however, concur with Brad Lookingbill, who asserted that this thesis of the importance of Alcatraz "overstates the results" and fails to pay due respect to the origins of Indian activism. Lookingbill, review of *The Occupation of Alcatraz Island*, 408. Historical accounts of Alcatraz include Costo, "Alcatraz"; Talbot, "Free Alcatraz"; DeLuca, "'We Hold the Rock!'"; Sklansky, "Rock Reservation and Prison"; T. R. Johnson, *You Are on Indian Land!*; and T. R. Johnson, *Occupation of Alcatraz Island*. For firsthand accounts of the occupation, see Blue Cloud, *Alcatraz Is Not an Island*; Fortunate Eagle, *Alcatraz! Alcatraz!*; and Fortunate Eagle with Findley, *Heart of the Rock*. In 1994 the *American Indian Culture and Research Journal* published a special edition devoted to Alcatraz, running some twelve articles by historians and participants. Most of these pieces were collected and reprinted in a single volume: T. R. Johnson, Nagel, and Champagne, *American Indian Activism*. Finally, Troy Johnson has collected poems and political statements regarding Alcatraz in *Alcatraz: Indian Land Forever*. See also Steiner, *New Indians*.

8. Cobb, *Native Activism*, 81.

9. Hazel Hertzberg's 1971 book, *The Search for an American Indian Identity*, remains the most exhaustive study of the Society of American Indians. Other scholars, however, have recently written on the organization and its origins, including D. Anthony Tyeeme Clark, who has traced the society's beginnings back to the late nineteenth century and has shown how the organization's founders helped establish a sense of intertribal identity. Others have written biographies on individual SAI leaders. Both Peter Iverson and Leon Sperloff have chronicled the life and legacy of Carlos Montezuma, Raymond Wilson and David Martinez wrote on Charles Eastman, and Doreen Rappaport's *Flight of Red Bird* (1997) traces the career of Gertrude Bonnin. See Hertzberg, *Search*; Clark, "Representing Indians"; D. Anthony Tyeeme Clark, "At the Headwaters of a Twentieth-Century 'Indian' Political Agenda: Rethinking the Origins of the Society of American Indians," in

Cobb and Fowler, *Beyond Red Power*; Iverson, *Carlos Montezuma*; Sperloff, *Carlos Montezuma, M.D.*; Wilson, *Ohiyesa*; Martinez, *Dakota Philosopher*; and Rappaport, *Flight of Red Bird*.

10. There are several works on John Collier and the Indian New Deal. Kenneth Philp's 1977 book remains the standard, while Lawrence Kelly's *Assault on Assimilation* offers a thorough examination of Collier's background and ideological development. Collier's autobiography provides a penetrating firsthand account of the Indian Reorganization Act from the man himself. See Philp, *John Collier's Crusade*; Kelly, *Assault on Assimilation*; and Collier, *From Every Zenith*. See also G. D. Taylor, *New Deal*. The literature on the American Indian Federation remains scant. There are a few articles and theses on the AIF and its leaders, but a full monographic treatment is lacking. See Hauptman, "American Indian Federation"; Hauptman, "Alice Jemison"; and Gracey, "Attacking the Indian New Deal."

11. Tom Holm, "Fighting a White Man's War: The Extent and Legacy of American Indian Participation in World War II," in Evans, *American Indians in American History*, 102–103. For more on Native people and World War II, see Bernstein, *American Indians and World War II*. Both historians and social scientists have thoroughly outlined the policy of termination. Probably the best historical account is Donald Fixico's *Termination and Relocation*. See also Philp, "Termination"; and Wilkinson and Boggs, "Evolution of the Termination Policy." Broader overviews on federal Indian policy in the twentieth century include T. W. Taylor, *Bureau of Indian Affairs*; Prucha, *Great Father* (1984); Deloria and Lytle, *Nations Within*; Burt, *Tribalism in Crisis*; Prucha, "American Indian Policy"; Lyden and Legters, *Native Americans and Public Policy*; Meyer, *American Indians and U.S. Politics*; Wilkins, *American Indian Politics*; and Deloria, *American Indian Policy*.

12. As with the American Indian Federation, the published literature on the National Congress of American Indians is surprisingly thin. Thomas Cowger's *National Congress of American Indians: The Founding Years*, stands as the only full monographic account of the oldest intertribal organization.

13. The published literature on the Regional Indian Youth Council is virtually nonexistent. Sociologist Robert C. Day touched upon the RIYC in a 1972 essay, while Sterling Fluharty delved more deeply into the councils in his 2003 master's thesis. See Robert C. Day, "The Emergence of Activism as a Social Movement," in Bahr, Chadwick, and Day, *Native Americans Today*; and Fluharty, "'For a Greater Indian America.'"

14. Until recently, the history of the Workshop on American Indian Affairs remained largely untold. Daniel Cobb first uncovered the significance of the workshops in his 2003 dissertation, "Community, Poverty, Power." Cobb's subsequent book, *Native Activism in Cold War America*, more thoroughly engages the workshops and their significance in preparing Native students for future leadership roles (pp. 23–27, 68–76).

15. The American Indian Chicago Conference has garnered greater attention from historians and social scientists than earlier gatherings have. Robert C. Day

set the tone for the importance of the conference in his essay "The Emergence of Activism as a Social Movement" (1972), when he called the meeting "probably the most important single event in the emergence of tribal nationalism as a social movement" (p. 512). Since then, nearly every book on Native politics or activism since World War II has addressed the Chicago Conference. Important studies that center exclusively on the Chicago Conference include R. P. Brown, "'Year One'"; and Shreve, "'We Must Become One People.'"

16. Farber, *Chicago '68*, 212; "National Indian Youth Council Highlights for 1963–64," 2; Mel Thom, "For a Greater Indian America," *Americans Before Columbus* 2, no. 1 (March 1964), 2; "Notes on the Fish-ins," n.d., ser. 1, box 28, folder 5, Stan Steiner Papers (hereafter Steiner Papers). As with the Chicago Conference, there is no shortage of accounts on the fishing crisis in the Pacific Northwest, but only a handful focus on the fish-in campaign. See Josephy, *Now That the Buffalo's Gone*, 177–211; Wilkinson, *Blood Struggle*, 160–73, 198–205; Sherry L. Smith, "Indians, the Counterculture, and the New Left," in Cobb and Fowler, *Beyond Red Power*, 142–60; and Shreve, "'From Time Immemorial.'"

17. Steiner, *New Indians*, 34.

18. For more on how Native activists used the Office of Economic Opportunity to their benefit, see Cobb, *Native Activism*, passim.

CHAPTER 1

1. "NIYC Annual Meeting," *Americans Before Columbus* 2, no. 4 (December 1964), in box 4, Shirley Hill Witt Papers (hereafter Witt Papers); Certificate of Incorporation, 26 September 1962, box 1, folder 1, NIYCR.

2. Timothy J. Shannon's *Iroquois Diplomacy on the Early American Frontier* (2008) shows how Iroquois peoples between the Great Lakes and the Atlantic Ocean united to form the Six Nations Confederacy in an effort to eliminate destructive intertribal warfare. After the European invasion, the confederacy used its might to open diplomatic relations with the newcomers. See Shannon, *Iroquois Diplomacy*, 26; and Fenton, *Great Law*. Many books have been written on the Algonquian intertribal alliances and Pontiac's Revolt. In *Pontiac's War*, Richard Middleton illustrates the great leader's "remarkable" ability to find common ground among diverse tribes throughout the Ohio country (p. 322). Even Howard Peckham, whose *Pontiac and the Indian Uprising* (1947) paints the Ottawa chief's efforts as a failed cause, acknowledges that Pontiac stood as a "warrior of heroic proportions who set in motion the most formidable Indian resistance" (p. 199). See also Dixon, *Never Come to Peace Again*. For more on the Shawnee-led war against the newly established United States, see Calloway, *Shawnees*.

3. In 1999, David Weber compiled five previously published essays and articles by various authors into the volume *What Caused the Pueblo Revolt?* The book gives various interpretations of the revolt and illuminates the many controversies and mysteries surrounding the revolt's origins and organization. Despite all of the disagreement, the contributing authors concur that the pueblos of the Rio Grande put

aside their differences to unite and confront a common non-Indian enemy. See also Folsom, *Red Power on the Rio Grande*. For more on nineteenth-century intertribal alliances on the Great Plains, see Calloway, "Intertribal Balance of Powers." In a 1996 essay, Colin Calloway complicates the narrative on intertribalism among Plains Indians by showing that the Crows, Arikaras, Pawnees, and Shoshones had their own agenda that led them to unite with the United States cavalry during the Great Sioux War. Calloway, "Army Allies or Tribal Survival? The 'Other Indians' in the 1876 Campaign," in Rankin, *Legacy*, 63–81.

4. Tecumseh and his political vision have been the subjects of many books. Bil Gilbert's *God Gave Us This Country* highlights the Shawnee chief's intellectual evolution and his uncanny ability to bring together people from diverse backgrounds (pp. 208–14, 336–37). See also Sugden, *Tecumseh*.

5. D. Anthony Tyeeme Clark maintains that the Indian Memorial Association preceded the Society of American Indians and gave rise to many of the latter organization's founders. Clark also shows how the Brotherhood of North American Indians—another intertribal association—worked contemporaneously alongside the SAI. Clark, "At the Headwaters of a Twentieth-Century 'Indian' Political Agenda."

6. Hertzberg, *Search*, 37, 60, 67, 117, 156.

7. Ibid., 32–35, 107; Clark, "At the Headwaters of a Twentieth-Century 'Indian' Political Agenda," 74; Carlos Montezuma, "Reservations," n.d., reel 5, frame 936, Supplement to the Papers of Carlos Montezuma, MD. For more on Carlisle and on Indian boarding schools in general, see Adams, *Education for Extinction*; and Johnston, *Indian School Days*.

8. Montezuma, reel 5, frames 1545–46, 1552, 1555, 1561, Supplement to the Papers of Carlos Montezuma, MD; Iverson, *Carlos Montezuma*, 95; Sperloff, *Carlos Montezuma, M.D.*, 360.

9. "Wassaja," which translated into "signaling" or "reckoning," was Montezuma's given Apache name. Iverson, *Carlos Montezuma*, 106, 108–109; Sperloff, *Carlos Montezuma, M.D.*, 382, 392.

10. Iverson, *Carlos Montezuma*, 37; Sperloff, *Carlos Montezuma, M.D.*, 206, 240; Hertzberg, *Search*, 139; Holm, *Great Confusion in Indian Affairs*, 79. For more on Bonnin's life and legacy, see Welch, "Zitkala-Sa"; and Hafen, "Zitkala-Ša." For more on the Native American Church and peyote, see Slotkin, *Peyote Religion*.

11. Crum, "Almost Invisible," 44–47.

12. Hertzberg, *Search*, 202; Sperloff, *Carlos Montezuma, M.D.*, 244; Gertrude Bonnin to John Collier, 3 March 1932, reel 1, frame 319, John Collier Papers, 1922–68 (hereafter Collier Papers).

13. Prucha, *Great Father* (1986), 277–79. The importance of the Meriam Report in influencing federal Indian policy cannot be overstated. See Prucha, *Great Father* (1984), 2:806–13, 836–39.

14. Connell Szasz, *Education and the American Indian*, 23–24.

15. Ekirch, *Ideologies and Utopias*, 77–85; Schlesinger, *Age of Roosevelt*, 556–57; McJimsey, *Presidency of Franklin Delano Roosevelt*, 19–23, 89–94.

16. Collier, *From Every Zenith*, 115, 123–24, 126; Philp, *John Collier's Crusade*, 23, 45–46, 58, 61.

17. Gertrude Bonnin to John Collier, 3 March 1932, reel 1, frame 320; and Collier to Bonnin, 4 March 1932, reel 1, frame 322, both in Collier Papers.

18. Philp, *John Collier's Crusade*, 120, 123–25, 131.

19. The stock reductions live on in the memories of Navajo people. Next to the Long Walk, the episode stands as the most painful and traumatic event in modern Navajo history. Ruth Roessel and Broderick H. Johnson's compilation *Navajo Livestock Reduction* relates dozens of Diné testimonies on the episode. See also Weisiger, *Dreaming of Sheep in Navajo Country*.

20. Prucha, *Great Father* (1986), 322. Collier held ten regional congresses in Rapid City, South Dakota; Hayward, Wisconsin; Chemawa, Oregon; Fort Defiance and Phoenix, Arizona; Santo Domingo, New Mexico; Riverside, California; and Anadarko, Muskogee, and Miami, Oklahoma. Prucha, *Great Father* (1984), 2:959.

21. Tribal leader quoted in Hauptman, *Iroquois and the New Deal*, 59.

22. Gracey, "Attacking the Indian New Deal," 7. Although a preponderance of the AIF's initial membership was from Oklahoma, other areas of Indian country were also well represented. Many members claimed affiliation with the Mission Indian Federation of California, New York's Intertribal Committee for the Fundamental Advancement of the American Indian, and the Black Hills Treaty Council of South Dakota. Hauptman, "American Indian Federation," 380.

23. Floyd LaRoche, notes on O. K. Chandler, n.d., reel 1, frame 374; O. K. Chandler to S. J. Montgomery, 18 March 1926, reel 4, frame 239; O. K. Chandler to John Collier, 11 July 1929, reel 4, frame 238; O. K. Chandler to John Collier, 1 June 1933, reel 4, frame 316; and "Report on O. K. Chandler and the AIF," n.d., reel 1, frame 374, all in Native Americans and the New Deal: The Office Files of John Collier (hereafter Collier Office Files).

24. John Collier to Joseph Bruner, 18 September 1933, reel 1, frame 588, Collier Office Files; A. R. Perryman to John Collier, 22 August 1938, reel 1, frame 734, Collier Office Files; "Report on O. K. Chandler and the AIF," n.d., reel 1, frames 372–74, Collier Office Files; Hauptman, "American Indian Federation," 382; Joseph Bruner to Harold Ickes, 16 October 1936, reel 1, frame 627, Collier Office Files.

25. House Committee on Indian Affairs, *Wheeler-Howard Act*, 165; Hauptman, "Alice Jemison," 15, 17, 21; Alice Jemison, "Freedom for the Indian," *Washington Evening Star*, 24 April 1933, reel 6, frame 381, Collier Office Files.

26. "A Memorial by American Indians," 21 December 1934, reel 1, frame 543, Collier Office Files.

27. Joseph Bruner, "The Indian Demands Justice," *National Republic* 22 (March 1935), 23–24, 31.

28. Statement by Joseph Bruner, n.d., reel 1, frame 465; Joseph Bruner to John Collier, 6 September 1935, reel 1, frames 456–58; and AIF statement to "the American citizenship," n.d., reel 1, frame 468, all in Collier Office Files.

29. "Resolution of 1936," 25 July 1936, reel 1, frame 592, Collier Office Files.

30. House Committee on Indian Affairs, *Wheeler-Howard Act*, 68–69, 73–74, 110, 166. Though Towner was a member of the AIF, others, such as Alice Lee Jemison, would later argue that he was an outsider and "troublemaker" who did not represent the federation. In hearings before the House Committee on Indian Affairs, Jemison further maintained that Towner unsuccessfully tried to usurp control of the AIF by redrafting the organization's constitution at the 1936 annual conference in Salt Lake City. Ibid., 166.

31. Chandler, *Now Who's Un-American?* 3–4, 17, 20, 22, 25.

32. Gracey, "Attacking the Indian New Deal," 38–40.

33. "A Proposed Bill by the American Indian Federation," n.d., reel 1, frame 777, Collier Office Files; "H.R. 6741," n.d., reel 2, frame 400, Collier Office Files; Hauptman, "American Indian Federation," 398–400.

34. Committee on Indian Affairs, *Wheeler-Howard Act*, 157–61, 66–86.

35. For more on the formation and evolution of the Indian Claims Commission, see Rosenthal, *Their Day in Court*.

36. For more on civic nationalism in post–World War II America, see Gerstle, *American Crucible*; Collier, *From Every Zenith*, 315–16, 362; John Collier, "The Inter-American Institute of the Indian and the Present Obligation and Opportunity of the United States," n.d., reel 57, frame 348, Collier Papers; Parker, *Singing an Indian Song*, 93, 106; and Cowger, *National Congress of American Indians*, 25–26, 31.

37. Cowger, *National Congress of American Indians*, 37–38; Constitution and By-laws of the National Council of American Indians, 27 May 1944, ser. 1, box 1, Records of the National Congress of American Indians (hereafter RNCAI).

38. D'Arcy McNickle, quoted in Cowger, *National Congress of American Indians*, 35; "Tribal Councils and Indian Leaders," 16 October 1944, box 1, RNCAI.

39. Cowger, *National Congress of American Indians*, 39; "Proceedings of the National Congress of American Indians," 1944, box 1, RNCAI.

40. Cowger, *National Congress of American Indians*, 40–42; "Proceedings of the National Congress of American Indians," 1944. Conference participants also resolved to elect the secretary and treasurer, rather appoint them; to create eight council seats rather than seven; and to have one vice president rather than two.

41. "Proceedings of the National Congress of American Indians," 1944.

42. Rickard with Graymont, *Fighting Tuscarora*, xxvi.

43. Cowger, *National Congress of American Indians*, 48, 56.

44. Ibid., 114–16; Beito, "Happy Birthday, Oswald Garrison Villard." See also Rosier, "'They Are Ancestral Homelands,'" 1305, 1308–1309.

45. *American Indian Development: A Project Sponsored by the National Congress of American Indians; First Annual Report*, 1952, reel 54, frame 758, Collier Papers. The Ford, Carnegie, Rockefeller, Whitney, and Marshall Field foundations were the primary contributors to AID. American Indian Development, Inc., *Second Annual Report*, 5, 27–28. Dorothy Parker summarized the formation and growth of AID during the 1950s and 1960s. See Parker, *Singing an Indian Song*; and Parker, "Choosing an Indian Identity."

46. Daniel M. Cobb, "Talking the Language of the Larger World: Politics in Cold War (Native) America," in Cobb and Fowler, *Beyond Red Power*, 162–63; Cobb, *Native Activism*, 23–24.

CHAPTER 2

1. "Report on Meeting with Indian Youth at Brigham Young University and Fort Yates," 1958, box 2 (9684), folder 41, Southwestern Association on Indian Affairs Records (hereafter SWAIAR).

2. Ibid.

3. In his book *Decolonization and Its Impact*, Martin Shipway investigates how World War II set the stage for the postwar wave of decolonization. The global nature of the conflict—one that was fought in both Europe and its colonies—and the Allied powers' efforts to define the war as one between democracy and fascism sowed the seeds for independence movements throughout the world. Once the decolonization process began, it snowballed. Newly independent nations collaborated within the United Nations and other international bodies to press colonial powers like Great Britain, France, and Belgium to withdraw from their imperial possessions and grant self-determination to colonized peoples. While Shipway's analysis deals primarily with European powers and their possessions in Asia and Africa, his explanation applies to other movements for self-determination and equality unfolding within nations such as the United States. Certainly, we must factor the Cold War into this equation. As Mary Dudziak shows, the ideological struggle between the West and the Soviet Union would force the United States to extend civil rights to African Americans. This logic can likewise be applied to Native peoples and their struggle for self-determination, sovereignty, and treaty rights, as Paul Rosier has recently argued. Although Native people never received the attention that their African-American counterparts garnered, the Soviets exploited the "Indian problem" and used the United States' failed policies in its propaganda campaign for global influence. Shipway, *Decolonization and Its Impact*; Dudziak, *Cold War Civil Rights*; Rosier, "'They Are Ancestral Homelands,'" 1301–1302.

4. There are numerous books on France's struggle to retain a hold on Indochina. Ellen Hammer's classic narrative, *The Struggle for Indochina* (1966), traces the conflict from the outbreak of World War II in the Pacific to the United States' co-optation of the conflict. Nicola Cooper's more recent study, *France in Indochina* (2001), offers a much more concise, yet penetrating, look at the dynamics of the struggle. For a brief history on the background of the Algerian struggle for independence, see Matthews, *War in Algeria*.

5. For an overview of India's long struggle for independence, see Patrick French, *Liberty or Death: India's Journey to Independence and Division* (1997). Robert Edgerton's *Mau Mau: An African Crucible* (1989) reassesses the Kenyan fight for independence by showing that Mau Mau brutality grew out of Britain's long-standing political and economic exploitation of Kenya. David Anderson's *Histories*

of the Hanged (2005) illustrates graphically the atrocities committed by both the British and the Mau Mau.

6. In his renowned book, *The Origins of the Civil Rights Movement* (1984), Aldon D. Morris shows that African Americans had employed bus boycotts in Baton Rouge, Louisiana, two years before the Montgomery Bus Boycott of 1955. However, Morris and most leading scholars of the early civil rights movement recognize that the Montgomery boycott served as the "watershed of the modern civil rights movement" due to its mass scale, the publicity it garnered, and its overwhelming success (p. 51).

7. Rosier, "'They Are Ancestral Homelands,'" 1302; Hauptman, *Iroquois and the New Deal*, 6; Steiner, *New Indians*, 281–82: Kersey, "Havana Connection," 496–97.

8. Cowger, *National Congress of American Indians*, passim.

9. Philp, *John Collier's Crusade*, 45–46; "Suggested Programme for Indian Education," n.d., box 2, folder 37, SWAIAR; "Executive and Publicity Committee Meeting," 21 June 1923, box 2, folder 37, SWAIAR; "Minutes of Board Meeting," 9 July 1958, box 2, folder 41, SWAIAR.

10. Kiva Club Memoir Book, "Kiva Club—1978" folder, Kiva Club Unprocessed Materials; notes on Herb Blatchford, ser. 1, box 23, folder 10, Steiner Papers; *New Mexico Association on Indian Affairs Newsletter* (*NMAIA Newsletter*), April 1954 and April 1955, both in box 29, folder 19, NIYCR.

11. Ann Pipkin, "Charter Member Recalls First Sequoyah Club," *Oklahoma Daily (Univ. of Okla.)*, 21 November 1964, 5; Sequoyah Club Constitution, 1936, box 5, folder 15, American Indian Institute Collection (hereafter AIIC).

12. Constitution of Ittanaha, 19 April 1947, box 5, folder 15, AIIC. See also Fluharty, "'For a Greater Indian America,'" 14.

13. "Indian Clubs Report," *Americans Before Columbus* 11, no. 1 (March 1964): 3, box 4, Witt Papers; "Program for the Third Annual Regional Indian Youth Council," April 1959, box 9688, folder 153, SWAIAR; "Report of the Executive Secretary," November 1959, box 9684, folder 42, SWAIAR. For more on World War II, the GI Bill, and Native college enrollment, see Bernstein, *American Indians and World War II*, 142–48.

14. *NMAIA Newsletter*, July 1954, box 29, folder 19, NIYCR. See also Steiner, *New Indians*, 32, 34.

15. "The Growth of the Youth Councils," *NMAIA Newsletter*, July 1958, box 29, folder 19, NIYCR; Minton, "Place of the Indian Youth Council," 29.

16. "Report for the Year 1958," n.d., box 9689, folder 168, SWAIAR; "Report on Meeting with Indian Youth at Brigham Young University and Fort Yates."

17. Minton, "Place of the Indian Youth Council," 32; "A Proposed Set of By-laws for the Southwestern Regional Indian Youth Council," n.d., box 5, folder 27, AIIC; "Report on Meeting with Indian Youth at Brigham Young University and Fort Yates."

18. "Third Annual Indian Youth Council," *NMAIA Newsletter*, February 1957, box 29, folder 19, NIYCR; "Minutes of June 12 Meeting," 12 June 1957, box 2, folder 40, SWAIAR; "Growth of the Youth Councils."

19. "Growth of the Youth Councils"; Steiner, *New Indians*, 32; "NMAIA Annual Report for 1956," n.d., box 9689, folder 168, SWAIAR; Gerald Brown, interview by author.

20. Letter of Herbert Blatchford, n.d., box 1, folder 11, NIYCR; Steiner, *New Indians*, 29; Charles Cambridge, interview by author; Herbert Blatchford, quoted in Dillon Platero, "Third Annual Indian Youth Council."

21. "Second Regional Indian Youth Council," 1958, box 2, folder 41, SWAIAR; "All in the Day's Work," Southwestern Association on Indian Affairs (hereafter SWAIA) Newsletter, January 1959, box 29, folder 19, NIYCR. In 1959 the Southwestern Association on Indian Affairs (formerly the NMAIA) earmarked $5,000 in disbursements for the RIYC and related scholarships, which amounted to more than that disbursed for salaries ($3,300) or office expenses ($3,500). "Budget for 1960," n.d., box 9686, folder 169, SWAIAR.

22. "Growth of the Youth Councils"; SWAIA Newsletter, July–October 1959, box 2, folder 42, SWAIAR; "Report of the Executive Secretary," April 1960, box 9684, folder 43, SWAIAR.

23. The figure for the RIYC mailing list is from 1959. "Report of the Executive Secretary," January 1959, box 2, folder 42; "Minutes of NMAIA Board Meeting," 13 November 1957, box 2, folder 40; and "Job Analysis," addendum to the board meeting minutes of 11 September 1957, box 2, folder 40, all in SWAIAR.

24. "Second Regional Indian Youth Council."

25. Vine Deloria, Jr., to Edward F. LaCroix, 11 December 1995, box 4, folder 4, NIYCR; Alfonso Ortiz to Charles Minton, 21 June 1961, box 9686, folder 118, SWAIAR; Gerald Brown, interview by author.

26. "The Fourth Southwestern Regional Indian Youth Council," SWAIA Newsletter, January 1961, box 55, folder 8, Clark S. Knowlton Collection, 1912–89 (hereafter CSKC); "Report of the Executive Secretary," April 1960; "Report of the Executive Secretary," April 1961, box 9688, folder 154, SWAIAR.

27. "Second Regional Indian Youth Council"; "Southwestern Regional Indian Youth Council," 29 March 1960, box 9684, folder 43, SWAIAR; SWAIA Newsletter, July–October 1959; "Fourth Southwestern Regional Indian Youth Council;" "Report of the Executive Secretary," April 1961; "Report of the Executive Secretary," January 1959.

28. "Report of the Executive Secretary," December 1957, box 2, folder 40, SWAIAR; SWAIA Newsletter, July–October 1959.

29. SWAIA Newsletter, July–October 1959; transcript of the Third Regional Indian Youth Council, n.d., 60–61, box 9688, folder 153, SWAIAR.

30. SWAIA Newsletter, July–October 1959; transcript of the Third Regional Indian Youth Council, 68–69, 73–74.

31. SWAIA Newsletter, July–October 1959; transcript of the Third Regional Indian Youth Council, 15–18.

32. SWAIA Newsletter, July–October 1959; transcript of the Third Regional Indian Youth Council, 23–24, 27–30, 34.

33. *NMAIA Newsletter*, January 1958, box 55, folder 8, CSKC.

34. Ibid.

35. "Report of the Executive Secretary," January 1959; "Report of the Executive Secretary," October [or November?] 1958, box 9684, folder 41, SWAIAR; NMAIA Board meeting agenda, 8 March 1960, box 9686, folder 122, SWAIAR.

36. Minton, "Place of the Indian Youth Council," 30–32; "All in the Day's Work"; "Report on Meeting with Indian Youth at Brigham Young University and Fort Yates"; "Farmington, Durango, and Provo, Utah, *Confidential*," 12–19 October 1958, box 2, folder 41, SWAIAR.

37. "Second Regional Indian Youth Council"; SWAIA Newsletter, July–October 1959; "Report of the Executive Secretary," April 1961; "Report on Meeting with Indian Youth at Brigham Young University and Fort Yates." Americans for the Restitution and Rightings of Old Wrongs (ARROW, Inc.) was the fund-raising branch of the NCAI. See Cowger, *National Congress of American Indians*, 69–71.

38. "Report on Meeting with Indian Youth at Brigham Young University and Fort Yates."

39. Ibid.

40. Mel Thom, "Indian Youth Councils," *Indian Voices*, 1963, box 3, folder 28; Don Ahshapanek to J. H. Belvin, 5 March 1962, box 5, folder 16, AIIC.

41. Charles Minton to Harry Getty, 22 November 1960, box 5, folder 18, AIIC; Minton, "Place of the Indian Youth Council," 30; Fluharty, "'For a Greater Indian America,'" 25–26; Alfonso Ortiz to Dave Timmons, 17 February 1961, box 5, folder 18, AIIC.

42. Biographical statement of Clyde Warrior, n.d., box 5, folder 30, NIYCR; P. C. Smith and Warrior, *Like a Hurricane*, 39, 53; resume of Clyde Warrior, n.d., box 2, folder 41, Murray Wax Papers (hereafter Wax Papers); "Fancy Dance Contest Honors World Champion Ponca Dancer," *Ponca City (Okla.) News*, 1 September 1996, 7-B; Shirley Hill Witt to author, e-mail correspondence, 17 January 2009.

43. Resume of Clyde Warrior; Karen Rickard Jacobson to author, e-mail correspondence, 27 October 2008; Della Warrior, interview by author.

44. Gerald Brown, interview by author.

45. Gerald Brown to Allan Quetone, 12 December 1960, box 5, folder 18, AIIC; Clyde Warrior, quoted in P. C. Smith and Warrior, *Like a Hurricane*, 42. Gerald Brown maintains that subsequent books and articles distorted Warrior's speech and that the Ponca never used the words "the sewage of Europe." According to Brown, Warrior stated, "There are no impurities in my veins." Gerald Brown interview by author.

46. The literature on the Student Nonviolent Coordinating Committee is rich and ever-growing. For the purposes of this study, I have relied primarily on Clayborne Carson's *In Struggle* (1981), which remains the foremost book on the ideological development of SNCC. Other important works on SNCC, the sit-in movement, and the rising tide of Black Power militancy include Zinn, *SNCC*; Lester, *Look Out Whitey!*; Forman, *Making of Black Revolutionaries*; Sellers with Terrell, *River of No Return*; Sellers, "From Black Consciousness to Black Power"; Stoper, *Student*

Nonviolent Coordinating Committee; Dittmer, *Local People*; Payne, *I've Got the Light of Freedom*; Lewis with Michael D'Orso, *Walking with the Wind*; Greenberg, *"A Circle of Trust"*; Murphree, *Selling of Civil Rights*; and Hogan, *Many Minds, One Heart.*

47. Herb Blatchford on the RIYC, n.d., Stan Steiner notebook, ser. 5, box 2, folder 1, Steiner Papers; Deloria to LaCroix, 11 December 1995.

48. "Report of the Executive Secretary," March 1961; and "Report of the Executive Secretary," May 1961, both in box 9688, folder 154, SWAIAR.

49. "Report of the Executive Secretary," June 1961, box 9688, folder 154, SWAIAR.

50. "Report of the Executive Committee to the Board of Directors of the Southwestern Association on Indian Affairs," 28 September 1959, box 2, folder 42; Oliver La Farge to Garfield C. Packard, 20 June 1961, box 9686, folder 128; Oliver La Farge to Charles Minton, 11 November 1957, box 9686, folder 130; "Report for the Year 1958," 31 December 1958, box 9686, folder 121; "Report of the Executive Secretary," October 1961, box 9688, folder 154, all in SWAIAR.

51. Herbert Blatchford to Clyde Warrior, 12 November 1961, box 1, folder 11, NIYCR; Herbert Blatchford to Joan Noble, 9 November 1961, box 1, folder 11, NIYCR; Gerald One Feather to Preston Keevama, 14 March 1962, box 5, folder 16, AIIC.

52. Gerald Brown, interview by author.

53. Viola Hatch, interview by author.

CHAPTER 3

1. D'Arcy McNickle to John Collier, 12 January 1963, reel 57, frame 357, Collier Papers.

2. A. D. Morris, *Origins of the Civil Rights Movement*, 124–25, 188–89, 215.

3. Isserman, *If I Had a Hammer*, 185, 195, 203–204.

4. Cobb, "Community, Poverty, Power," 52; Stucki, "Anthropologists and Indians," 300–301.

5. Stucki, "Anthropologists and Indians," 303–305, 307; Tax, "Values in Action," 168–70; Sol Tax, "The Fox Project," in Clifton, *Applied Anthropology*, 107, 109.

6. Tax, "Positive Program for the Indians," 4–5, 9.

7. Tax, "Importance of Preserving Indian Culture," 83–84, 86.

8. Ibid., 82; Tax, "Positive Program for the Indians," 4.

9. "Report on the Summer Workshop on American Indian Affairs," 16, file drawer 5, "Topical—Education—Summer Workshop—1956" folder, Robert Rietz Papers (hereafter Rietz Papers); Rosalie H. Wax, "A Brief History and Analysis of the Workshops on American Indian Affairs Conducted for American Indian College Students, 1956–1960, Together with a Study of Current Attitudes and Activities of Those Students," 1, box 33, folder 635, Wax Papers.

10. "Report on the Summer Workshop on American Indian Affairs," 16; R. Wax, "Brief History and Analysis of the Workshop on American India Affairs," 1; Cobb, *Native Activism*, 24.

11. "Workshop on American Indian Affairs 1962 Report," n.d., reel 57, frame 349, Collier Papers. McNickle tapped the Emil Schwartzhaupt Foundation for his Crownpoint Project—the same philanthropic foundation that bankrolled Tax's workshops. Parker, *Singing an Indian Song*, 138, 158, 166–67. In 1960, AID earmarked $20,000 for the Workshop on American Indian Affairs and $10,000 and $15,000 for projects in the Pacific Northwest and the Southwest, respectively. Royal B. Hassrick to John Collier, 7 June 1960, reel 57, frame 346, Collier Papers.

12. Cobb, *Native Activism*, 23–24; "Report on the Summer Workshop on American Indian Affairs," 9, 19; D'Arcy McNickle to Sol Tax, 19 February 1957, box 25, folder 214, D'Arcy McNickle Papers (hereafter McNickle Papers).

13. R. Wax, "Brief History and Analysis of the Workshops on American Indian Affairs," 1, 2, 15.

14. Frank Hole and Barbara Hole, "Evaluation of Summer Workshop, 1957," 21, 25, n.d., file drawer 5, "Topical—Education—Summer Workshop—1957" folder, Rietz Papers.

15. Pavlik, introduction to *A Good Cherokee*, xiii–xv; Vine Deloria, Jr., "Bob Thomas as Colleague," in Pavlik, *Good Cherokee*, 27; D'Arcy McNickle Diary, 2 August 1960, box 16, folder 121, McNickle Papers; Gerald Brown, interview by author; Rickard Jacobson to author, e-mail correspondence, 27 October 2008.

16. Wright, "American Indian College Student," 20; Bob Thomas, lecture on nationalism, 8 November 1960, ser. 1, box 28, folder 1, Steiner Papers; Parker, *Singing an Indian Song*, 184; Murray L. Wax, "Old Man Coyote: The Anthropologist as Trickster, Buffoon, Wise Man," in Pavlik, *Good Cherokee*, 21; Deloria, "Bob Thomas as Colleague," 28; Rosalie Wax, "Recommendations for Recruitment of Students," 6, 8, n.d., file drawer 5, "Topical—Education—Summer Workshops; Wax, Murray and Rosalie 1960–January 1961" folder (hereafter Wax folder), Rietz Papers.

17. "Request for Grant to Prepare Special Report on Workshop on American Indian Affairs for American Indian College Students," 1 August 1960, Wax folder, Rietz Papers; Murray Wax and Rosalie Wax, "Great Tradition, Little Tradition, and Formal Education," in M. Wax, Diamond, and Gearing, *Anthropological Perspectives on Education*, 4; D'Arcy McNickle Diary, 27 July–3 August 1960.

18. American Indian Development, Inc., *Education for Leadership: The Indian People See the Future in Their Children*, pamphlet, n.d., ser. 5, box 144, AID Workshop 1961–1966 folder, RNCAI; "Workshop on American Indian Affairs 1962 Report," reel 57, frame 349.

19. R. Wax, "Brief History and Analysis of the Workshops on American Indian Affairs," 1; "Workshop on American Indian Affairs 1962 Report," reel 57, frame 349; Hole and Hole, "Evaluation of Summer Workshop, 1957," 4.

20. "Report on the Summer Workshop on American Indian Affairs," 5–6. Rolland Wright's breakdown reported 88 students from the Southwest, 55 from the Dakotas, 52 from Oklahoma, 41 from the Midwest, 27 from the Great Basin, 23 from Alaska, 16 from the East, 14 from the Northwest, 11 from the Southeast,

7 from California, and 6 from Canada. Wright, "American Indian College Student," 16, 104–105; Modica, *Real Indians*, 70; Charles Cambridge, interview by author.

21. Karen Rickard Jacobson to author, e-mail correspondence, 26 October 2009.

22. Karen Rickard Jacobson to Shirley Hill Witt, e-mail correspondence forwarded to author, 26 October 2009.

23. Charles Cambridge, interview by author; R. Wax, "Recommendations for Recruitment of Students," 2–4; "Report on the Summer Workshop on American Indian Affairs," 3–4; Wright, "American Indian College Student," 128.

24. "Workshop on American Indian Affairs 1962 Report," reel 57, frame 349; Hole and Hole, "Evaluation of Summer Workshop, 1957," 5, 12; "Course Outline for 1961 Workshop," n.d., file drawer 5, "Topical—Education—Summer Workshop—1961" folder (hereafter 1961 folder), Rietz Papers; "Report on the Summer Workshop on American Indian Affairs," 10–11, 13–15; R. Wax, "Brief History and Analysis of the Workshops on American Indian Affairs," 10–12, October 1961.

25. R. Wax, "Brief History and Analysis of the Workshops on American Indian Affairs," 19, October 1961; Rosalie Wax Field Diary, 14, 19, n.d., file drawer 5, "Field Diary—1960 Workshop on American Indian Affairs" folder, Rietz Papers.

26. "Report on the Summer Workshop on American Indian Affairs."

27. See Collier, *Indians of the Americas*. Included in the syllabus for the 1962 workshop were such social scientific readings as *Heredity, Race, and Society*, by L. C. Dunn and Theodore Dobzhansky; "The Folk Society" and *The Primitive World and Its Transformations*, by Robert Redfield; *Where Peoples Meet*, by Everett C. Hughes and Helen M. Hughes; "The Stranger," by Alfred Schuetz; and *The Lonely Crowd*, by David Riesman. More politically oriented works included "Pluralism and the American Indian" (in *América Indígena*), by Robert A. Manners; "Colonialism: U.S. Style," by Felix Cohen; and "Report on the Kinzua Dam." Workshop instructors also assigned their own writings; Robert Thomas had students read his unpublished manuscripts "Cherokee Values and World View" and "The Social Problems of the Eastern Cherokee." Fred Gearing's piece "The Vicious Circle" was also included on the syllabus for 1962. "Workshop on American Indian Affairs 1962 Report," reel 57, frames 354–55. The readings for the first workshop in 1956 were similar in scope and content to those for subsequent workshops. "Report on the Summer Workshop on American Indian Affairs."

28. Fey and McNickle, *Indians and Other Americans*, 6–7, 72, 108, 143, 164, 168.

29. "Workshop on American Indian Affairs 1962 Report," reel 57, frames 354–55. Felix Cohen, "Colonialism: A Realistic Approach" (1945), in F. Cohen, *Legal Conscience*, 369, 378, 381–82.

30. Alfred Schuetz, "The Stranger: An Essay in Social Psychology," in Stein, Vidich, and White, *Identity and Anxiety*; Redfield, "Folk Society."

31. Benedict, *Patterns of Culture*, 206, 253, 256–57.

32. "Report on the Summer Workshop on American Indian Affairs," i; "Suggested List of Guest Speakers," 1962, 1962 folder, Rietz Papers; Hole and Hole, "Evaluation of Summer Workshop, 1957," 9–10; "Workshop on American Indian

Affairs 1962 Report," reel 57, frame 350; R. Wax, "Brief History and Analysis of the Workshops on American Indian Affairs," 18, October 1961; "Guest Speakers Listed," *Indian Progress: Newsletter of the Workshop on American Indian Affairs,* no. 7 (23 July 1962), 6, box 9, D'Arcy McNickle folder, American Indian Chicago Conference Records (hereafter AICCR).

33. Wax Field Diary, 1–2; Wright, "American Indian College Student," 24, 109; P. C. Smith and Warrior, *Like a Hurricane,* 40; Deloria, *Custer Died for Your Sins,* 86. Charles Cambridge, interview by Ned LaCroix, 9 June 1995, box 5, folder 20, NIYCR. There has been some discrepancy regarding the actual name of the students' after-hour parties. According to Shirley Hill Witt, they were known as "Forty-niners" rather than "forty-nines," as some have called them. The term came from a Sioux legend in which fifty warriors went off to battle but only forty-nine returned. The dance is a tribute to the one who was killed. Shirley Hill Witt to author, e-mail correspondence, 5 April 2009 and 17 March 2010. Regardless of the origin of the term, the forty-nine is a traditional Plains dance. Teenagers and young adults typically performed the forty-nine dance late in the evening following a powwow. The Forty-niners at the workshops were much more informal than a powwow, and alcohol consumption was not uncommon. See Feder, "Origin of the Oklahoma Forty-Nine Dance," 290–91.

34. Wax Field Diary, 7; Hole and Hole, "Evaluation of Summer Workshop, 1957," 13–14.

35. Wright, "American Indian College Student," 91, 94–95, 111, 113; "Workshop on American Indian Affairs 1962 Report," reel 57, frame 351.

36. Hole and Hole, "Evaluation of Summer Workshop, 1957," 13–14; "Request for Grant to Prepare Special Report on Workshop on American Indian Affairs for American Indian College Students," 3.

37. R. Wax, "Brief History and Analysis of the Workshops on American Indian Affairs," 15–16, n.d.; Wax Field Diary, 8.

38. "Workshop on American Indian Affairs 1962 Report," reel 57, frame 351; Wright, "American Indian College Student," 163; Rosalie Wax to Robert Rietz, 13 March 1961, 1961 folder, Rietz Papers; Wax Field Diary, 26. The work of sociologist Joane Nagel has further underscored this trend at the national level. She reported that from 1960 to 1990 the number of people claiming Indian ethnicity tripled, which she attributed to the Red Power movement and the new sociopolitical climate that emerged during the period. See Nagel, "American Indian Ethnic Renewal"; and Nagel, *American Indian Ethnic Renewal.*

39. Charles Cambridge, interview by author.

40. American Indian Development, Inc., *Education of Leadership;* "American Indian Development, Inc. Assessment of the Workshop," 7, n.d., file drawer 5, "Topical—Education in Summer Workshops—Student Assessments" folder (hereafter Assessments folder), Rietz Papers; R. Wax, "Recommendations for Recruitment of Students," 7; Wax Field Diary, 17.

41. R. Wax, "Recommendations for Recruitment of Students," 5, 7; "American Indian Development, Inc. Assessment of the Workshop," 1.

42. R. Wax, "Brief History and Analysis of the Workshops on American Indian Affairs," 24, October 1961; R. Wax, "Recommendations for Recruitment of Students," 6, 8; Karen Rickard Jacobson to author, e-mail correspondence, 27 October 2009; Modica, *Real Indians*, 70.

43. Exam of Clyde Warrior, 26 July 1962, file drawer 5, "Topical—Education—Summer Workshop 1962 Student Papers" folder (hereafter Student Papers folder), Rietz Papers; quiz of Clyde Warrior, n.d., Student Papers folder, Rietz Papers; Clyde Warrior, in "Indian Students Respond to 'Pluralism and the American Indian,'" 5, 1962, box 24, folder 212, McNickle Papers.

44. Bruce Wilkie, in "Indian Students Respond to 'Pluralism,'" 5.

45. Quiz of Bruce Wilkie, n.d., Student Papers folder, Rietz Papers; exam of Bruce Wilkie, 26 July 1962, Student Papers folder, Rietz Papers; Bruce Wilkie, in "Indian Students Respond to 'Pluralism,'" 5.

46. Exam of H. Browning Pipestem, 26 July 1962, Student Papers folder, Rietz Papers.

47. Wax Field Diary, 7, 9–10; Rosalie Wax to Robert Rietz, 6 February 1961, 1961 folder, Rietz Papers; *Indian Progress*, no. 5 (30 March 1962), box 3, folder 27, NIYCR; *Indian Progress*, no. 7 (23 July 1962), box 9, D'Arcy McNickle folder, AICCR.

48. Editorial clipping from *Indian Progress*, 1961, Student Assessments folder, Rietz Papers; *Indian Progress*, no. 7 (23 July 1962).

49. *Indian Progress*, no. 7 (23 July 1962).

50. American Indian Development, Inc., *Education for Leadership*.

51. The organizers of the AICC decided to hold the event in Chicago largely because Sol Tax, the chief organizer, taught at the University of Chicago and was able to secure conference space on the university's campus. Also, Chicago had a long tradition of intertribal organization, dating back to the early twentieth century. See LaGrand, *Indian Metropolis*; and Beck, "Developing a Voice."

52. Note on Witt, *Aborigine* 1, no. 1 (March 1962): 2 (El Paso, Tex.: Southwest Micropublishing, 1996).

53. Notes on Herbert Blatchford, n.d., ser. 1, box 23, folder 10, and ser. 3, box 15, folder 14, Steiner Papers; Shirley Witt to Herbert Blatchford, 28 June 1961, box 2, folder 25, Witt Papers; editor's note, *Aborigine* 1, no. 1 (1961) (El Paso, Tex.: Southwest Microfilming, 1996). It is unclear exactly how the youth caucus came into being. According to Blatchford, Vivian One Feather (Sioux) initially came up with the idea. Notes on Herbert Blatchford, n.d., ser. 3, box 15, folder 14, Steiner Papers.

54. Witt to author, e-mail correspondence, 4 December 2008.

55. Witt to Blatchford, 28 June 1961, box 2, folder 25, Witt Papers; Steiner, *New Indians*, 36–37; Gerald Brown, interview by author; R. P. Brown, "'The Year One,'" 65.

56. Witt to Blatchford, 28 June 1961, box 2, folder 25, Witt Papers; Witt to author, e-mail correspondence, 4 December 2008; John A. Anderson of Wisconsin, interview by Robert Paul Brown, Hayward, Wisconsin, 9 April 1993, in Brown, "'The Year One,'" 67; "Students Comment on American Indian Chicago Conference," *Indian Progress* (1961): 2, 3; file 5, Student Assessments folder, Rietz Papers.

57. AICC, "Declaration of Indian Purpose," box 1, folder 9, NIYCR.

58. Shirley Hill Witt to author, e-mail correspondence, 12 December 2008.

59. Gerald Brown, interview by author.

CHAPTER 4

1. Mel Thom, "For a Greater Indian America," *Americans Before Columbus* 1, no. 1 (October 1963): 2–3 (El Paso: Southwest Micropublishing, 1996).

2. Collins, *More*, 41; Farber, *Age of Great Dreams*, 8–9. For a penetrating look at how SNCC formed, as well as the founders' goals and motives, see Carson, *In Struggle*, 19–30.

3. For more on SNCC's voter registration campaign in the Deep South, see Dittmer, *Local People*; and Payne, *I've Got the Light of Freedom*.

4. T. H. Anderson, *Movement and the Sixties*, 62–65; Students for a Democratic Society, "The Port Huron Statement," reprinted in Albert and Albert, *Sixties Papers*, 181, 196.

5. Karen Rickard Jacobson to author, e-mail correspondence, 21 February 2009; Viola Hatch, interview by author; Della Warrior, interview by author.

6. Blatchford letter, n.d.; Steiner, *New Indians*, 29; Vine Deloria, Jr., to Edward LaCroix, 10 February 1997, box 4, folder 4, NIYCR; Witt to author, e-mail correspondence, 16 February 2009.

7. Herbert Blatchford to Melvin Thom, 28 June 1961; and Shirley Witt to Melvin Thom, 21 June 1961, both in box 1, folder 11, NIYCR.

8. Sam English, interview by author; Eugene Daniel Edwards, interview by author; Steiner, *New Indians*, 41; Melvin Thom to the Chicago Youth Caucus, 22 July 1961, box 1, folder 11, NIYCR.

9. Blatchford to Thom, 28 June 1961.

10. Ibid.

11. Ibid.; Herbert Blatchford to Shirley Witt, 28 June 1961, box 2, folder 25, Witt Papers; Shirley Witt to Herbert Blatchford, 2 July 1961, box 1, folder 11, NIYCR.

12. Melvin Thom to Tentative Charter Membership, 9 July 1961, box 1, folder 11, NIYCR.

13. Melvin Thom to the Tentative Charter Membership, 22 July 1961, box 1, folder 11, NIYCR.

14. John R. Winchester to Herbert Blatchford, 18 July 1961; Joan Noble to Herbert Blatchford, 23 July 1961; and Herbert Blatchford to the Chicago Conference Youth Group, 31 July 1961, all in box 1, folder 11, NIYCR. Included on Blatchford's list of those at the Chicago Conference were Clyde Warrior, John Winchester, Hattie T. Walker (Winnebago), Melvin Walker (Mandan), Mel Thom, Shirley Hill Witt, Bernadine Eschief, Ansel Carpenter, Jr., Reggie Sargeant (Klamath), Gerald L. Brown, Irving J. Eagle (Sioux), Robert Dominic (Chippewa), Teofilo Lucero (Chippewa), Patrick Duffy (Chippewa), Gerald DePerry (Chippewa), Norma Hayball (Shoshone-Bannock), Willie Ketcheshawno (Kickapoo), Tillie Walker (Mandan),

Gerald F. Burger (Chippewa), and Blatchford himself. Four others who left Chicago were added: Helen Maynor (Lumbee), Vivian Arviso (Navajo), Edison Real Bird (Crow), and Joan Noble. Of those targeted as charter members, there were sixteen men and eight women. Most were from reservations, rural areas, or small towns; just six of them lived in large cities. "Tentative Charter Membership," n.d., box 1, folder 11, NIYCR.

15. Melvin Thom to the Tentative Charter Membership, 6 August 1961, box 1, folder 11, NIYCR; Blatchford letter, n.d.; "Announcement of Appreciation," 11 September 1962, box 3, folder 27, NIYCR; Witt to author, e-mail correspondence, 17 January 2009; "Agenda: Chicago Conference Youth Council, August 10–11, 1961," n.d., box 1, folder 11, NIYCR.

16. Witt to author, e-mail correspondence, 17 January 2009.

17. "National India Youth Council, Inc., 1961–1975," n.d., box 1, folder 16, NIYCR; Witt to author, e-mail correspondence, 17 January 2009; "Agenda: Chicago Conference Youth Council, August 10–11, 1961." The ten charter members who attended were Shirley Hill Witt, Thomas and Bernadine Eschief (Shoshone-Bannock), Karen Rickard, Mary Natani, Clyde Warrior, Joan Noble, Howard McKinley, Jr. (Diné), Mel Thom, and Herb Blatchford. "Minutes of the National Indian Youth Council Meeting," 1–2, 10–11 August 1961, box 1, folder 11, NIYCR.

18. "Minutes of the National Indian Youth Council Meeting," 2–3, 10–11 August 1961.

19. Ibid., 4–5.

20. Ibid., 7–8.

21. Witt to author, e-mail correspondence, 17 January 2009; "Minutes of the National Indian Youth Council Meeting," 11–12, 10–11 August 1961.

22. "Minutes of the National Indian Youth Council Meeting," 13–14, 17, 10–11 August 1961.

23. Ibid., 20.

24. Ibid., 21–22.

25. Witt to author, e-mail correspondence, 17 January 2009.

26. Ibid.

27. Certificate of Incorporation, 26 September 1962.

28. Herbert Blatchford to Charter Membership, n.d.; and Herbert Blatchford to the Charter Membership, n.d., both in box 1, folder 11, NIYCR.

29. Helen Peterson to Melvin Thom, 12 August 1961, box 1, folder 11; Herbert Blatchford to Charter Membership, n.d.; Herbert Blatchford to E. Thomas Colosimo, 8 December 1961, box 1, folder 11; Herbert Blatchford to Shirley Witt, 17 April 1962, box 3, folder 27; Herbert Blatchford to Shirley Witt, 24 April 1962, box 3, folder 27; and Melvin Thom to Helen D. Maynor, 27 September 1961, box 1, folder 11, all in NIYCR. At its third annual meeting, the NIYC elected to change its newsletter's name from *Aborigine* to *American Aborigine*, believing the original title too "controversial." "Summation of the 1963 National Indian Youth Council," *American Aborigine* 3, no. 1 (1963): 27.

30. Shirley Hill Witt to author, e-mail correspondence, 10 January 2009; Blatchford to Noble, 9 November 1961; Blatchford to Warrior, 12 November 1961.

31. Shirley Witt to Herbert Blatchford, 17 November 1961 and 5 January 1962, box 1, folder 11; Herbert Blatchford to *Niagara Falls Gazette*, 30 January 1962, box 3, folder 27, NIYCR; "Report on the National Northeast Regional Youth Conference," n.d., box 3, folder 27; Herbert Blatchford to Shirley Witt, 12 January 1962, box 3, folder 27; and National Indian Youth Council, Inc., pamphlet, n.d., box 1, folder 16, all in NIYCR.

32. Herbert Blatchford to Shirley Witt, 29 August 1961 and 5 September 1961; Shirley Witt to Herbert Blatchford, 18 August 1961 and 24 August 1961; Melvin Thom to the U.S. Government Copyright Office, 16 August 1961; and Melvin Thom and Herbert Blatchford to the NIYC Charter Membership, 20 September 1961, all in box 1, folder 11, NIYCR.

33. Mel Thom, "Statement of the National Indian Youth Council," *Aborigine* 1, no. 1 (March 1962): 1.

34. "Summary of Minutes of the National Indian Youth Council, 1962"; Herbert Blatchford to Shirley Witt, 18 January 1962, 5 February 1962, and 2 May 1962; and Herbert Blatchford to Mel Thom, 23 March 1962, all in box 3, folder 27, NIYCR. The connection between the workshops and the NIYC remained strong well into the mid-1960s. Some NIYC founders, such as Warrior and Thom, continued to attend the workshops and recruit new members for the NIYC. In the words of Blatchford, the gatherings were "a good place to get a broad overview of Indian affairs in all its complexity." Blatchford to Witt, 5 February 1962.

35. "Summary of Minutes of the National Indian Youth Council," 1962.

36. Shirley Hill Witt to author, e-mail correspondence, 19 January 2009; Shirley Hill Witt to Edward F. LaCroix, 21 January 2000, box 1, folder 15, NIYCR.

37. Herbert Blatchford to members, subscribers, and friends, 28 December 1962, box 3, folder 27, NIYCR; "A Survey Outline of American Indian History," *Aborigine* 2, no. 1, passim; Shirley Hill Witt to members, 10 March 1963, box 3, folder 28, NIYCR; and Shirley Hill Witt to Chris Harrison, facsimile transmittal, 11 January 2000, box 1, folder 15, NIYCR.

38. Shirley Hill Witt to author, e-mail correspondence, 30 January 2009; "Summation of the 1963 National Indian Youth Council," 21, 25–27.

39. Witt to author, e-mail correspondence, 30 January 2009; "Summation of the 1963 National Indian Youth Council," 23.

40. "Summation of the 1963 National Indian Youth Council," 23; Rickard Jacobson to author, e-mail correspondence, 27 October 2008.

41. "Summation of the 1963 National Indian Youth Council," 22–24.

42. "Why *ABC*?" *Americans Before Columbus* 1, no. 1 (October 1963): 1.

43. Gerald Brown, interview by author; Charles Cambridge, interview by author; "After the Convention," *Americans Before Columbus* 1, no. 1 (October 1963): 6; "Law and Order—State of Washington," *Americans Before Columbus* 1, no. 1 (October 1963): 8. According to Vine Deloria, Jr., Walker and Poafpybitty were largely

responsible for the publication and distribution of *ABC*. Deloria noted they were "basically idealists who were content to do the work and let the men get credit for it." Vine Deloria, Jr., to Ned LaCroix, 13 March 1996, box 4, folder 4, NIYCR.

44. "Law and Order—State of Washington," 7; "Indian Fishing Rights," *Americans Before Columbus* 1, no. 2 (December 1963): 3–5.

45. "Washington State Shifts War Strategy," *Americans Before Columbus* 1, no. 2 (December 1963): 5.

46. Ibid.

47. "Notes on Bruce Wilkie and Hank Adams," *Americans Before Columbus* 1, no. 1 (October 1963): 1–2; Deloria to LaCroix, 13 March 1996.

48. "NIYC Board Meets in Denver," *Americans Before Columbus* 2, no. 1 (March 1964): 5; "National Indian Youth Council Highlights for 1963–64," *Americans Before Columbus* 2, no. 3 (27 July 1964): 2; Herbert Blatchford to Members of the National Indian Youth Council, 20 January 1964, file drawer 2, "National Indian Youth Council, 1964–1965" folder, Robert V. Dumont Papers (hereafter Dumont Papers). The NIYC used the Olin Hotel regularly for its midyear meetings, because the hotel was next door to the USS office, where *ABC* was published. Charles Cambridge, interview by author.

49. Olson, "Social Reform," 587; "National Indian Youth Council Highlights for 1963–64," 2; Thom, "For a Greater Indian America," 2.

CHAPTER 5

1. P. C. Smith and Warrior, *Like a Hurricane*, 37. For more on Iroquois activism, see Hauptman, *Iroquois Struggle for Survival*.

2. Hank Adams, "NIYC and Washington State," *Americans Before Columbus* 3, no. 2 (27 July 1964): 7.

3. A. D. Morris, *Origins of the Civil Rights Movement*, 188–93.

4. Ibid., 200, 203.

5. American Friends Service Committee, *Uncommon Controversy*, 14, 16, 19; Josephy, *Now That the Buffalo's Gone*, 180; Cohen with LaFrance and Bowden, *Treaties on Trial*, 24; J. E. Taylor, *Making Salmon*, 19–20, 28–37.

6. Cohen with LaFrance and Bowden, *Treaties on Trial*, 38. In her ethnography of the Puyallups and the Nisquallys, Marian Smith demonstrates that there was no formal political or tribal organization among the Salish-speaking peoples of the Puget Sound region. About the only thing that bound together the peoples of this region was a common geography, a shared language family, and some overarching cultural similarities. M. W. Smith, *Puyallup-Nisqually*, 4, 23. For more on ethnic identity, political organization, and artificial construction of the "tribe" among Salish-speaking peoples, see Harmon, *Indians in the Making*.

7. American Friends Service Committee, *Uncommon Controversy*, 25, 28; Josephy, *Now That the Buffalo's Gone*, 182; R. W. Johnson, "States versus Indian Off-Reservation Fishing," 212–13; "Treaty between the United States and the Nisqually and Other

Bands of Indians," box 80, folder 14, Frederick T. Haley Papers, 1933–2001 (hereafter Haley Papers); Cohen with LaFrance and Bowden, *Treaties on Trial*, xxiv, 38.

8. American Friends Service Committee, *Uncommon Controversy*, 54–55; Associate Solicitor of Indian Affairs to the Commissioner of Indian Affairs, "Status of the Puyallup Reservation in the State of Washington," memorandum, 26 March 1971, box 80, folder 8, Haley Papers.

9. Parman, "Inconsistent Advocacy," 168; Cohen with LaFrance and Bowden, *Treaties on Trial*, 42. The first commercial fish cannery opened in the Puget Sound area in 1877, the same year as the region's first conservation measures. Salmon quickly became a crux of the local and regional economy, and by 1900 the number of canneries had increased to nineteen. Boxberger, *To Fish In Common*, 38.

10. Wilkinson, *Messages from Frank's Landing*, 31; American Friends Service Committee, *Uncommon Controversy*, 58–67. Native fishers also experienced a severe decline in the number of fish harvested. In 1944, for example, the total poundage for the Nisqually salmon catch stood at 54,493. Twenty years later the figure had fallen to 12,123. Robison, Ward, and Nye, *1965 Fisheries Statistical Report*, 75. Although Janet McCloud claimed that the Sportsmen's Council controlled the Washington State Department of Game and Fish, neither the mainstream media nor Washington State legislators seriously investigated her accusations. A quick survey of the Sportsmen's Council papers, however, reveals a close relationship between its membership and the Game and Fish Department. See John A. Biggs, Director of the Department of Game, to Robert Pettie, President of the State Sportsmen Council, July 27, 1964, box 9, "Department of Game Finances, Reports and Resolutions, and Correspondence (1964)" folder, Washington State Sportsmen's Council Papers (hereafter WSSCP); John J. O'Connell, Attorney General, to Lowell Johnson of the Sportsmen Council, August 24, 1964, box 3, Indian Affairs folder, WSSCP; Walter Neubrech of the Game Department to Lowell Johnson, March 16, 1964, box 3, Indian Affairs folder, WSSCP. See also McCloud, "Indian Rights War Continues," 21.

11. "Minutes of the 84th Quarterly Meeting," 1955, 12–13, box 3, ascension 2580, WSSCP. One of the common refrains of the Sportsmen's Council was that Native fishers used modern fishing techniques and equipment, allowing them to harvest a greater number of fish than their ancestors who relied on cruder means. However, Joseph Taylor maintains that modern techniques were not solely responsible for the fishing success of Native people in the Puget Sound region; rather, the Native people were "frighteningly efficient" fishers, using a variety of methods that included the use of nets and dams. Taylor, *Making Salmon*, 20.

12. The other twelve states where PL 280 went into effect were Alaska, California, Florida, Idaho, Minnesota, Montana, Nebraska, Nevada, North Dakota, Oregon, South Dakota, and Wisconsin. Hobbs, "Indian Hunting and Fishing Rights," 506–507, 529; American Friends Service Committee, *Uncommon Controversy*, 51.

13. *State v. Satiacum*, 50 Wash.2d. 513, 314 P.2d 400 (1957); American Friends Service Committee, *Uncommon Controversy*, 90. Besides reading the respective

court verdicts on the numerous cases involving Native fishing rights, I have relied on several important and helpful secondary sources, including Hobbs, "Indian Hunting and Fishing Rights"; Hobbs, "Indian Hunting and Fishing Rights II"; R. W. Johnson, "States versus Indian Off-Reservation Fishing"; Parman, "Inconsistent Advocacy"; and Cohen with LaFrance and Bowden, *Treaties on Trial*.

14. "Two Indians Arrested in Fishing Controversy," *Seattle Times*, April 20, 1962, 16; "Skagits on Warpath? Shots, Violence Reported in Indian-Fishing Dispute," *Seattle Times*, January 8, 1963, 19; "Indian Netting Brings Outcry," *Bellingham (Wash.) Herald*, September 15, 1963, 1.

15. *State v. McCoy*, 63 Wash.2d, 387 P.2d 942 (1963); Hobbs, "Indian Hunting and Fishing Rights," 526.

16. Josephy, *Now That the Buffalo's Gone*, 192; "White Flag Lowered; India Group Ends Truce with State," *Yakama (Wash.) Morning Herald*, 22 January 1964, 1–2; Don Tewkesbury, "Court Orders Indians to Stop Fishing," *Tacoma (Wash.) News Tribune*, 23 January 1964, 1; Mike Conant, "Indians Net New Troubles," *Daily Olympian (Wash.)*, 4 March 1964, 1.

17. "Indians to Air Fishing Rights Here," *Seattle Times*, 12 February 1964, 49; "State Indians Reject Marches, Sit-In Tactics," *Seattle Post-Intelligencer*, 16 February 1964, 10; Bob Monahan, "Tribal Delegates Meet: Indians Urge Federal Study of Their Fishing Practices," *Seattle Times*, 16 February 1964, 63.

18. Notes on Mel Thom, n.d., ser. 1, box 28, folder 5, Steiner Papers.

19. Thom, "For a Greater Indian America," 2; Herbert Blatchford to Shirley Witt, telegram, 24 February 1964, box 19, folder 4, NIYCR; Larry Bush, "She Seeks Justice for Indians," *Ann Arbor (Mich.) News*, 30 April 1964, 1; Bruce Wilkie to NIYC members, memorandum, 12 March 1964, box 19, folder 4, NIYCR; Steiner, *New Indians*, 50–51.

20. Hank Adams, "Washington Tribes and NIYC," *Americans Before Columbus* 3, no. 2 (27 July 1964), 4; "Notes on the Fish-ins," n.d., ser. 1, box 28, folder 5, Steiner Papers; Mike Conant, "What Kind of a Guy Is This Actor Brando?" *Daily Olympian*, 3 March 1964, 1; Hunter S. Thompson, "The Catch Is Limited in Indians' Fish-in," *National Observer*, 9 March 1964, 13.

21. Thompson, "Catch Is Limited in Indians' Fish-in," 13; "Indians Tell Negroes to Stay Out of Fishing Case," *Seattle Post-Intelligencer*, 1 March 1964, 10. For more on tensions between Native activists and African American leaders, see Sherry L. Smith, "Indians, the Counterculture, and the New Left," in Cobb and Fowler, *Beyond Red Power*, 150–51.

22. "Notes on the Fish-ins"; Steiner, *New Indians*, 50.

23. Shirley Hill Witt to author, e-mail correspondence, 16 December 2008; "Notes on the Fish-ins"; Steiner, *New Indians*, 50.

24. Shirley Hill Witt to author, e-mail correspondence, 6 February 2009; "Marlon Brando, S.F. Cleric Arrested for Fishing Illegally," *Seattle Times*, 2 March 1964, 1; Conant, "What Kind of a Guy Is This Actor Brando?" 1; "Marlon Brando, Episcopal Minister Arrested, Released during Fish-In," *Bellingham Herald*, 2 March 1964, 1.

25. Witt to author, e-mail correspondence, 6 February 2009.

26. Ibid.

27. "Notes on the Fish-ins"; Bruce Wilkie to the NIYC, memorandum, 12 March 1964, box 19, folder 4, NIYCR; Steiner, *New Indians*, 57; "Governor Refuses to Yield to Pressure from Indians," *Daily Olympian*, 3 March 1964, 1; "Tribes Request Attention," *Americans Before Columbus* 1, no. 1 (5 May 1964): 4.

28. "Ponca Protests Treaty Breaking by Washington," *Americans Before Columbus* 1, no. 1 (5 May 1964): 3.

29. NIYC statement, 3 March 1964, box 19, folder 4, NIYCR.

30. Shirley Hill Witt to author, e-mail correspondence, 12 February 2009; Wilkie to NIYC, 12 March 1964; Adams, "Washington Tribes and NIYC," 4; C. J. Walker, "Quillayute Fishing Toot Lures Brando," *Daily Olympian*, 4 March 1964, 12.

31. "Remarks by Governor Albert D. Rosellini to a Gathering of Washington State Indians," 3 March 1964, box 3, Indian Affairs folder, WSSCP.

32. Ibid.

33. Thompson, "Catch Is Limited in Indians' Fish-in," 13; Walker, "Quillayute Fishing Toot Lures Brando," 12; Albert Rosellini to Lowell Johnson, 5 March 1964, box 3, Indian Affairs folder, WSSCP.

34. Lowell Johnson to Albert Rosellini, 10 March 1964, box 3, Indian Affairs folder, WSSCP; "Minutes to the Washington State Sportsmen's Council 120th Quarterly Meeting," 20–21 March 1964, box 2, 1964 Minutes and Resolutions folder, WSSCP; "Treaty between the United States and the Nisqually and Other Bands of Indians."

35. Adams, "NIYC and Washington State," 7; Wilkie to NIYC, 12 March 1964.

36. "Washington State Project Report," n.d., box 3, folder 30, NIYCR; "Judge Boldt Declines to Free Six Indians," *Seattle Times*, 12 March 1964; "Indian Youth Council Backs Court Defiance," *Seattle Times*, 16 March 1964, 3; "Fisheries Picketed by Indians," *Seattle Times*, 20 March 1964, 42.

37. Senate Committee on Interior and Insular Affairs, *Indian Fishing Rights*, 1–3.

38. Lowell Johnson to Senator Warren Magnuson, 12 May 1964, box 3, Indian Affairs folder, WSSCP; "Statement of the Washington State Sportsmen's Council," n.d., box 3, Indian Affairs folder, WSSCP.

39. Bob Hart to Fellow Sportsmen, n.d., box 3, Indian Affairs folder, WSSCP.

40. Bruce Wilkie, "Bills Offered in Congress Would Harm Fishing Rights," *Americans Before Columbus* 1, no. 1 (5 May 1964): 2; Senate Committee on Interior and Insular Affairs, *Indian Fishing Rights*, 24.

41. Senate Committee on Interior and Insular Affairs, *Indian Fishing Rights*, 13, 49, 76, 89, 91, 113.

42. Lowell Johnson to Walter Neubrech, 29 April 1964, box 3, Indian Affairs folder, WSSCP; Senate Committee on Interior and Insular Affairs, *Indian Fishing Rights*, 19, 25, 30, 44.

43. Robison, Ward, and Nye, *1965 Fisheries Statistical Report*, 74; American Friends Service Committee, *Uncommon Controversy*, 127. To be sure, many tribes

had enacted their own conservation regulations, recognizing—as they always had—that a healthy, sustainable salmon population was necessary for their subsistence. The Puyallups, for example, had established rules for the size and number of gillnets a tribal member could use. The Nisquallys, Muckleshoots, and eleven other recognized tribes likewise had regulations, including rules specifying when tribal members could cast their nets. Dennis Austin, *State of Washington Indian Tribal Fishing Regulations, 1960–1971* (State of Washington Department of Fisheries Management and Research Division, 1971), Fish and Ocean Library, University of Washington, Seattle (hereafter FOL), 1–6.

44. Hank Adams, "The Washington State Project," October 15, 1964, file drawer 2, NIYC—General File, 1965–68 folder, Dumont Papers.

45. Ibid., 2–4, 6, 8.

CHAPTER 6

1. Mel Thom to Board of Directors, memorandum, 20 June 1964, file drawer 2, National Indian Youth Council, 1964–65 folder (hereafter 1964–65 folder), Dumont Papers.

2. Herbert Blatchford to NIYC Members, 3 August 1964, 1964–65 folder, Dumont Papers. The first newspaper edition of *ABC* came out in May 1964. *American Aborigine* continued as a newsletter through 1965.

3. Mel Thom, "Indian War 1964," *American Aborigine* 3, no. 1 (1964): 5–7.

4. Shirley Hill Witt, "Right Flank and Left Flank," *American Aborigine* 3, no. 1 (1964): 10–12.

5. Dallek, *Flawed Giant*, 79, 226–27.

6. Payne, *I've Got the Light of Freedom*, 342–43.

7. Cobb, *Native Activism*, 124; "Rough Rock School OKd," *Navajo Times*, 17 August 1967. For more on the Office of Economic Opportunity and Native America, see Clarkin, *Federal Indian Policy*. See also Cobb, "Community, Poverty, Power."

8. "National Indian Youth Council Highlights for 1963–64," 2; Central Office to the members of the NIYC, memorandum, 26 May 1964, 1964–65 folder, Dumont Papers. The Senecas had litigated unsuccessfully in court, and President John Kennedy rejected their petitions to stop construction. Still, the tribe feared risking the $15 million the government had agreed to pay as compensation for lost lands. Further, conservative members of the tribe no doubt believed—as did so many others in Indian country—that protests and demonstrations were distasteful. Abrams, *Seneca People*, 100–101; Shirley Hill Witt, e-mail correspondence with author, 20 August 2009.

9. Eugene Daniel Edwards, interview by author; Blatchford to NIYC Members, 3 August 1964; Central Office to Directors, Members, and Subscribers, 26 May 1964, box 19, folder 4, NIYCR; William F. Weahkee to Clyde Warrior, 23 April 1964, box 19, folder 4, NIYCR.

10. Charles Cambridge, interview by author.

11. "National Indian Youth Council Highlights for 1963–1964," 2; Clyde Warrior, "Time for Indian Action," n.d., box 5, folder 30, NIYCR.

12. Robert Dumont to Hank Adams, 25 June 1964; and "Schedule of the International Indian Youth Conference," both in 1964–65 folder, Dumont Papers.

13. Witt to author, e-mail correspondence, 16 February 2009.

14. Tillie Walker to Robert Dumont, 6 April 1964, "NIYC American Indian Capital Conference on Poverty 1964" folder (hereafter Capital Conference folder), Dumont Papers; "American Indian Capital Conference on Poverty Findings," 9–12 May 1964, 2–7, box 3, folder 16, Witt Papers; Shirley Witt to Robert Dumont, 15 May 1964, Capital Conference folder, Dumont Papers; Clarkin, *Federal Indian Policy*, 113–17. Other notable attendees included Vine Deloria, Sr., and Vine Deloria, Jr., historian Alvin M. Josephy, Jr., folksinger Buffy Sainte-Marie, and future U.S. vice president Hubert Humphrey, who delivered the keynote address the opening night. For more on American Indian involvement in the Capital Conference on Poverty, see Cobb, *Native Activism*, 96–99.

15. "American Indian Capital Conference on Poverty Findings," 9–12 May 1964, 14–15, 17–19, box 3, folder 16, Witt Papers; Robert Dumont to Miss Reid, n.d., 1964–65 folder, Dumont Papers; *USS News* 1, no. 1 (1 September 1967): 3, box 3, folder 31, NIYCR.

16. Shirley Hill Witt to Edward LaCroix, e-mail correspondence, 20 September 2001, box 19, folder 4, NIYCR; speech of Clyde Warrior, 9 May 1964, box 19, folder 4, NIYCR.

17. Witt to Edward LaCroix, e-mail correspondence, 20 September 2001; and Karen Rickard to NIYC member, 14 May 1964, both in box 19, folder 4, NIYCR. Much has been made of the role alcohol played in the Red Power movement. Shirley Hill Witt, however, had this to say about it: "Alcohol and alcohol usage was a personal, individual tragedy, but in no ultimate way was it a tragedy for the National Indian Youth Council. If that were not so, how is it that we remain a vigorous, progressive engine for growth and development in the Indian World today? Individuals fell by the wayside, but NIYC always prevailed." Shirley Hill Witt to author, e-mail correspondence, 24 November 2008.

18. "Summary of the 1964 National Indian Youth Council, August 19–22, 1964," *American Aborigine* 5, no. 1 (1965): 11–13; "NIYC Annual Meeting."

19. "Summary of the 1964 National Indian Youth Council," 14–15; "NIYC Annual Meeting."

20. Ibid.; Robert Dumont to Mel Thom, 20 June 1964, 1964–65 folder, Dumont Papers; Gerald Brown to NIYC Board Members, memorandum, 19 January 1965, National Indian Youth Council 1965 folder (hereafter 1965 folder), Dumont Papers. When the NIYC signed up as a sponsor of the USS, it replaced the Association on Indian American Affairs.

21. Mel Thom to Robert Dumont, 12 February 1965, 964–65 folder, Dumont Papers; Steiner, *New Indians* (1968), 41. In 1965 the NIYC raised $21,651 in contributions earmarked specifically for the USS. The bulk of this came from Kettering.

Mel Thom to Ralph Bohrson, 19 September 1967, box 5, folder 38, NIYCR; Gerald Brown to NIYC Board of Directors, n.d., 1965 folder, Dumont Papers.

22. Clyde Warrior, "Which One Are You?" *Americans Before Columbus* 2, no. 4 (December 1964): 1, 7.

23. Ibid., 7.

24. "News Item," 8 January 1965, 1965 folder, Dumont Papers; Thom to Dumont, 12 February 1965.

25. Mel Thom to the Pentagon, 28 May 1965, box 29, folder 20, NIYCR.

26. Mel Thom to William Byler, 9 July 1965, 1965 folder, Dumont Papers; Mel Thom to Walter Houghton, 13 May 1965, box 29, folder 20, NIYCR.

27. Clyde Warrior, "Speech Presented at the Vermillion Conference, University of South Dakota," June 1965, box 5, folder 30, NIYCR. The United Church of Christ reprinted Warrior's speech in its journal in September 1966; see "Don't Take 'No' for an Answer," ser. 1, box 23, folder 13, Steiner Papers.

28. Gerald Brown to NIYC board members, memorandum, n.d., 1965 folder, Dumont Papers.

29. "NIYC Elects New Officers at Montana Summer Meeting," *Americans Before Columbus* 2, no. 6 (November 1965): 1.

30. Gerald Brown to NIYC Board Members, memorandum, 19 February 1965, 1965 folder, Dumont Papers; Tillie Walker to NIYC Board of Directors, memorandum, 16 February 1965, 1964–65 folder, Dumont Papers; Mel Thom to Robert Dumont, 2 July 1964, 1964–65 folder, Dumont Papers; Herb Blatchford to *ABC* staff, 26 April 1965, 1964–65 folder, Dumont Papers; Herbert Blatchford, quoted by Stan Steiner, ser. 3, box 15, folder 14, Steiner Papers.

31. Blatchford to *ABC* staff, 26 April 1965; Ted Rushton, "Community Center Helps Indians," *Gallup (N.Mex.) Independent*, 6 January 1968, 7; "NIYC Elects New Officers at Montana Summer Meeting," *Americans Before Columbus* 2, no. 6 (November 1965): 1; Witt to author, e-mail correspondence, 16 February 2009.

32. Thom, "For a Greater Indian America," 7.

33. Robert Dumont to Gerald Brown, n.d., NIYC—General File, 1965–68 folder (hereafter 1965–68 folder), Dumont Papers; Robert Dumont, "Education and the Community," *Americans Before Columbus* 2, no. 3 (27 July 1964): 3; Connell Szasz, *Education and the American Indian*, 157, 170–71.

34. "Participants in Upward Bound Indian Conference," 18–19 April 1966, Upward Bound 1966–67 folder (hereafter 1966–67 folder), Dumont Papers; Sarah A. Holden to Clyde Warrior, 13 April 1966, box 3, folder 29, NIYCR.

35. "Minutes to Upward Bound Meeting," 18 April 1966, 1–6, 8; and "Minutes to Upward Bound Meeting," 19 April 1966, 1, 3, both in 1966–67 folder, Dumont Papers.

36. "Minutes to Upward Bound Meeting," 18 April 1966, 4, 6, 1966–67 folder, Dumont Papers.

37. "Report on Upward Bound Project Directors—Indian Meetings," 17 May 1966, 1966–67 folder, Dumont Papers.

38. "Summary of Project," n.d., box 29, folder 12, NIYCR; "Draft Proposal for Indian Leadership Conference," 21–22 July 1966, 4, box 29, folder 12, NIYCR;

"Indian Leadership Planning Session," 21–22 July 1966, 2–3, 5, box 29, folder 12, NIYCR; "Preliminary Planning Grant Proposal to Develop Technical and Management Personnel from within the American Indian Community," n.d., 8–10, box 29, folder 12, NIYCR.

39. "Warrior Replaces Brown as NIYC Chief," *NCAI Sentinel* 11, no. 5 (1966), news clipping in box 3, folder 30, NIYCR; "Indian Youth Council Chooses New Officers," NIYC press release, 1966, box 3, folder 30, NIYCR; "Indian Youth Council Chooses New Officers," *Indian Voices*, October 1966, 7, box 3, folder 38, Witt Papers.

40. "Warrior Replaces Brown as NIYC Chief."

41. Charles Cambridge, interview by author; Mel Thom to Board of Directors, memorandum, 6 October 1966, 1965–68 folder, Dumont Papers; Mel Thom, "A Challenge to American Indians," *Americans Before Columbus* (December 1966): 2. Sam English, who served as office secretary of the NIYC in the late 1960s, recalled that Thom and Warrior "were like brothers." Sam English, interview by author.

42. Statement of Mel Thom before the U.S. Senate Subcommittee on Executive Reorganization, 12 December 1966, box 3, folder 30, NIYCR.

43. Josephy, Nagel, and Johnson, *Red Power*, 17.

44. Ibid., 19.

45. *Washington Post*, 5 February 1967, B7, news clipping in 1965–68 folder, Dumont Papers; statement of Hank Adams before the Senate Interior and Insular Affairs Sub-Committee on Indian Affairs, 15 February 1967, 1965–68 folder, Dumont Papers.

46. "Speech Given by Mel Thom to the Fifth Annual Wisconsin Indian Leadership Conference," 15–17 June 1967, box 3, folder 31, NIYCR; Charles Cambridge, interview by author.

47. Warrior remained so dedicated to Goldwater that he actually hitchhiked to the Los Angeles airport upon hearing on the radio that the presidential candidate would make a surprise stop there. The Ponca told Shirley Hill Witt that he arrived just in time to see Goldwater exit the plane. Warrior, who had donned a straw cowboy hat, a Hawaiian shirt, and cutoffs, told Witt, "Goldwater came through the line, shaking peoples' hands one by one, smiling and saying a few words as he went. He shook the hand of the guy right next to me, took one look at me, and skipped right over me to shake the hand of the next guy!" Shirley Hill Witt to author, e-mail correspondence, 18 February 2009.

48. Vine Deloria, Jr., would borrow Clyde Warrior's words "Custer died for your sins" for the title of his first book, which was published in 1968. Charles Cambridge, interview by author; Viola Hatch, interview by author.

CHAPTER 7

1. Jean Byrd to Clyde Warrior, 8 July 1966, box 3, folder 29, NIYCR; Stan Steiner to Clyde Warrior, 12 September 1966, box 3, folder 31, NIYCR; Steiner notebook; Steiner, *New Indians*, 4, 68, 95.

2. Certificate of Amendment of the National Indian Youth Council, November 1967, box 1, folder 2, NIYCR.

3. James Meredith, the first African American admitted to the University of Mississippi, had initiated his own one-man "March against Fear" on June 5, 1966. While marching through rural Mississippi, Meredith was fired upon, suffering several gunshot wounds. Though Meredith survived the ordeal, the event resulted in a flurry of meetings among civil rights leaders, who swiftly organized "the Meredith March" to protest the episode. See Payne, *I've Got the Light of Freedom*, 376–67; and Stokely Carmichael, "What We Want," *New York Review of Books*, 22 September 1966, reprinted in Chambers, *Chronicles of Black Protest*, 218–23. For more on SNCC and the Black Panthers' education stance, see Carson, *In Struggle*, 109–11, 119–21; and Black Panther Party, "What We Want, What We Believe," in Bloom and Breines, *"Takin' It to the Streets,"* 165. For an overview of the history of the Black Panther Party, see Alkebulan, *Survival Pending Revolution*.

4. Varon, *Bringing the War Home*, 52–53, 107–10, 123–31.

5. Cobb, "Community, Poverty, Power," 233, 236.

6. Murray Wax to the Industrial Areas Foundation, 20 February 1967, box 3, folder 31, Wax Papers; Dumont and Wax, "Cherokee School Society," 217–28.

7. Steiner notebook.

8. Connell Szasz, *Education and the American Indian*, 171–73; "Proposal for School Board Leadership Training and Bilingual Education Program," n.d., ser. 11, box 9, folder 34, Steiner Papers; "Rough Rock School OKd," *Navajo Times*, 17 August 1967, and "Rough Rock Offers Navajo Language Course," *Navajo Times*, 15 February 1966, news clippings in ser. 1, box 25, folder 1, Steiner Papers. For more on the Rough Rock School and its evolution, see House, "Historical Development of Navajo Community College." See also McCarty, *A Place to Be Navajo*.

9. Bob Dumont to Mel Thom, 6 November 1966, file drawer 2, "NIYC—Educational Planning" folder (hereafter Education folder), Dumont Papers.

10. Jack Forbes to Mel Thom, 13 May 1966, series F-2, box 3, Intertribal University Correspondence, 1966–71 folder (hereafter 1966–71 folder); Jack Forbes to Vice President Lyndon Johnson, December 1962, series F-2, box 1, Native American University Correspondence folder (hereafter NAU folder); Jack Forbes to Vice President Lyndon Johnson and the Secretary of the Interior, 1 May 1962, NAU folder; Jack Forbes to Sol Tax, 9 May 1961, NAU folder; W. W. Keeler to Jack Forbes, 29 October 1963, NAU folder; and Assistant Secretary of the Interior to Vice President Lyndon Johnson, 18 May 1962, NAU folder, all in Jack Forbes Collection (hereafter Forbes Collection).

11. "News on the Workshop on American Indian Affairs," *Indian Progress*, no. 12 (25 July 1966): 3, in box 29, folder 13, NIYCR; D'Arcy McNickle to Jack Forbes, 20 June 1966, 1966–71 folder, Forbes Collection; Jack Forbes to Robert K. Thomas, 20 February 1967, series F-2, box 2, Indian Education Correspondence, 1966–68 folder (hereafter 1966–68 folder), Forbes Collection; "Far West Laboratory Report," *Carnegie Quarterly* 17, no. 2, n.d., in box 1, folder 39, NIYCR.

12. "Proposal for Programmatic Support for a Long-Term Research and Development Program to Improve Indian Education," 6 April 1967, box 5, folder 38, NIYCR; "Proposal to the Carnegie Corporation for Funding Continuation of the Indian Education Survey Project," n.d., file drawer 2, Francis McKinley—Indian Education—Carnegie folder, Dumont Papers. Far West and NIYC chose locations throughout Indian country for the demonstration schools, including White Eagle, Oklahoma; the Fort Berthold Reservation in North Dakota; the Crow reservation in Montana; Naknek and Nondalton in Alaska; Pine Ridge Oglala Sioux reservation in South Dakota; the Mescalero Apache Reservation in New Mexico; and the Hopi and Tohono O'odham reservations in Arizona. "First Quarter Report," 1 January–21 April, 1968, box 1, folder 38.

13. Mel Thom to Charles Kettering, 18 April 1967, box 5, folder 38; Charles Kettering to Mel Thom, 24 April 1967, box 5, folder 38; and Mel Thom to Members and Friends of NIYC, 18 January 1968, box 1, folder 38, all in NIYCR.

14. "Bennett Keynotes Conference, Warrior Re-elected Prexy," *Americans Before Columbus* (November 1967): 1; Robert Dumont, "The Quality of Indian Education and the Search for Tradition," 24–26 August 1967, 1–3, box 5, folder 38, NIYCR. Robert Bennett was the first Native commissioner of Indian Affairs since 1871, when Ely Parker (Seneca) served during Ulysses S. Grant's administration.

15. Dumont, "Quality of Indian Education," 3–5, 7–8.

16. Jack Forbes to Emil Koledin, 11 April 1967, 1966–68 folder, Forbes Collection; Thom to Members and Friends of NIYC, 18 January 1968.

17. Robert Dumont to Bob Loescheo, 29 January 1968, box 3, folder 332, NIYCR; Sam English, interview by Ned LaCroix, 27 May 1996, box 5, folder 22, NIYCR. English himself was a product of relocation, his parents having moved to Phoenix, Arizona, from their home among the Chippewas in North Dakota and Minnesota.

18. Gerald Brown, interview by author; Della Warrior, interview by author; Charles Cambridge, interview by author.

19. Bob [Dumont?] to Clyde Warrior, 27 November 1967, box 3, folder 31, NIYCR; "NIYC Educational Planning and the Indian Education Study," 9 April 1968, box 1, folder 38, NIYCR; Steiner notes on Browning Pipestem, n.d., ser. 5, box 2, folder 7, Steiner Papers.

20. Charlie Cambridge, interview by Ned LaCroix, 9 June 1995; Browning Pipestem to Jack Forbes, 18 July 1968, series F-2, box 3, Indian-Chicano Higher Education Correspondence, 1965–72 folder (hereafter 1965–72 folder), Forbes Collection. See also Wright, "American Indian College Student," 28–30.

21. Clyde Warrior to James Wilson, 11 December 1967, box 3, folder 31, NIYCR; NIYC Institute for American Indian Studies, 11 December 1967, box 37, folder 688, Wax Papers; L. Madison Coombs to Sidney M. Carney, 13 February 1968, box 3, folder 32, NIYCR; William Bennett to Clyde Warrior, 29 January 1968, box 3, folder 32, NIYCR.

22. "Proposed General Course Outline" and "American Indian Reader," n.d., file drawer 5, "Topical—Education—Summer Workshop—1969" folder, Rietz Papers;

Charles Cambridge, interview by author; Pipestem to Forbes, 18 July 1968; Institute for American Indian Studies, n.d., file drawer 2, NIYC—Educational Planning folder, Dumont Papers.

23. Wright, "American Indian College Student," 15; "American Indian Development, Inc.: The First Evaluation and Planning Conference," 2–4, 29 July 1968, file drawer 5, "Topical—Education—Summer Workshop—1968" folder, Rietz Papers.

24. Wright, "American Indian College Student," 31–33.

25. Steiner, *New Indians*, 37, 39, 66, 93. Native perspectives on Steiner's account vary, but most give the journalist high marks for accuracy and integrity. Former NIYC board member Charles Cambridge called *The New Indians* "the book to read" about early NIYC history. Shirley Hill Witt agreed with Cambridge, noting, "Stan Steiner was inordinately thorough. . . . You may bank on anything else he wrote there or elsewhere. . . . I saw him work. He was, I repeat, thorough." The *NCAI Sentinel* called Steiner an "eloquent, forceful writer" who brought out the Indian voice "loud and clear." However, the review also stated that Steiner's "tendency toward the dramatic at times causes him to sacrifice clarity for color." Charlie Cambridge, interview by Ned LaCroix, 9 June 1995; Witt to Harrison, facsimile transmittal, 11 January 2000; review of *The New Indians*, *NCAI Sentinel* (Winter–Spring 1969), news clipping in ser. 3, box 15, folder 4, Steiner Papers.

26. Ted Rushton, "Indian Center Director Is Featured in New Book," *Gallup Independent*, 22 March 1968, 8; Wayne Gregory, "'New Indians' Frown on Paternalism, UNM Student Featured in Book Says," *Albuquerque Tribune*, 4 April 1968, D-1. See also Charles T. Powers, "Uses of Red Power," *Kansas City Star*, March 1968, news clipping in box 2, folder 28, NIYCR.

27. P. C. Smith and Warrior, *Like a Hurricane*, 54; Clyde Warrior to Shirley Witt, 15 March 1966, box 3, folder 31, NIYCR.

28. Murray Wax to Clyde Warrior, 24 November 1966, box 2, folder 41, Wax Papers.

29. Murray Wax to Clyde Warrior, 4 September 1966, box 2, folder 41, Wax Papers.

30. Murray Wax to Clyde Warrior, 7 July 1967, box 2, folder 41, Wax Papers.

31. William E. Cadbury, Jr., to Tillie Walker, 27 March 1967; Stuart Levine to Clyde Warrior, 15 May 1967; Wax to Industrial Areas Foundation, 20 February 1967; D'Arcy McNickle to Florence Dickerson, 21 January 1967; and Florence Dickerson to Clyde Warrior, 6 April 1967, all in box 3, folder 31, NIYCR.

32. Powers, "Uses of Red Power."

33. Deloria, "Bob Thomas as Colleague," 30; P. C. Smith and Warrior, *Like a Hurricane*, 57.

34. Shirley Hill Witt to author, e-mail correspondence, 19 February 2009.

35. Mel Thom, "A Tribute to Clyde Warrior," n.d., box 2, folder 41, Wax Papers.

36. Mel Thom to Friends of the Late Clyde Warrior, 30 July 1968, box 2, folder 41, Wax Papers; "Personnel, Policy, and Procedures Manual," n.d., box 5, folder 30, NIYCR.

37. "NIYC–Educational Planning and the Indian Education Study," 9 April 1968, box 1, folder 38, NIYCR.

38. "Second Quarter Report," 2 April–8 July 1968; and "Third Quarter Report," 1 July 30–September 1968, both in box 1, folder 38, NIYCR. According to Shirley Hill Witt, Hank Adams was the "star of the Poor People's Campaign." Indeed, as a member of the campaign's national steering committee, Adams was instrumental in organizing the Coalition of American Indian Citizens' protest march and in drafting the statement presented to Interior Secretary Stewart Udall. Witt to Edward F. LaCroix, e-mail correspondence, 20 September 2001, box 28, folder 6, NIYCR; Olson, "Social Reform," 217. For more on the Poor People's Campaign from the viewpoint of a participant, see Fager, *Uncertain Resurrection*.

39. "American Indian Statement of the Poor People's Campaign," 1 May 1968, box 28, folder 6, NIYCR; Sam English, interview by Ned LaCroix, 2 November 1999, box 5, folder 22, NIYCR; "Second Quarter Report," 2 April–8 July 1968, For a full treatment of American Indian involvement in the Poor People's Campaign, see Cobb, *Native Activism*, 161–92.

40. Sam English, interview by author.

41. Ford Foundation to Mel Thom, 5 October 1967, box 5, folder 38, NIYCR; "Terms of Grant," 5 October 1967, box 5, folder 38, NIYCR; Ralph Bohrson to Mel Thom, 25 July 1968, box 3, folder 32, NIYCR; "What Is National Indian Youth Council?" *Americans Before Columbus* (October 1969): 3; Sam English, interview by author; Jack Forbes to Franklyn Johnson, 21 August 1968, 1966–71 folder, Forbes Collection; Franklyn Johnson to Jack Forbes, 31 October 1968, 1966–71 folder, Forbes Collection.

42. Pipestem to Forbes, 18 July 1968; Charles Cambridge, interview by author.

43. Sam English, interview by author; Shirley Hill Witt to author, e-mail correspondence, 20 February 2009.

44. Witt to author, e-mail correspondence, 20 February 2009; Sam English, interviews by Ned LaCroix, 2 November 1999 and 27 May 1996, both in box 5, folder 22, NIYCR; "NIYC Third Quarter Report," 1 July–30 September 1968, box 1, folder 38, NIYCR; Sam English, interview by author. NIYC officers after the 1968 election included Richard Nichols (president), Bernard Second (first vice president), Bill Pensoneau (second vice president), and Barbara Walkingstick (secretary). The executive board consisted of Gillis Chapela (Navajo), David Redhorse (Navajo), Della Warrior (Otoe-Missouria), Browning Pipestem (Otoe), Thomas Eaglestaff (Sioux), and Diane Porter (Pima). The new board appointed Thomas G. Lentz as executive secretary and Ted Holappa (Ojibwe) as educational coordinator.

CHAPTER 8

1. Sam English, interview by author.

2. Sam English, interview by Ned LaCroix, 27 May 1996; Charlie Cambridge, interview by Ned LaCroix, 9 June 1995; "National Indian Youth Council Proposal

for Emergency Grant," n.d., box 5, folder 39, NIYCR; "NIYC Statement of Policy," *Indian Truth* 45, no. 3 (Winter 1968): 10.

3. NIYC Organization report, 1979, box 2, folder 10, NIYCR.

4. Rossinow, *Politics of Authenticity*, 202. See also Varon, *Bringing the War Home*. Two memoirs that give insiders' perspectives on Weatherman operations are Wilkerson, *Flying Close to the Sun*; and Rudd, *Underground*.

5. Carson, *In Struggle*, 292, 295.

6. "El Plan de Aztlán," in Bloom and Breines, *"Takin' It to the Streets,"* 181; Vigil, *Crusade for Justice*, 97–100, 164–15; Acuña, *Occupied America*, 365, 390.

7. Wei, *Asian American Movement*, 15–20, 132.

8. "Colonialist BIA Exposed," *Warpath* 1, no. 2 (1968): 9; "Bureau of White Affairs," *Warpath* 1, no. 2 (1968): 6.

9. "Petition for American Indian National Center," n.d.; "American Indian Nation's Petition for Tax Exemption," n.d.; and "American Indian Nation to the President's Commission on the Disposition of Alcatraz," n.d., all in ser. 1, box 26, folder 7, Steiner Papers.

10. Jack Forbes to Sol Tax, 10 January 1966, series F-2, box 3, "Correspondence, 1966" folder. For more on the United Native Americans' role in the Alcatraz takeover, see Jack D. Forbes, "The Native Struggle for Liberation: Alcatraz," in T. R. Johnson, Nagel, and Champagne, *American Indian Activism*, 132–33.

11. "Alcatraz Island Reclaimed by Indians," *Americans Before Columbus* 2, no. 1 (December 1969–January 1970): 8; "Indians of All Tribes Proclamation," in Josephy, Nagel, and Johnson, *Red Power*, 40–3.

12. See Fortunate Eagle, *Alcatraz! Alcatraz!*; P. C. Smith and Warrior, *Like a Hurricane*; T. R. Johnson, *Occupation of Alcatraz Island*; T. R. Johnson, Nagel, and Champagne, *American Indian Activism*; Josephy, Nagel, and Johnson, *Red Power*; and Fortunate Eagle with Findley, *Heart of the Rock*.

13. NIYC news release, 4 August 1970, box 2, folder 30; NIYC press release, 24 March 1972, box 2, folder 33; and Gerald Wilkinson to Jim Cantrill, 7 January 1971, box 3, folder 34, all in NIYCR. Although the NIYC publicly claimed 5,000 members in 1970, the organization's own records indicate that the membership base may not have been as extensive. Records show that in 1970 there were fewer than thirty NIYC chapters, with each having between 10 and 30 members. On top of this base were 256 others who were enrolled as "honorary members." "NIYC Membership Lists," 1970, box 1, folder 20, NIYCR.

14. Sam English, interview by Ned LaCroix, 27 May 1996; resume of Gerald Thomas Wilkinson, n.d., box 5, folder 32, NIYCR; Jim Anaya, "In Memory of Gerald Thomas Wilkinson," 3 May 1989, box 5, folder 32, NIYCR; "Gerald Wilkinson, NIYC Leader Passes On," NIYC press release, 15 May 1989, box 5, folder 32, NIYCR; Sam English, interview by author; Vine Deloria, Jr., to Edward LaCroix, 12 January 1996, box 4, folder 4, NIYCR.

15. James Nez, interview by author.

16. Charles Cambridge, interview by author.

17. Gerald Wilkinson to Scott McLemore, 8 September 1969, box 3, folder 33, NIYCR; letter to Board Members, 22 February 1974, box 1, folder 45, NIYCR.

18. NIYC form letter, 11 April 1972, box 1, folder 20, NIYCR; Gerald Wilkinson to Randy Lewis, 7 January 1971, box 3, folder 34, NIYCR.

19. "Summer Programs," *United Scholarship News*, May 1969, box 27, folder 19, NIYCR; NIYC memorandum, n.d., box 27, folder 18, NIYCR.

20. Untitled letter, n.d.; and "Prospectus to the U.S. Bureau of Indian Affairs," n.d., both in box 27, folder 20, NIYCR.

21. Viola Hatch, interview by author; "A Brief Summary of Activities," 12 September 1973, box 1, folder 44, NIYCR.

22. Viola Hatch, interview by author; letter to Board Members, 22 February 1974.

23. "NIYC Sues BIA at Intermountain Indian School," *Americans Before Columbus* 3, no. 1 (January–July 1971): 1; NIYC news release, 6 May 1971, box 2, folder 32, NIYCR; "Brief Summary of Activities."

24. "NIYC Protests BIA Discrimination," *Americans Before Columbus* 1, no. 1 (October 1969): 1; NIYC news release, 8 October 1969, box 28, folder 8, NIYCR; "Charter of AMERIND," n.d., box 28, folder 8, NIYCR.

25. "Struggle at Fort Totten," *Americans Before Columbus* 1, no. 1 (October 1969); "NIYC Sponsors Protest Pow-wow," *Americans Before Columbus* 2, no. 1 (December 1969–January 1970).

26. Gerald Wilkinson to Clyde Bellecourt, 3 December 1969, box 3, folder 33, NIYCR; Clyde Bellecourt to Gerald Wilkinson, 7 January 1970, box 3, folder 34, NIYCR; Sam English interview by author.

27. Steiner, *New Indians*, 189, 223; "Brief History of AIM," n.d., box 3, folder 4, Witt Papers; Akard, "Wocante Tinza," 15–16. The literature on the American Indian Movement rivals that on Alcatraz in its scope. While it would be next to impossible to cite every source on AIM, the following are among the best: P. C. Smith and Warrior, *Like a Hurricane*; Akard, "Wocante Tinza"; and Stern, *Loud Hawk*. Russell Means and Dennis Banks' autobiographies also offer firsthand accounts of AIM's numerous campaigns and misadventures. See Means with Wolf, *Where White Men Fear to Tread*; and Banks with Erdoes, *Ojibwa Warrior*.

28. "Brief History of AIM"; Akard, "Wocante Tinza," 16; "American Indian Task Force Statement Presented to Vice President Spiro Agnew," in Josephy, Nagel, and Johnson, *Red Power*, 94–97.

29. NIYC press release, 26 March 1970, box 2, folder 30, NIYCR; "NIYC Files Complaint in Colorado," *Americans Before Columbus* 2, no. 2 (February–March 1970): 1, 4–5; "Statement of Support of the Littleton 12," n.d., box 2, folder 31, NIYCR.

30. William L. Claiborne, "26 Indians Arrested in D.C. Protest," *Washington Post*, 23 September 1971, B-1, B-11.

31. "Summary of the Twenty Points," in Josephy, Nagel, and Johnson, *Red Power*, 45–47.

32. P. C. Smith and Warrior, *Like a Hurricane*, 153–62. Vine Deloria, Jr., details the occupation of the BIA building and the aftermath in his classic *Behind the Trail of Broken Treaties*, 43–62.

33. "NIYC Statement on Takeover of Bureau of Indian Affairs, Washington, D.C.," press release, 16 November 1972, box 2, folder 33, NIYCR; James Nez, interview by author.

34. Weyler, *Blood of the Land*, 58–96; P. C. Smith and Warrior, *Like a Hurricane*, 194–217. To portray AIM as an organization that solely wreaked havoc through occupation and vandalism would be unfair. Julie Davis's recent dissertation shows that AIM, like the Black Panthers or SNCC, focused much energy on establishing survival schools in an effort to promote Native culture and pride. See Davis, "American Indian Movement Survival Schools."

35. Shreve, "Up Against Giants," 25.

36. Nagel, *American Indian Ethnic Renewal*, 5, 13. More specifically, 523,591 people reported Indian ethnicity in 1960, and 1,878,285 in 1990. After statistically analyzing the data, Nagel noted that such a change could not be due to a natural increase in the population. Nagel, "American Indian Ethnic Renewal," 947.

37. *Sequoyah v. TVA*, 620 F.2d 1159 (U.S. Court of Appeals, 6th Circuit 1980); *Badoni v. Higginson*, 455 F.Supp. 641 (U.S. District Court, Utah D. 1977). See also B. E. Brown, *Religion, Law, and the Land*.

38. Shreve, "Of Gods and Broken Rainbows," 377–78.

39. Ibid., 379.

40. "Annual Report to the Field Foundation," 1977, box 2, folder 4; letter to Board Members, 22 February 1974 and 7 March 1974, box 1, folder 45, all in NIYCR.

41. NIYC to Leslie Dunbar, 29 April 1974, box 1, folder 45, NIYCR.

42. "Annual Report," 1977, box 2, folder 4; letter to Board, 31 July 1974 and 29 September 1974, box 1, folder 45; and "Annual Report," 1975, box 2, folder 1, all in NIYCR.

43. "Annual Report," 1977; "Annual Report to the Field Foundation," 1977; James Nez, interview by author; "NIYC Employment and Training Project Consolidated Expenditure Statement," 1982, box 2, folder 12, NIYCR.

44. Carlos Salazar, "Indians Lose a Dedicated Friend," *Albuquerque Tribune*, 29 April 1989; James Nez, interview with author; NIYC news release, 15 May 1989, box 5, folder 32, NIYCR.

45. "Annual Report," 1975.

EPILOGUE AND CONCLUSION

1. Barack Obama, "Barack Obama's Principles for Stronger Tribal Communities," n.d., manuscript in possession of author.

2. NIYC, "The New Self Determination Act: A Plan to Provide Services to *All* American Indians," n.d., manuscript in possession of author.

3. Norman Ration, Shirley Hill Witt, Cecelia Belone, and James W. Zion, "International Activity Report, National Indian Youth Council: Expert Mechanism on the Rights of Indigenous Peoples, Second Session, 10–14 August 2009, Palais des Nations, Geneva, Switzerland," manuscript in possession of author; Cecelia Belone, "Expert Mechanism on the Rights of Indigenous Peoples, Item 4(a), Program of Work, Implementation of the Declaration at the Regional and National Level, Submission of the National Indian Youth Council," n.d., manuscript in possession of author.

4. Shirley Hill Witt to author, e-mail correspondence, 21 January 2009; Deloria to LaCroix, 13 March 1996; Viola Hatch, interview by author; Sam English interview by author; Charles Cambridge, interview by author; Della Warrior, interview by author.

5. Karen Rickard Jacobson to author, e-mail correspondence, 17 March 2009.

6. Della Warrior, interview by author.

7. Gerald Brown, interview by author.

8. Survival of American Indians Association to "Friend," n.d., box 80, folder 6 Haley Papers; Lyle E. Smith to Hank Adams, 31 March 1971, box 80, folder 8 Haley Papers; *United States v. Washington* 384 F.Supp. 312 (W.D. Wash. 1974); Richard A. Finnigan, "Indian Treaty Analysis and Off-Reservation Fishing Rights: A Case Study," *Washington Law Review* 51 (1975), 87, 89; Prucha, *Great Father* (1986), 389.

9. Shirley Hill Witt to author, e-mail correspondence, 23 February 2009.

10. Edward LaCroix to Vine Deloria, Jr., 5 January 1995 and 13 February 1997, box 4, folder 4, NIYCR; Bill Donovan, "Fire Claims Life of Early Activist," *Navajo Times*, 5 December 1996, A-7.

11. "Melvin Thom, 1938–1984," box 5, folder 30, NIYCR; Sam English, interview by author; Vine Deloria, Jr., to Edward LaCroix, 16 July and 7 June 1996, box 4, folder 4, NIYCR.

BIBLIOGRAPHY

ARCHIVAL COLLECTIONS

American Indian Chicago Conference Records (AICCR). National Anthropological Archives, Smithsonian Institution, Suitland, Md.

American Indian Institute Collection (AIIC). Western History Collections. University of Oklahoma. Norman,.

American Indian Oral History Collection. Center for Southwest Research, Zimmerman Library. University of New Mexico, Albuquerque.

Collier, John, Papers, 1922–68. Sanford, N.C.: Microfilming Corporation of America, 1980. Center for Southwest Research, Zimmerman Library, University of New Mexico, Albuquerque.

Dumont, Robert V., Papers. Native American Educational Service College Archives. Chicago.

Forbes, Jack, Collection. Special Collections, Shields Library. University of California, Davis.

Haley, Frederick T., Papers, 1933–2001. Special Collections University Archives, Allen Library South, University of Washington, Seattle.

Kiva Club Unprocessed Materials. Native American Studies Department, Mesa Vista Hall, University of New Mexico, Albuquerque.

Knowlton, Clark S., Collection (CSKC), 1912–89. New Mexico State Records Center and Archives, Santa Fe.

McNickle, D'Arcy, Papers. Edmund E. Ayer Manuscript Collection. Newberry Library, Chicago.

Montezuma, Carlos, MD. Supplement to the Papers of. Edited by John W. Larner, Jr. Scholarly Resources, Wilmington, Del., 2001. Center for Southwest Research, Zimmerman Library, University of New Mexico, Albuquerque.

National Congress of American Indians, Records of the (RNCAI). National Anthropological Archives, Smithsonian Institution, Suitland, Md.

National Indian Youth Council Records (NIYCR). Center for Southwest Research, Zimmerman Library, University of New Mexico, Albuquerque.

Native Americans and the New Deal: The Office Files of John Collier. Edited by Robert E. Lester. Bethesda, Md.: University Publications of America, 1993. Center for Southwest Research, Zimmerman Library, University of New Mexico, Albuquerque.

Rietz, Robert, Papers. Native American Educational Service College Archives. Chicago.

Southwestern Association on Indian Affairs Records (SWAIAR). New Mexico State Records Center and Archives, Santa Fe.

Steiner, Stan, Papers. Department of Special Collections, Green Library, Stanford University, Palo Alto, Calif.

Underground Newspaper Collection. Center for Southwest Research, Zimmerman Library, University of New Mexico, Albuquerque.

Washington State Sportsmen's Council Papers (WSSCP). Special Collections University Archives, Allen Library South, University of Washington, Seattle.

Wax, Murray, Papers. Edmund E. Ayer Manuscript Collection. Newberry Library, Chicago.

Witt, Shirley Hill, Papers. Center for Southwest Research, Zimmerman Library, University of New Mexico, Albuquerque.

GOVERNMENT DOCUMENTS

Robison, Robert, Dale Ward, and Gene Nye. *1965 Fisheries Statistical Report*. Department of Fisheries, State of Washington, 1965. Available Fish and Ocean Library, University of Washington, Seattle.

U.S. Congress. House. Committee on Indian Affairs. *Wheeler-Howard Act—Exempt Certain Indians: Hearing before the Committee on Indian Affairs*. 76th Cong., 3rd sess., 10–20 June 1940.

U.S. Congress. Senate. Committee on Interior and Insular Affairs. *Indian Fishing Rights: Hearings before the Subcommittee on Indian Affairs of the Committee on Interior and Insular Affairs*. 88th Cong., 2nd sess., 5–6 August 1964.

AUTHOR INTERVIEWS

Brown, Gerald (Flathead). Telephone interview, 1 October 2009.

Cambridge, Charles (Diné). Telephone interview, 6 October 2009.

Edwards, Eugene Daniel (Yurok). Telephone interview with author, 12 March 2010.

English, Sam (Ojibwe). Albuquerque, 27 February 2007.

Hatch, Viola (Arapaho). Telephone interview, 2 November 2009.

Jacobson, Karen Rickard (Tuscarora). E-mail correspondence, 2008–2010.

Nez, James (Diné). 10 March 2009.

Ration, Norman (Diné-Laguna). Correspondence, 2006–2010

Warrior, Della (Otoe-Missouria). Telephone interview, 3 March 2010.

Witt, Shirley Hill (Mohawk). E-mail correspondence, 2008–2010.
Zion, James. E-mail correspondence, 2009.

NEWSPAPERS AND PERIODICALS

Aborigine (NIYC newsletter)
Akwesasne Notes
Albuquerque Journal
Albuquerque Tribune
American Aborigine
Americans Before Columbus
Ann Arbor (Mich.) News
Bellingham (Wash.) Herald
Catholic Worker
Chicago Sun-Times
Chicago Tribune
Commentary (New York)
Daily Olympian (Wash.)
Gallup (N.Mex.) Independent
Indian Voices
Kansas City Star
Nation
National Observer
Navajo Times
New Republic
Newsweek
New York Times
Oklahoma Daily (Univ. of Okla.)
Ponca City (Okla.) News
Ramparts
Seattle Post-Intelligencer
Seattle Times
Tacoma (Wash.) News Tribune
Time
U.S. News and World Report
Warpath
Washington Post
Yakima (Wash.) Morning Herald

PUBLISHED SOURCES, THESES, AND DISSERTATIONS

Ablon, Joan. "The American Indian Chicago Conference." *Journal of American Indian Education* 1, no. 2 (January 1962): 3–9.
Abrams, George H. J. *The Seneca People.* Phoenix: Indian Tribal Series, 1976.

Acuña, Rodolfo. *Occupied America: A History of Chicanos*. 4th ed. New York: Longman, 2000.

Adams, David Wallace. *Education for Extinction: American Indians and the Boarding School Experience, 1875–1928*. Lawrence: University of Kansas Press, 1995.

Akard, William Keith. "Wocante Tinza: A History of the American Indian Movement." Ph.D. diss., Ball State University, 1987.

Albert, Judith Clavir, and Steward Edward Albert. *The Sixties Papers: Documents of a Rebellious Decade*. New York: Praeger, 1984.

Alkebulan, Paul. *Survival Pending Revolution: The History of the Black Panther Party*. Tuscaloosa: University of Alabama Press, 2007.

American Friends Service Committee. *Uncommon Controversy: Fishing Rights of the Muckleshoot, Puyallup, and Nisqually Indians*. Seattle: University of Washington Press, 1970.

American Indian Development, Inc. *American Indian Development: Second Annual Report*. Library of Congress, Washington, D.C., 1953.

Anderson, David. *Histories of the Hanged: The Dirty War in Kenya and the End of Empire*. New York: W.W. Norton and Company, 2005.

Anderson, Terry H. *The Movement and the Sixties*. New York: Oxford University Press, 1995.

———. *The Sixties*. New York: Longman, 1999.

Bahr, Howard M., Bruce A. Chadwick, and Robert C. Day, eds. *Native Americans Today: Sociological Perspectives*. New York: Harper and Row, 1972.

Banks, Dennis, with Richard Erdoes. *Ojibwa Warrior: Dennis Banks and the Rise of the American Indian Movement*. Norman: University of Oklahoma Press, 2004.

Beck, David R. M. "Developing a Voice: The Evolution of Self-Determination in an Urban Indian Community." *Wicazo Sa Review* 17, no. 2 (2002): 117–41.

Beito, David T. "Happy Birthday, Oswald Garrison Villard." History News Network. http://hnn.us/blogs/entries/10744.html.

Benedict, Ruth. *Patterns of Culture*. New York: Mentor Books, 1949.

Bernstein, Alison R. *American Indians and World War II: Toward a New Era in Indian Affairs*. Norman: University of Oklahoma Press, 1991.

Blansett, Kent. "A Journey to Freedom: The Life of Richard Oakes, Ranoies—'Big Man,' 1942–1972." M.A. thesis, University of New Mexico, 2004.

Bloom, Alexander, and Wini Breines, eds. *"Takin' It to the Streets": A Sixties Reader*. New York: Oxford University Press, 1995.

Blue Cloud, Peter. *Alcatraz Is Not an Island*. Berkeley, Calif.: Wingbow Press, 1972.

Borstelmann, Thomas. *The Cold War and the Color Line: American Race Relations in the Global Arena*. Cambridge, Mass.: Harvard University Press, 2001.

Boxberger, Daniel L. *To Fish in Common: The Ethnohistory of Lummi Indian Salmon Fishing*. Seattle: University of Washington Press, 1999.

Brown, Brian Edward. *Religion, Law, and the Land: Native Americans and the Judicial Interpretation of Sacred Land*. Contributions in Legal Studies, no. 94. Westport, Conn.: Greenwood Press, 1999.

Brown, Robert Paul. "'The Year One': The American Indian Chicago Conference of 1961 and the Rebirth of Indian Activism." M.A. thesis, University of Wisconsin–Eau Claire, 1993.

Bruner, Joseph. "The Indian Demands Justice." *National Republic* 22 (March 1935): 23–31.

Burt, Larry W. *Tribalism in Crisis: Federal Indian Policy, 1953–1961*. Albuquerque: University of New Mexico Press, 1982.

Butts, Michele Tucker. "Red Power: Indian Activism, 1960–1973." M.A. thesis, Austin Peay State University, 1974.

Calloway, Colin G. "The Intertribal Balance of Powers on the Great Plains, 1760–1850." *Journal of American Studies* 16, no. 1 (April 1982): 25–47.

———. *New Directions in American Indian History*. Norman: University of Oklahoma Press, 1988.

———. *The Shawnees and the War for America*. Penguin Library of American Indian History, edited by Colin G. Calloway. New York: Viking, 2007.

Carmichael, Stokely, and Charles V. Hamilton. *Black Power: The Politics of Liberation in America*. New York: Vintage Books, 1967.

Carson, Clayborne. *In Struggle: SNCC and the Black Awakening of the 1960s*. Cambridge, Mass.: Harvard University Press, 1981.

Chambers, Bradford, comp. and ed. *Chronicles of Black Protest*. New York: Mentor Books, 1968.

Chandler, O. K. *Now Who's Un-American? An Expose of Communism in the United States Government*. Pamphlet. Washington, D.C.: American Indian Federation, n.d.

Clark, D. Anthony Tyeeme. "Representing Indians: Indigenous Fugitives and the Society of American Indians in the Making of Common Culture." Ph.D. diss., University of Kansas, 2004.

Clarkin, Thomas. *Federal Indian Policy in the Kennedy and Johnson Administrations, 1961–1969*. Albuquerque: University of New Mexico Press, 2001.

Clifton, James A., ed. *Applied Anthropology: Readings in the Uses of the Science of Man*. Boston: Houghton Mifflin, 1970.

Cobb, Daniel M. "Community, Poverty, Power: The Politics of Tribal Self-Determination, 1960–1968." Ph.D. diss., University of Oklahoma, 2003.

———. *Native Activism in Cold War America: The Struggle for Sovereignty*. Lawrence: University Press of Kansas, 2008.

Cobb, Daniel M., and Loretta Fowler, eds. *Beyond Red Power: American Indian Politics and Activism since 1900*. Santa Fe: School for Advanced Research Press, 2007.

Cohen, Fay G., with Joan LaFrance and Vivian L. Bowden. *Treaties on Trial: The Continuing Controversy over Northwest Indian Fishing Rights*. Seattle: University of Washington Press, 1986.

Cohen, Felix. *The Legal Conscience: Selected Papers of Felix S. Cohen*. Edited by Lucy Kramer Cohen. New Haven, Conn.: Yale University Press, 1960.

Collier, John. "Amerindians: Problems in Psychic and Physical Adjustments to a Dominant Civilization." *Pacific Affairs* (March 1929): 116–22.

——. *From Every Zenith: A Memoir and Some Essays on Life and Thought*. Denver: Sage Books, 1963.

——. *The Indians of the Americas*. New York: Norton, 1947.

Collins, Robert M. *More: The Politics of Economic Growth in Postwar America*. New York: Oxford University Press, 2000.

Commission on the Rights, Liberties, and Responsibilities of the American Indian. *A Program for Indian Citizens: A Summary Report*. Albuquerque: Fund for the Republic, 1961.

Connell Szasz, Margaret, ed. *Between Indian and White Worlds: The Cultural Broker*. Norman: University of Oklahoma Press, 1994.

——. *Education and the American Indian: The Road to Self-Determination since 1928*. 3rd ed. Albuquerque: University of New Mexico Press, 1999.

Cooper, Nicola. *France in Indochina: Colonial Encounters*. New York: Oxford University Press, 2001.

Cornell, Stephen. *Return of the Native: American Indian Political Resurgence*. New York: Oxford University Press, 1988.

Costo, Rupert. "Alcatraz." *Indian Historian* 3, no. 1 (1970): 4–12.

Cowger, Thomas W. *The National Congress of American Indians: The Founding Years*. Lincoln: University of Nebraska Press, 1999.

Crum, Steven. "Almost Invisible: The Brotherhood of North American Indians (1911) and the League of North American Indians (1935)." *Wicazo Sa Review* 21 (Spring 2006): 43–59.

Dallek, Robert. *Flawed Giant: Lyndon Johnson and His Times, 1961–1973*. New York: Oxford University Press, 1998.

Davis, Julie L. "American Indian Movement Survival Schools in Minneapolis and St. Paul, 1968–2002." Ph.D. diss., Arizona State University, 2004.

De La Torre, Joely. "From Activism to Academics: The Evolution of American Indian Studies at San Francisco State, 1968–2001." *Iroquois Nations Studies Journal* 2, no. 1 (2001): 11–20.

Deloria, Vine, Jr., ed. *American Indian Policy in the Twentieth Century*. Norman: University of Oklahoma Press, 1985.

——. *Behind the Trail of Broken Treaties: An Indian Declaration of Independence*. Austin: University of Texas Press, 1985.

——. *Custer Died for Your Sins: An Indian Manifesto*. New York: Macmillan, 1969.

Deloria, Vine, Jr., and Clifford M. Lytle. *The Nations Within: The Past and Future of American Indian Sovereignty*. New York: Pantheon Books, 1984.

DeLuca, Richard. "'We Hold the Rock!' The Indian Attempt to Reclaim Alcatraz Island." *California History* 62, no. 1 (1983): 2–22.

Dittmer, John. *Local People: The Struggle for Civil Rights in Mississippi*. Urbana: University of Illinois Press, 1995.

Dixon, David. *Never Come to Peace Again: Pontiac's Uprising and the Fate of the British Empire in North America*. Norman: University of Oklahoma Press, 2005.

Dudziak, Mary L. *Cold War Civil Rights: Race and the Image of American Democracy*. Politics and Society in Twentieth Century America, edited by William Chafe,

Gary Gerstle, and Linda Gordon. Princeton, N.J.: Princeton University Press, 2000.

Dumont, Robert, and Murray Wax. "Cherokee School Society and the Intercultural Classroom." *Human Organization* 28, no. 3 (Fall 1969): 217–26.

Edgerton, Robert B. *Mau Mau: An African Crucible*. New York: Free Press, 1989.

Ekirch, Arthur A., Jr. *Ideologies and Utopias: The Impact of the New Deal on American Thought*. Chicago: Quadrangle Books, 1969.

Evans, Sterling, ed. *American Indians in American History, 1870–2001: A Companion Reader*. Westport, Conn.: Praeger, 2002.

Fager, Charles. *Uncertain Resurrection: The Poor People's Washington Campaign*. Grand Rapids, Mich.: William B. Eerdmans, 1969.

Farber, David. *The Age of Great Dreams: America in the 1960s*. New York: Hill and Wang, 1994.

———. *Chicago '68*. Chicago: University of Chicago Press, 1988.

———, ed. *The Sixties: From Memory to History*. Chapel Hill: University of North Carolina Press, 1994.

Feder, Norman. "Origin of the Oklahoma Forty-Nine Dance." *Ethnomusicology* 8, no. 3 (1964): 290–94.

Fenton, William N. *The Great Law and the Longhouse: A Political History of the Iroquois Confederacy*. Norman: University of Oklahoma Press, 1998.

Fey, Harold, and D'Arcy McNickle. *Indians and Other Americans: Two Ways of Life Meet*. Rev. ed. New York: Harper and Row, 1970.

Finnegan, Richard A. "Indian Treaty Analysis and Off-Reservation Fishing Rights: A Case Study." *Washington Law Review* 51, no. 1 (November 1975): 61–95.

Fixico, Donald L. *Termination and Relocation: Federal Indian Policy, 1945–1960*. Albuquerque: University of New Mexico Press, 1986.

Fluharty, Sterling Ray. "'For a Greater Indian America': The Origins of the National Indian Youth Council." M.A. thesis, University of Oklahoma, 2003.

Folsom, Franklin. *Red Power on the Rio Grande: The Native American Revolution of 1680*. Albuquerque: University of New Mexico Press, 1973.

Forbes, Jack. *Native Americans and Nixon: Presidential Politics and Minority Self-Determination, 1969–1972*. Los Angeles: University of California American Indian Studies Center, 1981.

Forman, James. *The Making of Black Revolutionaries*. New York: Macmillan, 1972.

Fortunate Eagle, Adam. *Alcatraz! Alcatraz! The Occupation of 1969–1971*. Berkley, Calif.: Heyday Books, 1992.

Fortunate Eagle, Adam, with Tim Findley. *Heart of the Rock: The Indian Invasion of Alcatraz*. Norman: University of Oklahoma Press, 2002.

Fraser, Steve, and Gary Gerstle, eds. *The Rise and Fall of the New Deal Order, 1930–1980*. Princeton, N.J.: Princeton University Press, 1989.

French, Patrick. *Liberty or Death: India's Journey to Independence and Division*. London: Harper Collins, 1997.

Fuchs, Lawrence H. *The American Kaleidoscope: Race, Ethnicity, and the Civic Culture*. Middletown, Conn.: Wesleyan University Press, 1990.

Gerstle, Gary. *American Crucible: Race and Nation in the Twentieth Century*. Princeton, N.J.: Princeton University Press, 2001.

Gilbert, Bil. *God Gave Us This Country: Tekamthi and the First American Civil War*. New York: Atheneum, 1989.

Gómez-Quiñones, Juan. *Chicano Politics: Reality and Promise, 1940–1990*. Albuquerque: University of New Mexico Press, 1990.

Gordon-McCutchan, R. C. *The Taos Indians and the Battle for Blue Lake*. Santa Fe, N.Mex.: Red Crane Books, 1991.

Gracey, Marci Jean. "Attacking the Indian New Deal: The American Indian Federation and the Quest to Protect Assimilation." M.A. thesis, Oklahoma State University, 2003.

Greenberg, Cheryl, ed. *"A Circle of Trust": Remembering SNCC*. New Brunswick, N.J.: Rutgers University Press, 1998.

Grossman, Mark. *The ABC-CLIO Companion to the Native American Rights Movement*. Santa Barbara, Calif.: ABC-CLIO, 1996.

Hafen, Jane. "Zitkala-Ša: Sentimentality and Sovereignty." *Wicazo Sa Review* 12 (1997): 31–41.

Hammer, Ellen J. *The Struggle for Indochina, 1940–1955*. Stanford, Calif.: Stanford University Press, 1966.

Harmon, Alexandra. *Indians in the Making: Ethnic Relations and Indian Identities around Puget Sound*. Berkeley: University of California Press, 1998.

Hauptman, Laurence M. "Alice Jemison: Seneca Political Activist, 1901–1964." *Indian Historian* 12 (Summer 1979): 15–22, 60.

———."The American Indian Federation and the Indian New Deal: A Reinterpretation." *Pacific Historical Review* 52 (November 1983): 378–402.

———. *The Iroquois and the New Deal*. Syracuse: Syracuse University Press, 1981.

———. *The Iroquois Struggle for Survival: World War II to Red Power*. Syracuse, N.Y.: Syracuse University Press, 1986.

Hauptman, Laurence M., and Jack Campisi. "The Voice of Eastern Indians: The American Indian Chicago Conference of 1961 and the Movement for Federal Recognition." *Proceedings of the American Philosophical Society* 132, no. 4 (1988): 316–29.

Hertzberg, Hazel W. *The Search for an American Indian Identity: Modern Pan-Indian Movements*. Syracuse, N.Y.: Syracuse University Press, 1971.

Herzog, Stephen J., comp. *Minority Group Politics: A Reader*. New York: Holt, Rinehart, and Winston, 1971.

Hobbs, Charles A. "Indian Hunting and Fishing Rights." *George Washington Law Review* 32, no. 3 (March 1964): 504–32.

———. "Indian Hunting and Fishing Rights II." *George Washington Law Review* 37, no. 5 (July 1969): 1251–73.

Hogan, Wesley C. *Many Minds, One Heart: SNCC's Dream for a New America*. Chapel Hill: University of North Carolina Press, 2007.

Holm, Tom. *The Great Confusion in Indian Affairs: Native Americans and Whites in the Progressive Era*. Austin: University of Texas Press, 2005.

———. *Strong Hearts, Wounded Souls: Native American Veterans of the Vietnam War.* Austin: University of Texas Press, 1996.

House, Lloyd Lynn. "The Historical Development of Navajo Community College." Ph.D. diss., Arizona State University, 1974.

Isserman, Maurice. *If I Had a Hammer: The Death of the Old Left and the Birth of the New Left.* New York: Basic Books, 1987.

Iverson, Peter. *Carlos Montezuma and the Changing World of American Indians.* Albuquerque: University of New Mexico Press, 1982.

———, ed. *Plains Indians of the Twentieth Century.* Norman: University of Oklahoma Press, 1985.

———. *"We Are Still Here": American Indians in the Twentieth Century.* Wheeling, Illinois: Harlan Davidson, 1998.

Johnson, Ralph W. "The States versus Indian Off-Reservation Fishing: A United States Supreme Court Error." *Washington Law Review* 47 (1972): 207–37.

Johnson, Troy R., ed. *Alcatraz: Indian Land Forever.* Los Angeles: University of California American Indian Studies Center, 1994.

———. *The Occupation of Alcatraz Island: Indian Self-Determination and the Rise of Indian Activism.* Urbana: University of Illinois Press, 1996.

———. "The Roots of Contemporary Native American Activism." *American Indian Culture and Research Journal* 20, no. 2 (1996): 127–54.

———. *You Are on Indian Land! Alcatraz Island, 1969–1971.* Los Angeles: University of California American Indian Studies Center, 1995.

Johnson, Troy R., Joane Nagel, and Duane Champagne, eds. *American Indian Activism: Alcatraz to the Longest Walk.* Urbana: University of Illinois Press, 1997.

Johnston, Basil H. *Indian School Days.* Norman: University of Oklahoma Press, 1988.

Josephy, Alvin M., Jr. *Now That the Buffalo's Gone: A Study of Today's American Indians.* New York: Alfred A. Knopf, 1982.

———, ed. *Red Power: The American Indians' Fight for Freedom.* New York: American Heritage Press, 1971.

Josephy, Alvin M., Jr., Joane Nagel, and Troy Johnson, eds. *Red Power: The American Indians' Fight for Freedom.* 2nd ed. Lincoln: University of Nebraska Press, 1999.

Kelly, Lawrence C. *The Assault on Assimilation: John Collier and the Origins of Indian Policy Reform.* Albuquerque: University of New Mexico Press, 1983.

Kersey, Harry A., Jr. "The Havana Connection: Buffalo Tiger, Fidel Castro, and the Origin of Miccosukee Tribal Sovereignty, 1959–1962." *American Indian Quarterly* 25, no. 4 (2001): 491–507.

Koppes, Clayton R. "From New Deal to Termination: Liberalism and Indian Policy, 1933–1953." *Pacific Historical Review* 46 (November 1977): 543–66.

LaGrand, James B. *Indian Metropolis: Native Americans in Chicago, 1945–1975.* Urbana: University of Illinois Press, 2002.

Lake, Randall A. "Enacting Red Power: The Consummatory Function in Native American Protest Rhetoric." *Quarterly Journal of Speech* 69 (May 1983): 127–42.

Lester, Julius. *Look Out, Whitey! Black Power Gon' Get Your Mama!* New York: Dial Press, 1968.

Levine, Stuart, and Nancy O. Lurie, eds. *The American Indian Today.* Baltimore: Penguin Books, 1974.

Lewis, John, with Michael D'Orso. *Walking with the Wind: A Memoir of the Movement.* New York: Simon and Schuster, 1998.

Liberty, Margot. *American Indian Intellectuals of the Nineteenth and Early Twentieth Centuries.* Norman: University of Oklahoma Press, 2002.

Lookingbill, Brad. Review of *The Occupation of Alcatraz Island,* by Troy R. Johnson. *American Indian Quarterly* 22 (Summer 1998): 408.

Lurie, Nancy O. "Sol Tax and Tribal Sovereignty." *Human Organization* 58, no. 1 (1999): 108–17.

———. "The Voice of the American Indian: Report on the American Indian Chicago Conference." *Current Anthropology* 2 (1961): 478–500.

Lyden, Fremont J., and Lyman H. Legters, eds. *Native Americans and Public Policy.* Pittsburgh: University of Pittsburgh Press, 1992.

Martinez, David. *Dakota Philosopher: Charles Eastman and American Indian Thought.* St. Paul: Minnesota Historical Society Press, 2009.

Matthews, Tanya. *War in Algeria: Background for Crisis.* Fordham: Fordham University Press, 1961.

McCarty, Teresa L. *A Place to Be Navajo: Rough Rock and the Struggle for Self-Determination in Indigenous Schooling.* Mahwah, N.J.: Lawrence Erlbaum, 2002.

McCloud, Janet. "Indian Rights War Continues in Defense of 1854 Treaty Laws." *Indian Historian* 4, no. 1 (January–February 1967): 15–21.

McJimsey, George. *The Presidency of Franklin Delano Roosevelt.* Lawrence: University Press of Kansas, 2000.

Means, Russell, with Marvin J. Wolf. *Where White Men Fear to Tread: The Autobiography of Russell Means.* New York: St. Martin's Press, 1995.

Meyer, John M., ed. *American Indians and U.S. Politics: A Companion Reader.* Westport, Conn.: Praeger, 2002.

Middleton, Richard. *Pontiac's War: Its Causes, Course and Consequences.* New York: Routledge, 2007.

Miller, Bruce. "The Press, the Boldt Decision, and Indian-White Relations." *American Indian Culture and Research Journal* 17, no. 2 (1993): 75–97.

Minton, Charles. "The Place of the Indian Youth Council in Higher Education." *American Indian Education* 1, no. 1 (July 1961): 29–35.

Modica, Andrea. *Real Indians: Portraits of Contemporary Native Americans and America's Tribal Colleges.* New York: Melcher Media, 2003.

Morris, Aldon D. *The Origins of the Civil Rights Movement: Black Communities Organizing for Change.* New York: Free Press, 1984.

Morris, Charles E., and Stephen H. Browne. *Readings on the Rhetoric of Social Protest.* State College, Pa.: Strata Publishers, 2001.

Murphree, Vanessa. *The Selling of Civil Rights: The Student Nonviolent Coordinating Committee and the Use of Public Relations*. New York: Routledge, 2006.

Nagel, Joane. "American Indian Ethnic Renewal: Politics and the Resurgence of Identity." *American Sociological Review* 60, no. 6 (1995): 947–65.

———. *American Indian Ethnic Renewal: Red Power and the Resurgence of Identity and Culture*. New York: Oxford University Press, 1996.

Nielsen, Nancy J. *Reformers and Activists*. New York: Facts on File, 1997.

Olson, Mary B. "Social Reform and the Use of the Law as an Instrument of Social Change: Native Americans' Struggle for Treaty Fishing Rights." Ph.D. diss., University of Wisconsin–Madison, 1984.

Parker, Dorothy Ragon. "Choosing an Indian Identity: A Biography of D'Arcy Mc-Nickle." Ph.D. diss., University of New Mexico, 1988.

———. *Singing an Indian Song: A Biography of D'Arcy McNickle*. Lincoln: University of Nebraska Press, 1992.

Parman, Donald L. "Inconsistent Advocacy: The Erosion of Indian Fishing Rights in the Pacific Northwest, 1933–1956." *Pacific Historical Review* 53 (1984): 163–89.

Pavlik, Steve, ed. *A Good Cherokee, A Good Anthropologist: Papers in Honor of Robert K. Thomas*. Contemporary American Indian Issues Series. Los Angeles: American Indian Studies Center, University of California at Los Angeles, 1998.

Payne, Charles. *I've Got the Light of Freedom: The Organizing Tradition and the Mississippi Freedom Struggle*. Berkeley: University of California Press, 1995.

Peckham, Howard H. *Pontiac and the Indian Uprising*. Princeton, N.J.: Princeton University Press, 1947.

Philp, Kenneth R. *John Collier's Crusade for Indian Reform, 1920–1954*. Tucson: University of Arizona Press, 1977.

———. "Stride toward Freedom: The Relocation of Indians to Cities, 1952–1960." *Western Historical Quarterly* 14 (April 1983): 165–80.

———. "Termination: Legacy of the Indian New Deal." *Western Historical Quarterly* 14, no. 2 (1983): 165–80.

———. *Termination Revisited: American Indians on the Trail to Self-Determination, 1933–1953*. Lincoln: University of Nebraska Press, 1999.

Prucha, Francis Paul. "American Indian Policy in the Twentieth Century." *Western Historical Quarterly* 15, no. 1 (1984): 4–18.

———. *The Great Father: The United States Government and the American Indians*. 2 vols. Lincoln: University of Nebraska Press, 1984.

———. *The Great Father: The United States Government and the American Indians*. Abridged ed. Lincoln: University of Nebraska Press, 1986.

Rankin, Charles E., ed. *Legacy: New Perspectives on the Battle of the Little Bighorn*. Helena: Montana Historical Society Press, 1996.

Rappaport, Doreen. *The Flight of Red Bird: The Life of Zitkala-Sa*. New York: Puffin Books, 1997.

Redfield, Robert. "The Folk Society." *American Journal of Sociology* 52, no. 4 (January 1947): 293–308.

Rickard, Clinton, with Barbara Graymont. *Fighting Tuscarora: The Autobiography of Clinton Rickard*. Syracuse, N.Y.: Syracuse University Press, 1973.

Riggs, Christopher. "American Indians, Economic Development, and Self-Determination in the 1960s." *Pacific Historical Review* 69, no. 2 (August 2000): 431–63.

Roessel, Ruth, and Broderick H. Johnson. *Navajo Livestock Reduction: A National Disgrace*. Chinle, Navajo Nation: Navajo Community College Press, 1974.

Rosenthal, Harvey. *Their Day in Court: A History of the Indian Claims Commission*. New York: Garland Press, 1990.

Rosier, Paul C. "'They Are Ancestral Homelands': Race, Place, and Politics in Cold War Native America." *Journal of American History* 92, no. 4 (2006): 1300–1326.

Rossinow, Doug. *The Politics of Authenticity: Liberalism, Christianity, and the New Left in America*. New York: Columbia University Press, 1998.

Rudd, Mark. *Underground: My Life with SDS and the Weathermen*. New York: William Morrow, 2009.

Schlesinger, Arthur M., Jr. *The Age of Roosevelt: The Coming of the New Deal*. Boston: Houghton Mifflin, 1958.

Schusky, Ernest Lester. *The Right to Be Indian*. San Francisco: Indian Historian Press, 1965.

Sellers, Cleveland. "From Black Consciousness to Black Power." *Southern Exposure* 9, no. 1 (1981): 64–67.

Sellers, Cleveland, with Robert Terrell. *The River of No Return: The Autobiography of a Black Militant and the Life and Death of SNCC*. New York: William Morrow and Co., 1973.

Senese, Guy B. *Self-Determination and the Social Education of Native Americans*. Westport, Conn.: Praeger, 1991.

Shannon, Timothy, J. *Iroquois Diplomacy on the Early American Frontier*. Penguin Library of American Indian History, edited by Colin G. Calloway. New York: Viking, 2008.

Shipway, Martin. *Decolonization and Its Impact: A Comparative Approach to the End of the Colonial Empires*. Malden, Mass.: Blackwell, 2008.

Shreve, Bradley Glenn. "'From Time Immemorial': The Fish-in Movement and the Rise of Intertribal Activism." *Pacific Historical Review* 78, no. 3 (2009): 403–34.

———. "Of Gods and Broken Rainbows: Native American Religions, Western Rationalism, and the Problem of Sacred Lands." *New Mexico Historical Review* 82, no. 3 (2007): 369–90.

———. "Up Against Giants: The National Indian Youth Council, the Navajo Nation, and Coal Gasification, 1974–77." *American Indian Culture and Research Journal* 30, no. 2 (2006): 17–34.

————. "'We Must Become One People, United, with a Singleness of Purpose': The American Indian Chicago Conference of 1961." *Journal of Illinois History* 12, no. 2 (Summer 2009): 107–28.

Sklansky, Jeff. "Rock Reservation and Prison: The Native American Occupation of Alcatraz Island." *American Indian Culture and Research Journal* 13, no. 2 (1989): 29–68.

Slotkin, James Sydney. *The Peyote Religion: A Study in Indian-White Relations.* Glencoe, Ill.: Free Press, 1956.

Smith, Marian W. *The Puyallup-Nisqually.* Columbia University Contributions to Anthropology, vol. 32. New York: AMS Press, 1969.

Smith, Paul Chaat, and Robert Allen Warrior. *Like a Hurricane: The Indian Movement from Alcatraz to Wounded Knee.* New York: New Press, 1996.

Sperloff, Leon. *Carlos Montezuma, M.D., a Yavapai American Hero: The Life and Times of an American Indian, 1866–1923.* Portland, Ore.: Arnica, 2003.

Spicer, Edward H. *Cycles of Conquest: The Impact of Spain, Mexico, and the United States on the Indians of the Southwest, 1533–1960.* Tucson: University of Arizona Press, 1962.

Srupp, C. Mathew, ed. *Public Policy Impacts on American Indian Economic Development.* Albuquerque: Native American Studies Institute for Native American Development, University of New Mexico, 1988.

Stein, Maurice R., Arthur J. Vidich, and David Manning White, eds. *Identity and Anxiety: Survival of the Person in Mass Society.* Glencoe, Ill.: Free Press, 1960.

Steiner, Stan. *The New Indians.* New York: Harper and Row, 1968.

Stern, Kenneth S. *Loud Hawk: The United States versus the American Indian Movement.* Norman: University of Oklahoma Press, 1994.

Stoper, Emily. *The Student Nonviolent Coordinating Committee: The Growth of Radicalism in a Civil Rights Organization.* Martin Luther King, Jr. and the Civil Rights Movement, edited by David J. Garrow. Brooklyn, N.Y.: Carlson, 1989.

Stucki, Larry R. "Anthropologists and Indians: A New Look at the Fox Project." *Plains Anthropologist* 12, no. 36 (1967): 300–317.

Sturm, Circe. *Blood Politics: Race, Culture, and Identity in the Cherokee Nation of Oklahoma.* Berkeley: University of California Press, 2002.

Sugden, John. *Tecumseh: A Life.* New York: Henry Holt and Co., 1997.

Talbot, Steve. "Free Alcatraz: The Culture of Native American Liberation." *Journal of Ethnic Studies* 6, no. 3 (1978): 83–96.

Taylor, Graham D. *The New Deal and American Indian Tribalism: The Administration of the Indian Reorganization Act, 1934–1945.* Lincoln: University of Nebraska Press, 1980.

Taylor, Joseph E. *Making Salmon: An Environmental History of the Northwest Fisheries Crisis.* Seattle: University of Washington Press, 1999.

Taylor, Theodore W. *The Bureau of Indian Affairs.* Boulder, Colo.: Westview, 2002.

Tax, Sol. "The Importance of Preserving Indian Culture." *América Indígena* 26, no. 1 (January 1966): 81–86.

———. "A Positive Program for the Indians." *American Indian* 8, no. 1 (Spring 1958): 3–10.

———. "Values in Action: The Fox Project." *Eastern Anthropologist* 11, no. 3–4 (March–August 1958): 168–74.

Treat, James. *Around the Sacred Fire: Native Religious Activism in the Red Power Era.* New York: Palgrave Macmillan, 2003.

Varon, Jeremy. *Bringing the War Home: The Weather Underground, the Red Army Faction, and Revolutionary Violence in the Sixties and Seventies.* Berkley: University of California Press, 2004.

Vigil, Ernesto B. *The Crusade for Justice: Chicano Militancy and the Government's War on Dissent.* Madison: University of Wisconsin Press, 1999.

Wax, Murray, Stanley Diamond, and Fred O. Gearing, eds. *Anthropological Perspectives on Education.* New York: Basic Books, 1971.

Weber, David J., ed. *What Caused the Pueblo Revolt?* Boston: Bedford/St. Martin's, 1999.

Wei, William. *The Asian American Movement.* Philadelphia: Temple University Press, 1993.

Weisiger, Marsha L. *Dreaming of Sheep in Navajo Country.* Seattle: University of Washington Press, 2009.

Welch, Deborah. "Zitkala-Sa: An American Indian Leader, 1976–1938." Ph.D. diss., University of Wyoming, 1985.

Weyler, Rex. *Blood of the Land: The Government and Corporate War against First Nations.* Philadelphia: New Society Publishers, 1992.

Wilkerson, Cathy. *Flying Close to the Sun: My Life and Times as a Weatherman.* New York: Seven Stories Press, 2007.

Wilkins, David E. *American Indian Politics and the American Political System.* Lanham, Md.: Rowman and Littlefield, 2002.

Wilkinson, Charles. *Blood Struggle: The Rise of Modern Indian Nations.* New York: W. W. Norton and Co., 2005.

———. *Messages from Frank's Landing: A Story of Salmon, Treaties, and the Indian Way.* Seattle: University of Washington Press, 2000.

Wilkinson, Charles F., and Eric R. Boggs. "The Evolution of the Termination Policy." *American Indian Law Review* 5 (1980): 139–84.

Wilson, Raymond. *Ohiyesa: Charles Eastman, Santee Sioux.* Urbana: University of Illinois Press, 1983.

Wright, Rolland H. "The American Indian College Student: A Study in Marginality." Ph.D. diss., Brandeis University, 1972.

Zinn, Howard. *SNCC: The New Abolitionists.* Boston: Beacon Press, 1965.

INDEX

Page numbers in italics refer to illustrations.

Women's National Indian Association, 18

Work, Hubert, 22

Workshop on American Indian Affairs, 65–93, 213n14; assimilation discussion at, 72, 77, 81, 82; attendance at, 75, 76; as brainchild of Sol Tax, 68, 70; debate between integrationists and traditionalists at, 82–83; discussion on Indian education at, 162; founding of, 65–66; funding for, 74; ideological agenda of, 12, 66, 76, 77, 81, 84, 88; Institute for American Indian Studies and, 169; instructors and guest speakers at, 72–73, 81; intertribal spirit at, 75, 83, 85, 92; photos, *78, 86*; politicization of participants at, 83–84, 88; readings and curriculum, 77, 79–81, 224n27; support to self-determination and tribal sovereignty, 66, 69, 71, 72, 77, 80; trains future NIYC leaders, 111

Works Progress Administration, 24

Wounded Knee occupation (1973), 184, 195–96

Wovoka, 99

Wright, Rolland, 82, 83, 169–70

Yakama Nation, 26, 88, 135

Yaryan, John J., 127, 128

Young People's Socialist League, 67

Zitkala-Ša. *See* Bonnin, Gertrude

CPSIA information can be obtained at www.ICGtesting.com
Printed in the USA
LVOW060129180712

290509LV00002B/2/P

9 780806 141787